Philosophy and Psychoanalytic Theory

Bert Olivier

Philosophy and Psychoanalytic Theory

Collected Essays

PETER LANG
Oxford • Bern • Berlin • Bruxelles • Frankfurt am Main • New York • Wien

Bibliographic information published by Die Deutsche Bibliothek
Die Deutsche Bibliothek lists this publication in the Deutsche Nationalbibliografie; detailed bibliographic data is available on the Internet at <http://dnb.ddb.de>.

A catalogue record for this book is available from The British Library.

Library of Congress Cataloging-in-Publication Data:

Olivier, Bert, 1946-
Philosophy and psychoanalytic theory : collected essays / Bert Olivier.
p. cm.
Includes bibliographical references and index.
ISBN 978-3-03911-901-1 (alk. paper)
1. Psychoanalysis and philosophy. I. Title.
BF175.4.P45O45 2009
150.19'5--dc22
2009007627

Cover design: Mette Bundgaard, Peter Lang Ltd
ISBN 978-3-03911-901-1

Printed in Germany

To Andrea,
my preternatural philosophical muse

Contents

Acknowledgements

The essays collected here originally appeared in various peer-reviewed academic journals. I wish to express my appreciation for editorial permission to reprint them in the present volume. Their initial publication details are as follows:

Chapter 1: 'Discourse, agency and the question of evil'. *South African Journal of Philosophy*, Vol. 22 (4), December 2003, pp. 329–348.

Chapter 2: 'Lacan and narrative identity: *The Piano Teacher*'. In: *Word, (wo)man, world: Essays on literature. Festschrift for Ina Gräbe*. Oliphant, A.W. & Roos, H. (eds). Pretoria: UNISA Press, 2005, pp. 94–112.

Chapter 3: 'Lacan and the question of the psychotherapist's ethical orientation'. *South African Journal of Psychology* 35 (4), 2005, pp. 657–683.

Chapter 4: 'The contemporary context of relativity and relativism'. *Acta Academica Supplementum*, 2005 (2) (special edition on relativity and relativism), pp. 73–104.

Chapter 5: 'The question of an appropriate philosophical response to "global" terrorism: Derrida and Habermas'. *Freiburger Zeitschrift für Philosophie und Theologie* 54 (1/2) 2007, pp. 146–167.

Chapter 6: 'Nature as "abject", critical psychology, and "revolt": The pertinence of Kristeva'. *South African Journal of Psychology*, Vol. 37, No. 3, 2007, pp. 443–469.

Chapter 7: 'Negotiating the "paranoiac structure" of human knowledge: Fowles's *The Magus* and Lacan'. *South African Journal of Psychology* 38 (1), April 2008, pp. 176–199.

Chapter 8: 'Trauma and literature: Derrida, *9/11* and Hart's *The reconstructionist*'. *Journal of Literary Studies* 24 (1), March 2008, pp. 32–58.

Preface

The essays brought together here are written from the dual perspectives of philosophy and psychoanalytic theory. Sometimes more weight is given to the one perspective than the other and *vice versa*, but always with the conviction that the rational, argumentative and hermeneutic-interpretive approach of philosophy requires the sobering influence of psychoanalytic theory's conception of the human being as a split subject, prone to the laws of the unconscious, no less than to those of reason.

In practice this consideration therefore means that, in the interpretation of human actions – whether these are historically experienced or historiographically documented, on the one hand, or fictionally elaborated, on the other – it is not sufficient to depend on the traditional argumentative and hermeneutic-interpretive approach of philosophy. (I deliberately avoid using the term 'method(s)', given the connotation of 'guarantee of truth or validity' that accompanies it.) Philosophy has to be augmented by psychoanalysis, or – as I prefer to say, because clinical practice is not at stake here – by psychoanalytic theory, with its understanding of human subjectivity in universalistic 'structural' terms, that is, in terms that are predicated on the principle that the subjectivity of all human beings, regardless of culture or race, is structurally shaped in the same manner. This happens along a trajectory of developmental stages which leave their structural psychic imprint ineradicably on the individual subject, even if every person appropriates these 'structures' differently, in accordance with what Freud and Lacan thought of as the individual person's singular 'desire'.

What makes psychoanalytic theory uniquely valuable for philosophy from a heuristic perspective, therefore, is its 'quasi-transcendental' orientation according to both the universal and the particular at the same time – universal structures (of subjectivity), as well as a singularising 'desire', are constitutive of each and every human being, and these exceed the transcendental rational forms attributed by Immanuel Kant (1724–1804) to all human beings. In short, the essays in this volume are predicated on the assumption that the constitution of human beings, while certainly including rationality (articulated conceptually in language), also includes registers which surpass the rational. What these are, and how they help one in understanding human actions and behaviour, the different essays in the present volume are elaborations of, sometimes with reference to actual historical events, and sometimes by way of analyses of exemplary fictional (literary or cinematic) instantiations of such actions.

Although they therefore display a similarity in thinking-style, as it were, the essays cover a wide thematic spectrum. Topics range from the question concerning the relation between discourse, evil and the agency of the subject to that of the non-relativistic ethical positioning of the psychotherapist, from the problem of overcoming relativism by way of a post-structuralist understanding of language to that of a cogent (Derridean) philosophical response to global 'terrorism', and from a Lacanian understanding of narrative identity, of human knowledge as 'paranoiac', and of 'trauma literature' to a Kristevan perspective on nature as 'abject' in the light of the degradation of ecosystems globally. By means of these articles I hope to have contributed in a modest manner to the understanding of our complex (human) species.

To conclude, I wish to thank Hannah Godfrey, my editor, as well as Shirley Walker Werrett, the office manager at Peter Lang, Oxford, for their able and efficient communication in the course of the publication of this volume and its companion volumes *Philosophy and Communication* and *Philosophy and the Arts*.

Bert Olivier
Port Elizabeth
January 2009

CHAPTER 1

Discourse, agency and the question of evil

Joan Copjec's penetrating essay on Kant's notion of 'radical evil' brings into focus what is at stake when one confronts the question of the relationship between the human will and evil – whether the former should be regarded as irredeemably tainted by evil ('diabolical' or 'absolute' evil), or whether it is inhabited by 'radical' evil – the ineradicable tendency to do evil despite the concomitant possibility of choosing good. The latter possibility means that humans would be unable to instantiate the (Kantian) moral law *consistently* in the moral actions that issue from the will, notwithstanding their sense of guilt in the face of moral transgressions or their best efforts to conform to this moral law. 'Diabolical evil', in contrast, would entail the ineluctable perpetration of evil deeds, without *any* choice in the matter. Correspondingly, one would have no reason to expect any sign of guilt or remorse on the part of humans capable of such diabolical evil, either. If there were evidence that one has to assume humans[1] incapable of resisting evil, they would be, as Kant (1960: 30) put it, 'devilish' beings. Kant's originality in this regard, Copjec shows (1996:

1 It is conceivable, of course, that one need not choose between these alternatives, namely 'radical' and 'diabolical' evil in a generalized manner, that is, to assume that, all human beings are subject to either the one or the other. It is quite conceivable that some people – those who are susceptible to guilt – are subject to 'radical' evil, while others, presumably those impervious to guilt and remorse, are subject to 'diabolical' evil. I would venture the hypothesis that so-called psychopaths, who are recognizable by various behavioural traits, including the apparent absence of an active conscience or a sense of guilt, are capable of 'diabolical' evil. It is a moot question whether psychopaths are the outcome of 'nature' or 'nurture'. From what I have found in my research, it seems to me that a psychopathic disposition is rooted in the former, namely a genetic condition, which would locate the 'source' of psychopathy in what Lacan (1977: 299–302) calls the 'real', as instantiated in

x–xi), was to depart from the customary view, that evil was nothing real, that it should be conceived of negatively as issuing from the limitations of human understanding or of humanity's inability to resist its own passions. Instead, by linking evil to (historically achieved) freedom, Kant thought of it as something positive (p. xi): '… Kant sees evil as uniquely the product of a free humanity, and it is this which is new in his thought.'

One could take issue with Copjec on whether Kant was indeed the first to attribute positive ontological value to evil – it seems to me that, on this score, Cusanus (Windelband 1958: 335–337; 345–347) preceded Kant in a certain sense. Specifically, Cusanus went against the historical/philosophical grain by arguing that evil should not merely be regarded in privative terms as the absence of good, but should, if God were indeed seen as Creator, be understood as already ('positively') present in the infinite divine itself, albeit as part of a 'coincidence of opposites' that exceeds human cognition. Kant does seem to have added another item to his 'Copernican Revolution', though, by showing that evil, positively conceived, enters the finite realm of history through human freedom. In *Religion within the limits of reason alone* (1960: 50), he remarks:

> To become morally good it is not enough merely to allow the seed of goodness implanted in our species to develop without hindrance; there is also present in us an active and opposing cause of evil to be combatted.

In other words, for Kant – the same thinker who had earlier valorized 'a *good will*' as the only thing in the world ('or even out of it') that may be called good without qualification (1983: 7) – the human will is itself corrupted, and does not merely have to combat human inclinations to do evil, as the Stoics, for example, believed. '… genuine evil consists in this', he says (1960: 51, note), 'that a man does not *will* to withstand those inclinations when they tempt him to transgress – so it is really this disposition that is the true enemy.' Evil is to be sought 'in freedom itself'. One way of putting this is to say, following Derrida (Bennington 1993: 276–277),

---

the human body in so far as it surpasses any symbolic interpretation of it. Cf. in this regard Cornwell 2002: 26–29. Cf. also notes 14 and 18, below.

that for Kant freedom of the will has the status of a 'quasi-transcendental'; it is the condition of the possibility of moral goodness as well as of its impossibility, that is, of evil actions. As Bennington explains: '... in Derrida what makes possible immediately makes impossible the purity of the phenomenon made possible.' As a 'quasi-transcendental' free will, which enables humans to choose what is morally good, also prevents the actualization of 'pure' goodness, or enables one to do evil. In other words, as long as humans are free (and that would be for as long as they are human), evil, as well as good, is a 'real' possibility, or a possibility to be realized, in every situation which requires moral choice (cf. also note 1, below).

Copjec's appropriation of Kant's argument has the purpose of recuperating his ethical insights in the face of various positions which, in their respective readings of Kant or their conceptions of the subject, tend to reduce the latter (erroneously, in her view) to the product of historical circumstance, thus assimilating 'ought' to 'is'. What interests me about her position are its implications for a certain problem that one encounters in the context of Foucault's theory of discourse: his notion of discourse seems to suggest that, because human subjects are discursively constituted, their actions can only be grasped in terms and on the basis of the (historical) discourses that comprise subjects' subjectivity exhaustively. The way I read Copjec's argument, she provides a way out of such a historicist-deterministic discourse-theoretical dilemma by demonstrating that Kant's notion of 'radical evil', because it is predicated on the freedom of human will, posits an ethical subject 'in excess of itself' (1996: xvi). This subject would have access to a quasi-discursive[2] realm, as it were,

2 I use the term 'quasi-' here in conjunction with 'discursive' to suggest something analogous to its function in combination with '(quasi-)transcendental' in Derrida's work, where a whole range of terms, including '*différance*' (as the condition of the possibility *and* the impossibility of meaning) and a 'justice to come' (as the condition of the possibility *and* the impossibility of just actions) may be referred to as having a 'quasi-transcendental' status (Bennington 1993: 276–277). Similarly, by claiming that the 'excessive' subject has access to a 'quasi-discursive' realm or mode of action, I want to suggest that, while I believe that the subject is discursively

that enables it to intervene in the practical functioning of discourses or to confront the effects of (as well as to oppose) those discursive practices that may impel us to act in apparently pre-determined ways. This is important for more than merely 'theoretical' reasons: theory is, in my view, epistemically (if not aesthetically) worthless except when it passes the test of making experience intelligible,[3] whether it is the experience of remorse, cruelty, expiation or (moral) guilt – which, as Copjec reminds us, is the only manifestation of the Kantian 'moral law' to which we are privy. The experience in question here is crime – a particularly violent crime that seems to deserve the epithet 'evil' as much as any instance of virtually incomprehensible cruelty ever has. The question which I will raise concerns the status of the 'evil' perpetrated in this crime, notoriously known as the 'ripper-rapist' case (Thamm 1998). Does it issue from 'radical'

---

constituted, I agree with Kant, Lacan and Copjec that it surpasses the discourses in terms of the convergence of which it is constituted. This is what Copjec means when she talks of a subject 'in excess of itself', which, in turn, corresponds with Kant's notion of the free subject (1960: 51) and Lacan's distinction (1977: 298) – one which also has a recognizable Kantian provenance – between the subject of the enunciation or '*Je*', 'I' (which is always in excess of any qualities or attributes which may be assigned to the concrete self), and the subject of the enunciated (statement) or '*moi*', 'me', (which is precisely the concrete, empirical, identifiable self or ego). Unless one assumes such a quasi-discursive moment on the part of the subject, it would indeed coincide with the discourses by which its subjectivity is structured at any given time, and hence it would be incapable, at any moment, to position itself differently in relation to these, or to appropriate a novel discursive position which may be critical of its own former position(s).

3 It is worth recalling that the term 'theory' is derived from the ancient Greek term *theoros*, which referred to a spectator at a drama or religious festival. The important point is that such an 'onlooker' was not considered to be neutral, but to be a spectator only to the degree that she or he shared or participated in the religious-dramatic events. Analogously, 'theory' is far from neutral – it allows the theoretician to 'participate' in the 'events' (whatever these are called: reality, being, history, etc.) which constitute the focus of theoretical attention. In the process one is enabled to overcome possible epistemic alienation, despite the 'distance' that 'looking on' implies. Importantly, however, it presupposes that the theory in question is suitable for the 'event' or field that one is investigating, just as a *theoros* could fail to do justice to the events confronting her or him (Gadamer 1982: 111).

evil, or from what deserves to be called 'diabolical' evil? And how should one articulate this difference in terms of discourse-theory?

But, before returning to Copjec's argument and its relevance for the criminal case that will be considered here, why should Foucault's notion of discourse be of interest here, in the context of violent criminal actions? The reason is that, for him, 'discourse' denotes the convergence of language, knowledge and power; hence his concept of 'genealogy' as a mode of analysis which focuses on discursive practices with a view to articulating, not simply their 'rules of formation', but more especially the power-relations in which they are embedded (Davidson 1986: 227; Carroll 1987: 107).[4] It follows that such a mode of analysis would enable one to come to grips with the relations of power and knowledge – the discursive terrain – within which certain actions are located, inasmuch as, according to this model, action cannot be separated from knowledge and *vice versa*. Criminal actions are no exception here.

One of the most illuminating instances of such discourse-analytical scrutiny that Foucault (1982) and his seminar group have provided, is a reading of the Pierre Riviere dossier that dates back to 1835. All the court documents pertaining to the appalling multiple murder, by a young peasant, of his mother, brother and sister, are reproduced in the dossier, together with an exceptionally eloquent memoir by Riviere himself (despite his rudimentary education), as well as a number of critical essays by Foucault and members of his group. They showed that Riviere's memoir became a battleground where emerging, competing modern discourses such as the juridical and the psychiatric confronted each other in an attempt to demarcate their respective domains of 'power-knowledge' and establish their own legitimacy (1982: x–xi; Macey 1994: 248; Miller 1994: 225). Regarding Riviere's own act, however, Foucault expressed the discursive link between actions and knowledge as follows (1982: 209):

4 Elsewhere, I have examined the pertinence of Foucault's genealogical model for the understanding of and possible intervention regarding crime. Cf. Olivier 2000 and 2001.

> Riviere, there is little doubt, accomplished his crime at the level of a certain discursive practice and of the knowledge bound up with it. In the inextricable unity of his parricide and his text he *really* played the game of the law, the murder and the memoir ...

Moreover, as the following remark by Edith Kurzweil (reprinted on the back cover of Foucault 1982) testifies, the Riviere case was set in an historical context characterized by major social changes:

> For Foucault, Riviere provides the 'excuse' to examine power structures and social institutions, to question the scientificity of medical science, and to delineate the chaos of values and beliefs, of knowledge and power as it existed 150 years ago – a chaos we have not yet eliminated.

What appears to me to be different today, compared to the early nineteenth century, is that the Riviere case was set at the time when some of the major discursive constituents of modernity were struggling for recognition; a time which had turned (or at least tried to turn) its back on religious 'superstition' (Baumer 1977: 314–323). By contrast, the present, 'postmodern' era, with its proliferation of 'language games', discursive pluralism and cultural eclecticism (Anderson 1996: 1–11), has opened the way once again for the resurrection of discourses that were once discredited by modernity's tendency to organize knowledge exlusively in terms of the three 'rational' spheres of cognition, morality and art (Habermas 1985: 8–9). Hence, the 'eventalization' (Foucault 1988)[5] of the crimes in question by the discourse analyst, today, would seem to be able to draw on a qualitatively different, but also perhaps more complex, multiplicity of forces to uncover their singularity.

In the so-called 'ripper-rapist' case of 1995 (see Appendix to this chapter, p. 27) in Port Elizabeth, the familiar discursive confrontation between the juridical and the psychological is complicated by the emergence of a quasi-religious discourse, namely that of 'satanism' – not simply

5 Foucault's term for the strategy of inscribing one's subject or object of research into as many particular relationships or contexts as possible to achieve an optimal grasp of its specificity.

as a factor for consideration in determining the 'causal' psychological elements relating to the crime of raping and attempting to murder a young woman, 'Alison', but as a premodern (myth-informed) discourse of justification making its claim to legitimacy in the accommodating context of postmodernity. Whether or not the cult of 'satanism', as it is practised in contemporary societies – and there is ample evidence that its practice is widespread (cf. Peters 1994: 2–3) – should be understood as a premodern discourse, as I do here, or whether it is part and parcel of modernity as one of its 'metanarratives' (in Lyotard's sense, in *The postmodern condition* [1984], of a 'grand' discourse of legitimation), or of postmodernity (as one of many competing 'language games', again in the sense that Lyotard gives it), is a matter for debate. It is indeed possible to argue that, in so far as Lyotard regards any grand discourse of (epistemic or ontological) legitimation as 'modern' (1984: xxiii), Christianity, and therefore also satanism as parasitic counter-metanarrative, should count, paradoxically, as 'modern'. However, because modernity is characterized by the collapse of the historically premodern Christian-Platonic value-system, I prefer satanism to be understood, together with many other cultural phenomena ranging from art movements to political ideologies and even a revivalist Christianity itself in multifarious forms (reduced, now, to just another language game among others) as being among the attempts to fill the vacuum left by this collapse.[6] It is therefore possible to think of it as 'premodern' in light of the mythology it draws on, 'modern' as 'counter-metanarrative', while, again paradoxically, it is simultaneously 'postmodern' as a contemporary phenomenon, in so far as postmodernity comfortably accommodates the premodern, the modern, and the post-modern, side by side. This is, after all, part and parcel of the heterogeneity and fragmentation (Jameson 1993: 14) characteristic of postmodernity.

The extent to which satanism already enjoys credibility or a kind of *de facto* legitimacy in South Africa – a country where pre-modernity,

6 I would argue, though, that satanism is too closely tied to the very premodern axiological system – the one that has collapsed, namely Christianity – that made it possible in the first place, to be convincingly treated as a candidate for filling the void left by this collapse. Needless to say, the same goes for Christianity itself.

modernity and postmodernity co-exist in a precarious configuration[7] – is apparent from the fact that an 'expert' witness, Colonel Jonker of the Occult Crime Unit, South African Police Service (1995), testified at length on its characteristics, the strength of its support, the validity of its claims, and so on, at the 'ripper-rapist' trial. One of the two accused (and convicted) rapists and would-be murderers, Frans du Toit, was a self-confessed satanist, who claimed in his testimony (1995: 20, 23) that this allegiance enhanced his sexual potency and that a demon called Incubus – a medieval (!) name for a demon believed to have sexual intercourse with women in their sleep – exercised control over his actions by urging him irresistibly to inflict rape on women. From his testimony, but also from that of two specialist witnesses – Colonel Jonker and a clinical psychologist, Ian Meyer (1995: 65) – it is evident that the satanist discourse belongs in the category of fundamentalist religions or cults.[8]

7 Just how precarious this configuration is, may be gathered from an African provincial minister of security being interviewed on a radio news programme on the topic of graves having been robbed of corpses for 'muti' (medicine-) purposes in South Africa's Northern Province a few years ago. (Local witchdoctors use amputated body parts such as ears, noses and genitals to prepare 'muti' sold to customers who wish to cast spells on their enemies.) In the interview he first reassured the listening public, as any efficient, 'modern' politician should, that there was nothing to be concerned about – the investigation into the grave robberies was proceeding smoothly and the police service had everything under control. Then he added, almost as an afterthought, that, besides, 'muti' only worked when it was made from body parts amputated while the 'donor' was alive – a remark which evinced a conspicuously anomalous, 'premodern' belief in the efficacy of witchcraft. Remarkably, the juxtaposition of these (and other) heterogeneous cultural beliefs makes the whole thing paradigmatically postmodern.

8 It is interesting to note that Hardt and Negri (2001: 146–150) understand the rise of fundamentalist religions as a manifestation of the failure of modernization – an interpretation which seems, on the one hand, to be compatible with my argument in this paper, insofar as I see it as something curiously and atavistically 'premodern' in a postmodern culture, with the complexity of which fundamentalism's adherents cannot cope, and hence flee into the 'simple', 'cut and dried' environment of something like satanism or Islamic fundamentalism. A closer look, however, reveals that they prefer to understand it as being *postmodern* in the sense that, like other forms of postmodernism, it opposes the modern – for them, it is anti-modern

Significantly, as Meyer (p. 65; following Ivey) points out, such 'religions' provide '... unambiguous and simple answers' to the question concerning the meaning of life. Moreover, they provide 'Instant community identity' for alienated or marginalized individuals (p. 65), and satanism, in particular, 'legitimates rebellion against traditional orthodox or authority figures and moral systems' (p. 66).

One notices a parallel, here, between these recorded events in the late twentieth century and certain narrated events in the Riviere case from the early nineteenth century. In his memoir, Riviere remarked (Foucault 1982: 108):

> ... in former times one saw Jaels against Siseras, Judiths against Holoferneses, Charlotte Cordays against Marats; now it must be men who employ this mania, it is the women who are in command now in this fine age which calls itself the age of enlightenment, this nation which seems to be so avid for liberty and glory obeys women, the Romans were far more civilized ... never have they debased strength, it has always been the stronger in body who have laid down the law among themselves. I thought it would be a great glory to me to have thoughts opposed to all my judges, to dispute against the whole world, I conjured up Bonaparte in 1815. I also said to myself: that man sent thousands to their death to satisfy mere caprices, it is not right therefore that I should let a woman live who is disturbing my father's peace and happiness ...

The woman referred to here was his mother, who – as the rest of the memoir testifies – was regarded by him as a tyrant to his father, much to the young Pierre's chagrin. In answer to the question, in court, why he had killed the three members of his family, he maintained (Foucault 1982: 23–24):

'... in its refusal of modernity as a weapon of Euro-American hegemony ...' (p. 149). Because they place it (fundamentalism) in the context of processes of globalization in political, economic and cultural terms, Hardt and Negri's argument will not be pursued further here. Suffice it to say that, for them, postmodernist positions attract those who are 'winners' in terms of globalization, while fundamentalist positions attract those who are the 'losers'.

> … I did it to help my father out of his difficulties. I wished to deliver him from an evil woman who had plagued him continually ever since she became his wife, who was ruining him, who was driving him to … despair … I killed my sister … because she took my mother's part. I killed my brother by reason of his love for my mother and my sister.

Riviere's opinion appears to be corroborated by several of the villagers in the sense that his mother figures as a shrew in their testimony (cf. for example the mayor's, the doctor's and the carpenter's – although it may be significant that these are all male witnesses; Foucault 1982: 24, 25, 27). What is significant, however, is the fact that Riviere perceived his mother, by virtue of his logic of power, as representing a social and political order which had to be challenged to be able to reinstate those more powerful in body. It is important to remember, however – in accordance with Foucault's insight (1982: 209), that Riviere's crime was executed 'at the level of a certain discursive practice and of the knowledge bound up with it' – that questions concerning the 'stronger in body' are intimately tied up with the discursive constitution of subjects. This would prevent one from falling into the trap of naively assuming that deeds such as Riviere's (or Du Toit's and Kruger's) can be adequately understood in isolation from discursive practices, in this way reducing them to their 'symptomatic dimension', and the killers to 'the abstraction of a clinical case' (Peter & Favret 1982: 191).

The parallel in question pertains, therefore, in the first instance to the assumption and therefore the promise of power in and through a certain discursive practice – in Riviere's case that of the 'stronger in body' (with all that it entails), and in the case of the 'ripper-rapists' that of satanism, which promised them sexual and occult power (*Staat teen Du Toit en Kruger*; Meyer 1995: 67; Du Toit 1995: 20). If Riviere gloried prematurely in the thought of being opposed, through his knowing actions, to the whole world, Du Toit and Kruger relished the thought of being empowered, through 'satanic knowledge', to challenge traditional authority in all its guises. This is importantly consonant with Foucault's observation (1980: 105–106) that, while deviant forms of sexuality come into existence simultaneously with and on the same discursive basis as 'normal' ones (and therefore cannot be construed as representing a significant threat to 'normality'), sexuality does indeed constitute one of the sites of resistance to 'power', that is, to dominant discourses. The fact that they would not really pose a threat to established practices, and that they would simply be exchanging subordination to one hierarchical system for another, does not seem to have crossed these two criminals' minds. Given their own alienation from 'normal' society (*Staat teen Du Toit en Kruger*; Meyer 1995: 64–68; Du Toit 1995: 2–6), what seems to have mattered was that satanist practices and beliefs sanctioned their defiance of orthodoxy. In its most extreme form this defiance manifested itself as coercive power over their victim(s), the representatives of traditional society – a power that was experienced by them as being inseparable from their satanistic commitment, their 'contract' with the demonic.[9]

One could argue that, by treating satanistic practices seriously, the juridical as well as the scientific-psychological discourse gave it a measure of credibility, even renewed factual, if not normative legitimacy – a 'legitimacy' that it would be denied by the modern or Enlightenment discourse of rationality, but which (as I argued earlier), has been made possible by the pluralistic discursive space of postmodernity. It is important to note, however, that in this court battle legal and psychological discourses persistently denied satanism *de jure* status (cf. Advocate Buchler's remark in the evidence of Jonker 1995: 29).[10] The simultaneous treatment of satanism as something that has to be taken seriously as a factor in human motivation, that is, granted a certain credibility, *and* as something which should be denied normative standing, therefore has the effect of rendering it

9 Du Toit was convicted and sentenced to life-imprisonment on multiple counts of rape as well as on charges of indecent assault and attempted murder; Kruger on one of rape as well as indecent assault and attempted murder (Thamm 1998: 158, 188).

10 Whether this exclusion of the satanic from the normative domain will continue successfully in the multicultural space of postmodernity is an interesting question, if one considers Paul Feyerabend's exhaustively argued claim that there should be no epistemic differentiation between science, voodoo, magic and witchcraft. Cf. Feyerabend 1980: 50, 298–299.

undecidable to a certain degree, and of exacerbating or complicating the axiological 'chaos' alluded to by Kurzweil (quoted earlier).

One should add to this the fact that, from both Jonker's (1995: 7) as well as Du Toit's (1995: 2–10) evidence it is apparent that satanism has a relatively large following in South Africa, suggesting an axiological-cultural situation of severe alienation[11] or what Durkheim called *anomie* (Baumer 1977: 395). After all, given that the satanist discourse is one of extreme opposition to the *status quo*, especially in so far as the latter represents (parental) authority in various guises, and that it displays a quasi-religious, and therefore ideological nature (in Thompson's [1990: 56] sense of 'meaning in the service of power or relations of domination'), it embodies a complete rejection of those values which, psychologically speaking, members of 'mainstream' society have 'internalized' (cf. the evidence of Meyer 1995: 67). Add to this the consideration that, like fundamentalist religions, it provides '... unambiguous and simple answers' (Meyer 1995: 65) to questions or problems in a social and cultural situation which has become unmanageably complex to many people (cf. Meyer 1995: 81), then the force of its attraction is more easily comprehensible. The distribution of satanistic 'cells' over many parts of South Africa therefore reflects a cultural, or more specifically, an axiological crisis of sorts – one which may be expected to be manifested in conflicting discursive practices that, parallel to the Riviere case, have the appearance of battles or struggles over meaning, as the 'ripper-rapist' trial testifies.

What constituted the 'ripper-rapist' case, then? Where did the cross-fire within which it took shape, issue from? The curiously anachronistic, and yet apparently newly credible satanistic discourse was certainly a major constituent, issuing from both Colonel Jonker's 'authoritative' testimony

11 A defensible alternative view is that, instead of alienation, it reflects the fragmentation (Jameson 1993: 14–16) typical of postmodernity, in so far as the human subject is not so much alienated from an indifferent world and from other subjects, but rather that it is scattered over disjointed, fragmented 'feelings' or 'intensities' which display a 'free-floating' character. There is evidence in the court transcripts used for the present analysis that the two convicted rapists drifted from one 'intensity' (such as drug use or rape) to another.

as well as from that of Du Toit as discursive subject; but, moreover, also from the testimony of Meyer, the psychologist, although it is here subordinated to the evaluative scrutiny of the scientific psychological discourse. While Du Toit (1995: 20) as subject of satanistic discourse could boast that (my translation): 'The Incubus [demon] enabled me to make good love (make love well?); I would be attractive to the female sex, which was indeed the case because I never had a shortage of girls'; psychology construed the rapists' contract with the demonic along the axes of scientific categories. These included a 'Psychosocial Predisposition to Satanic Involvement', 'pre-satanism', as well as predispositional factors such as 'lack of cohesive identity' and 'pathogenic familial interaction' (Meyer 1995: 64–65), in this way paving the way for the more encompassing and telling categories of 'defective self-structure', 'chronic lack of self-esteem' (p. 68) and 'Borderline Personality Disorder' (p. 81; categories that were applied to Kruger). Psychological discourse – which is, after all, an exemplary 'modern' discourse – could thus by implication relativize the epistemic value of the satanistic discourse as articulated under the aegis of self-understanding and -justification by Du Toit, were it not for the credulity displayed towards it (the satanistic) by Colonel Jonker's quasi-legal, pseudo-psychological, 'expert' account of this cultic phenomenon (1995: 5; my translation):

> Your Honour, you know me ... I was in Murder and Robbery Branch for years: I used to go only by reality. But the last three years things have happened in front of me, too ... then you see the reality of it, that Satan is a reality as I am standing here in the dock and as God is too.

The *de facto* credibility – if not *de jure* legitimacy – bestowed on the satanistic in this way, despite the suspicion cast on it by psychology forging a link between the satanists' behaviour and a disorder of some kind, therefore has the effect of constituting the crime (rape and attempted murder) as a multi-layered, bizarre event. Culpability – while assumed or maintained by the judge in his verdict and sentence of the accused – may nevertheless seem to slip somewhere through the cracks between personal volition and the sway of a trans-individual, premodern, mythical discourse over individual actions. The question is therefore threefold:

first, it concerns the culpability of the two convicted rapists; second, the related question of the 'evil' of their deed(s) – was it 'radical', chosen, or 'diabolical', inevitable? And third: how are their deeds connected with discourse?

Discourse and agency

There is the rub, after all: if human subjectivity is indeed discursively constituted – if we, as one of the cardinal insights on the part of discourse theorists indicates, do not only speak, but 'are spoken' by the discourses which constitute our subjectivity (cf. e.g. Derrida 1973: 145) – is it far-fetched to understand actions like those of Du Toit and Kruger (but also everyday, 'normal' actions on the part of most people) as being performed under the sway or in the grip of discourses which 'speak' us?[12] This would have far-reaching implications for culpability, an issue which unavoidably obtrudes itself at this point, regardless of so-called 'extenuating circumstances'. I would argue, however, that anyone (including Du Toit or Kruger), who is an agent of the 'logic' of a certain discourse, is not for that reason exempted from responsibility for his/her actions, with the important proviso that such a person shows him- or herself as being susceptible to guilt or remorse (the signs of an active conscience). Whatever the specific character of the multiple discourses – such as legal, economic, educational, gender-, political and cultural – by which our subjectivities are constructed, they are bound to include the moral discourse

12 A particularly striking instance of a theoretical stance which seems to me to stress the extent to which one underestimates the force with which humans are 'spoken' by the discourses – and here specifically the discourses of law, or legal discourses, and of institutions – by which subjects' subjectivity is structured, is that of the French psychoanalytic and legal theorist, Pierre Legendre. Cf. the important text which introduces his work to English readers, *Law and the unconscious: A Legendre reader* (1997).

of 'free will' in various guises, whether it is in the language of personal choice, of decision, responsibility, accountability or some other notion which presupposes freedom of volition (cf. for example the invocation of this discourse in terms of 'decision of will' ['wilsbesluit'] in Jonker 1995: 12–13). As such, these volitional discursive spaces provide a foothold, at least potentially, from which a dominant discourse (such as satanism, or patriarchy) may be challenged and/or defused by the very subject who enacts its 'logic' or functions as the agent of its power. As Foucault puts it (1990: 84): 'There is no power without potential refusal or revolt'. Moreover, as intimated at the outset of this paper, I agree with Copjec (1996: xvi), Silverman (1992: 2) and other psychoanalytic theorists that the human psyche is always more than or 'in excess' of the 'vehicle[s]' – such as discourses – by which it is 'inserted' into reality.

The important question that obtrudes itself here is nevertheless one alluded to at the beginning of this paper. It concerns the adequacy of the Foucaultian discursive model: Does the claim that Riviere's deeds as well as deeds like those of the 'ripper-rapists' are indissolubly bound up with the discursive constitution of the agents in question, convincingly show that, at the level of perpetration, deed, 'knowledge', subjectivity and agency form a continuum? Even if, as I argued earlier, subjects are never exclusively constituted by one discourse, in this way enabling them to draw on intersecting alternative or counter-discourses which allow them to escape the straitjacket of monodiscursive determination, is it sufficient to escape the conclusion of discursive determinism of a more encompassing kind, which effectively prevents subjects from 'positioning' themselves vis-á-vis the discourses that 'claim' them?

Foucault's notion of the 'pastoral' may add a much needed explanatory moment here. In John Forrester's (1997) insightful assessment of Foucault's attempt to trace the emergence of the modern individual, he demonstrates that 'the pastoral' functioned as a kind of bridging concept between the notion of power-knowledge as constitutive of the subject (which I have focused on here) and traditional political theory. Succinctly stated, Foucault contended that the political model inherited from the Greeks – pertaining to the public relationship between citizens and the polis or state – was incapable of providing guidance regarding a different form of power, namely the relationship of state care for individuals (Forrester 1997: 123–124). This required a different model, introduced to the west by the Hebrews, namely the 'pastoral', that is, the image of a shepherd guarding over and caring for the well-being of its flock. The crucial moment of this model is that each individual in the 'flock' only becomes what it is in and through the caring bestowed on it by the 'shepherd'. It is therefore a model of 'positive', as opposed to 'negative' power, and emphasises individualisation (Foucault, quoted in Forrester 1997: 124):

> This form of power is salvation orientated (as opposed to political power). It is oblative or altruistic (as opposed to the principle of sovereignty); it is individualising (as opposed to legal power); it is coextensive and continuous with life; it is linked with a production of truth – the truth of the individual himself.

As Forrester points out, this contrast between political and pastoral power is easily integrated with the rest of Foucault's work on the period from the eighteenth century on (p. 124). In fact, although the Christian church, according to Foucault, embodied pastoral power through practices such as spiritual exercises and confession, it was only in the modern era with its urban cultures that the pastoral appeared fully fledged: the modern states, according to Foucault (quoted in Forrester 1997: 125; cf. Foucault 1990: 71–72), 'combine[d] those two games – the city-citizen game and the shepherd-flock game …' Moreover, the 'elements' of the latter game 'are life, death, truth, obedience, individuals, self-identity …' Crucially, in modern states pastoral power was no longer the exclusive domain of the church; it was diffused throughout society in '… a series of powers: those of family, medicine, psychiatry, education, and employers' (Foucault, quoted in Forrester 1997: 126). In this way, Forrester shows (p. 126), the modern individual is linked to those 'closed institutions' on which Foucault's work focuses, such as the hospital and the prison. Interestingly, Forrester takes Foucault's contrast between 'open' institutions (the market, law, the state) and 'closed' institutions (schools, the military, etc.) further by contrasting (pp. 127–128) 'two different sorts of modern individuals: open individuals, participants in civic society, atomised property-holders and taxpayers; and closed individuals, with private lives, secrets of the soul, inner sensibilities and thoughts'. While liberal political theory concerns itself with the open, public individual, the 'closed individuals' that emerge in Foucault's genealogies (listed by Forrester 1997: 128; cf. also Foucault 1980: 39–49), include: 'the child, the pervert, the hysterical woman, the madman, the Romantic genius, the dandy, and the most private and quintessentially modern individual of all, the fantasising masturbator'. Finally, although their genealogies are separate, according to Foucault, open (or public) and closed individuals interact in complex and historically contingent ways (Forrester 1997: 128).

Does this notion of 'pastoral power' cast any light on the question of agency? If we consider the incomprehensibly violent acts performed by Du Toit and Kruger in relation to especially the woman called Alison, could one not discern in them the manifestations of 'identities' forged in the crucible of satanistic 'pastoral' relationships of authority and obedience[13] that produced 'closed' individuals of a certain kind – the kind that would assert their 'pastorally' shaped selves by way of transferring their masturbatory fantasies to a suitable object (cf. Du Toit 1995: 22–23)? Do their actions, constituted as criminal acts in the force-field of countervailing discourses, not exemplify the problem which, according to Foucault, had preoccupied him from his earliest work on insanity, namely (1990: 71):

> ... the relations between experiences (like madness, illness, transgression of laws, sexuality, self-identity), knowledge (like psychiatry, medicine, criminology, sexology, psychology), and power (such as the power which is wielded in psychiatric and penal institutions, and in all other institutions which deal with individual control).

13 Evidence of this is found in Alison Collier's (1995: 14) testimony on the discussion by Du Toit and Kruger of different options concerning the question, what to do with her after having raped her: 'Then they also mentioned what would old Nick want us to do with her ... I knew then that Old Nick is another name for Satan, and the answer to that question was that he would want us to kill her ...' Clearly, authority was vested in the mythical figure of Satan, represented by the hierarchy of satanistic followers, to whose 'pastoral' guidance and teachings Du Toit and Kruger owed obedience.

I cannot – nor could anyone – single out conclusively the discursive, pastorally engendered threads of individual subjectivities that were instrumental in moving Du Toit and Kruger to their violent (some would prefer to say 'evil') deeds. What Foucault's pastoral-discursive model enables one to grasp, however, is that their 'transgression of laws', their crimes, cannot be divorced from the productive discursive nexus of language and power-knowledge, itself produced by 'pastoral' relationships of individualising, subordinating and identifying. This is the case even if these (satanistic) relationships were 'counter-productive' in the sense of simultaneously depending upon and opposing the network of dominant or traditional relations of power-knowledge centred around institutions like schools, churches, the military, and so on. Nor should we forget that Foucault (1990: 71) insisted that western 'societies proved to be really demonic since they happened to combine those two games – the city-citizen game and the shepherd-flock game ...' 'Demonic' is the apposite term here, no doubt, issuing as it does from a complex interplay of 'political' and 'pastoral' powers – in so far as the political ultimately concerns the relations of unity or disunity between citizens and the state, and the pastoral pertains to the 'technology of power' which, in the exchange between individuals and their authorities or mentors, as well as between individuals and 'themselves', produces identities or subjectivities.

The problem concerning the status of the crime in question may therefore be phrased in different ways. One could ask whether one should see in the actions of Du Toit and Kruger the outcome of the hold that a pastorally cultivated (counter-) discourse had on them, or one could inquire if their deeds were the expression of an 'intrinsic' or 'diabolical' kind of evil – one that somehow pre-empts all moral choice. Here one should recall Copjec's (1996: xiv) reminder that Kant regarded this as being impossible for humankind, who characteristically acknowledges the non-universalizability of evil deeds, even in the case of the perpetrators themselves when they affirm their own culpability.[14] Recall that instead

14 I am well aware that this statement opens up a can of worms, so to speak, in so far as violent crimes or 'evil deeds' are sometimes attributed to individuals who, for some or other reason, don't show a sense of guilt or remorse (and that Du

Kant imputed to humankind a 'radical evil', which manifests itself in actions that are freely chosen, and *always* remains a possibility. To see in the actions of these two criminals the embodiment of irredeemably devilish evil would seem to ignore the moment of 'excess' (on which freedom is predicated) in their subjective make-up, which might have enabled them to refrain from these actions.[15] In terms of discourse, on the other hand,

---

Toit and Kruger felt such remorse is by no means clear) – who, in short, don't seem to have a 'conscience' (as psychopaths are sometimes described). It seems to follow, therefore, that some people do not exhibit precisely those characteristics that would qualify them as morally accountable, 'free' human beings. But – and here's the rub – unless this absence of guilt, or of a conscience, is demonstrably rooted in the (Lacanian) 'real' of the symbolically unsaturated body (whether this be articulated in genetic or in other terms), such individuals may be described as morally 'damaged' human beings, where some set of experiences may be uncovered which prevented him or her from developing a conscience, or, in Freudian terms, a superego. In cases where one is led to conclude that genetic factors are *causally* linked to criminal (or 'evil') deeds, however, it seems to me that it would be misleading to refer to such individuals as morally 'damaged' human beings, because they could not be said to be free and hence could not be deemed capable of 'evil' deeds of the 'radical' evil variety, either, because that would presuppose freedom of will. On the other hand, the evil they do would resort under the rubric of 'diabolical' evil. Cf. in this regard the important study by Andrea Hurst, *Killer in our midst*, Parts 1 & 2 (2003 & 2003a), where she approaches a serial killer's deeds in terms of the question raised in the press: is he 'sick or evil?' Cf. also notes 1, above, and 18, below.

15 It is noteworthy that a recent *film noir* – *Minority Report* – directed by Steven Spielberg, is predicated on this Kantian notion of 'radical evil', which presupposes a morally free subject through whom evil enters the world as a positive phenomenon, as explained by Copjec. In this futuristic neo-*noir*, a 'pre-crime' unit of the police prevents murders by following the clues provided by three 'pre-cognitives' – clairvoyants who 'dream' the future – and arresting the would-be perpetrators of the killings *before* they happen. The head of the unit, Captain John Anderton (Tom Cruise), is implicated in such a 'pre-cognized' murder, and in an effort to prove his innocence, has no choice but to seek out his would-be victim, and, confronting him (and this is the point), exercise his freedom of choice by *not* committing the murder. Needless to say, he confirms his moral status as a free individual (although the would-be victim dies in the process anyway). The mastermind behind this, who further happens to be the murderer of two other people, confirms the

humans are thus conceivable as beings who are never the mere functionaries of the discursive imperatives to whose authority they have submitted (except in those cases which I refer to in note 14). Criticising the later Foucault[16] for what she terms his 'historicist ... reduction of society to its indwelling network of relations of power and knowledge' (Copjec 1995: 6) – another way of formulating the claim that social agents are merely the functionaries of discursive imperatives – Copjec puts this insight as follows (1995: 7): 'Yet some notion of transcendence is plainly needed if one is to avoid the reduction of social space to the relations that fill it'. (This restates what she says elsewhere [1996: xvi], citing Kant, about the subject being 'in excess' of itself, to account for freedom of choice.)

And yet, a close reading of the court transcripts pertaining to the 'ripper-rapist' case shows, I believe, that one has grounds for challenging Kant (1960: 31) regarding his claim that the general affirmation of culpability on the part of perpetrators of wickedness proves that 'diabolical evil' is out of the question, humanly speaking. In discursive terms, it

---

'minority report' (that the future is not absolutely predictable for humans; not even by clairvoyants or technology – a theme that also features in another neo-*noir* film, *Terminator II – Judgement Day*) by also contradicting a pre-cognition by the three clairvoyants or 'pre-cogs' when he turns his revolver on himself in the end instead of shooting Anderton (as the pre-cogs predicted he would). These two neo-*noir* films, at least, seem to me to be underpinned by the principle that evil is not predetermined, but enters the world through freely chosen human actions. There are other *films noirs*, however, including Polanski's *Chinatown* and *The 9th Gate*, which evince a belief in 'diabolical evil'. Cf. Olivier 2004 in this regard.

16 While I think one cannot argue against Copjec with regard to the instances she points to on the later Foucault's part (*Discipline and punish*, *The history of sexuality*, etc.; cf. Copjec 1995: 4) where he (questionably) appears to be claiming that the subject of discourse is at any given time coterminous with the discourses or power-relations which comprise a society – keeping in mind that she does not claim that this is the case throughout his work – I believe that even in his later work he sometimes puts forward a notion of the subject which exempts him from this charge. I am thinking especially of his views in Vol. 3 of *The history of sexuality* concerning the care of the self by the self (Foucault 1988a: 39–67), which seems to me to be unthinkable without a conception of a 'divided' subject, or one characterized by a moment of excess.

would mean that Kant did not think it was possible for humans to be unilaterally 'spoken' by discourse (to the point of performing evil deeds), nor did he seem to grant that some criminals deny (or at least do not affirm) culpability. I would argue that the following is, at least, a claim on the part of Du Toit to being subject to such discursive determinism (or inescapability of 'diabolical evil') and concomitantly an implicit denial of culpability (1995: 20–21; my translation):

> ... it was also a short time afterwards that I started getting these terrible urges; the Incubus [medieval sex demon] which told me in my head what I should do and I am absolutely powerless against what he says to me ... I was absolutely powerless against these urges which he put in my head. At times I could really hear him talk in my head and he did say to me, I want you to go and rape someone for me ...

To be sure, it could be that Du Toit is here merely 'passing the buck', so to speak, in order to fool the court into believing that he could not be held accountable (something Alison suspected; Thamm 1998: 182). But it is also conceivable that this 'discourse of powerlessness' in the face of a superior power evinces an inability to challenge a dominant discourse, that is, allowing oneself to be spoken by it (cf. Olivier 2001). And, given that rape and murder are sanctioned by this discourse, is that not an avowal of the absence of guilt (and hence of free will), in other words, of the sway of 'diabolical evil' on his part? Recall that, for Kant, the moral law only manifests itself negatively, that is, in the form of the moral feeling of guilt (Copjec 1996: xiv–xvi; Kant 1960: 31, 66). These are difficult judgements to make, but it does seem to me significant that several witnesses, as well as the judge in the case, remarked on the fact that the two accused did not show any sense of guilt or remorse, or displayed a 'lack of conscience', in Judge Jansen's words (Thamm 1998: 105, 177, 187). One could easily infer that Du Toit and Kruger are psychopaths with no 'moral capacity' because they showed no sign of remorse or guilt[17] (cf. Cornwell

17 It is interesting to note (Marsh 1999: 17) that serial killers are usually men who do not show any signs of a conscience either, and whose deeds would therefore also appear to fall into the category of 'diabolical evil'. Although one could not know this with certainty, it may be significant that Du Toit and Kruger had planned

2002: 26–29), were it not for evidence that satanism actively discourages guilt (Meyer 1995: 67) on the part of Satan-worshippers, and hence that their lack of remorse was merely a function of their satanistic pastoral-discursive subjectivization.

To summarize, one may conclude that the upshot of the preceding investigation or argument consists in acknowledging that, contrary to what Kant believed, there appear to be instances of both 'radical', freely chosen evil and of 'diabolical', compulsive, ineluctable evil on the part of human agents, although it is difficult to say with clarity what motivates the actions of the latter. It seems to me that, in a certain sense, such individuals do not have freedom of (moral) choice. In terms of discourse theory, they are invariably 'spoken' by discourse(s), unlike 'free' individuals who *sometimes* 'allow themselves' to be 'spoken' by discourse(s), and *sometimes* position themselves critically or questioningly within a discourse or from the perspective of another discourse in a manner which instantiates their freedom from unilateral discursive domination. I have pointed to the significance of conscience, remorse and guilt as indicators of moral capacity in this respect, as well as to the possibility that the absence of guilt may be rooted in the (Lacanian) 'real' of the symbolically unsaturated body (cf. notes 1 and 14).[18] In order to pre-empt possible objections to the effect that I am here (supposedly) putting forward an argument in favour of what is sometimes referred to as 'linguistic determinism', suffice it to stress, once again, that having investigated such a possibility,

---

to kill another woman the day after they had raped Alison and left her for dead (Thamm 1998: 176).

18 It should be added, though, that another possibility is that deeds which seemingly stem from 'diabolical' evil may in fact issue from the failure on the part of the subject to develop a conscience, for instance because of traumatic experience(s). Marsh (1999: 17) refers to this as a factor in serial killing. In terms of Lacanian psychoanalytic theory it could then be said that trauma leads, not merely to repression, but to 'foreclosure' in the sense of the complete rejection of the traumatic event by the psyche, with the result that its effect registers only as a physical or somatic phenomenon, for example the compulsive 'enactment' of nonsensical behaviour such as murder or mutilation. Cf. in this regard Benvenuto & Kennedy 1986: 151–153; Olivier 1998: 137–138.

I have pointed to evidence that *one* of the possible grounds for action on the part of perpetrators of 'evil' deeds does seem to fall into this category. This would correspond to what Kant termed 'diabolical evil'. On the other hand, however, the investigation has also adduced evidence, I believe, that although one's actions may sometimes (or even most of the time) be consistent with the axiological priorities embedded in a particular, 'dominant', discourse, there is room for taking a stand against such a discourse in counter-discursive fashion. This would correspond to something related to what Kant termed 'radical evil', namely freedom of the will, which (as far as moral choice is concerned) entails that one may choose against evil on particular occasions, despite the impossibility of eradicating the likelihood of doing evil once and for all. In a nutshell: Kant's distinction between two types of evil focuses one's attention on *two* possible 'grounds of action', only *one* of which presupposes freedom. This is as much as saying that it seems to me a mistake to believe that *all* individuals are morally free. There is no contradiction here. In terms of discourse theory, some individuals (including those who are termed 'psychopaths') seem to be the mere instruments of the discourse(s) which has (have) decisively shaped their subjectivity,[19] while others, presumably the vast majority of the human race, are capable of 'freely' taking a stand against (even) those dominant discourses.

Before concluding, however, one should not overlook a certain irony which operates here, in the ripper-rapist case as well as in that of Pierre Riviere. Peter and Favret articulate it as follows (1982: 191):

> To his father, who played in good faith, but blindly, at a fallacious emancipation by collecting plots of land, Pierre Riviere wished to oppose, at the cost of his life, the radical violence of the liberated word. He would have chosen rightly if, in so doing, he had not happened to cut down his mother and his sister, two other rebels, engaged in the same confused struggle for emancipation, women desper-

19 See in this regard my 'Discourse, space and violence' (Olivier 2001), for another discourse-theoretical investigation – this time in relation to two criminal cases where men murdered women – into the phenomenon of 'being spoken by' discourse, the discourse in question here being patriarchy.

> ate to undermine from one side (their own) an unjust order at which Pierre was aiming from the other.

Similarly, in their criminal 'revolt' against traditional society, Du Toit and Kruger aimed their destructive activity at women, the very people who have every reason to exert their energies towards the transformation (if not the subversion) of traditional, *patriarchal* society (Olivier 2001). It is an interesting question, whether an alliance between them and their victims in this regard would be precluded by their own possible complicity with patriarchal practices within satanistic discourse, or whether the latter accords women (in the guise of 'witches') a position that is incompatible with patriarchy, in this way allowing for an alliance of sorts. Whatever the answer to this may be, it appears that a discourse-analytical approach to documents pertaining to crime in South Africa uncovers – or perhaps: reconstructs – a social space fraught with tensions between divergent, competing discursive practices; a social space so precarious that it seems, at times, to approach a condition of 'meltdown'.

It is worth noting that Susan Faludi's book, *Stiffed: The betrayal of the American man* (1999a) enables one to place the preceding analysis in a broader social context that is compatible with it – one which combines Copjec's work on Kant's notion of 'radical evil' with Foucault's notions of discourse, power and the pastoral in an attempt to arrive at an understanding of the motive forces behind the terrible crime committed by the 'ripper rapists'. On the basis of six years' work aimed at unravelling the reasons for the perceived crisis of masculinity in the United States, Faludi argues that it flows from the inability of men, today, to find or experience their masculinity in terms derived from the ideal image bequeathed to them by their World War II and Korean war veteran fathers, who won and safeguarded the world for them, but could not foresee the emergence of a culture that would double-cross them by failing to honour these traditional codes of manhood. While the enemy and what it represented had been clear in those wars, the Vietnam War was marked by no such clarity or victory from which clarity could be reconstructed. Instead it was marked by moral obscurity and collective-psychological confusion, reflected on US soil by rebellion and social upheavals. These, while bringing indisputable gains in the realm of civil and women's rights, further dented the traditional image of 'the man' as someone who, above all, should be 'in control', even if this required the violent exertion of such control.

Faludi's odyssey to find the soul of the American male took her to everything from woman-batterer rehabilitation groups and terrorist militiamen to the Promise Keepers and the media domains of 'commodified' manhood. One encounter with a woman batterer gave her a significant clue: in the course of being counselled, following initial denials and an insistence that the assault on his girlfriend had been the result of loss of control, he finally reversed this testimony and admitted, on the contrary, that it had provided him with the rare, if fleeting, experience of being in control, of feeling powerful – but only '"until they put the cuffs on"'. Faludi's comment on this incident gives one an important indication concerning the grounds of so much violent behaviour on the part of contemporary men – including the ripper-rapists (1999a: 9):

> He was typical in this regard. The men I got to know in the group had, without exception, lost their compass in the world. They had lost or were losing jobs, homes, cars, families. They had been labeled outlaws but felt like castoffs ... There was something almost absurd about these men struggling, week after week, to recognize themselves as dominators when they were so clearly dominated, done in by the world.[20]

In Foucaultian discursive terms, the crisis regarding 'masculine identity' in the US therefore derives from the fact that the formative male discourse of power and control (which is at the basis of traditional patriarchy, and

20 Although this is not the place to pursue the issue, it is interesting that Faludi (1999a: 3–47) identifies the sources of the disempowerment of contemporary men not by pointing to the women's movement (as some commentators argue), but to the 'ornamental culture' spawned by multinational corporations in whose interest it is, for example, to promote the politically powerless (and communally irrelevant) 'cool look' of designer clothes and accessories. The neo-*noir* film, *Fight Club*, seems to me to be a highly significant instance of a popular cultural artifact which registers this 'castration effect' of the 'ornamental culture', on the one hand, and, in fictional terms, the violent shape of a possible rebellion against it on the part of men.

was given a specific historical configuration by the collective image of the generation of men who fought in the Second World War), no longer applies across the board in the contemporary world, although it has shaped the identities of the vast majority of men who live in this world. (And it should be clear from what was said earlier that this applies to South Africa as well, although the social and political reasons are different here.) Is it at all surprising that these men find themselves in a condition of crisis? As Faludi (1999: 58) points out, the only effective way to deal with this, would be for men to realize that '… their task is not, in the end, to figure out how to be masculine – rather, their masculinity lies in figuring out how to be human'. This does not have to mean being permanently disempowered, but it does entail facing the question of articulating power differently – as she found, for instance, in the case of the many men she encountered who '… were seeking something worthwhile to do. Their sense of their own manhood flowed out of their utility in a society, not the other way around' (p. 58).

Faludi thus enables one to see the ripper-rapist case as just one of many criminal cases that are symptomatic of the fact that men – in South Africa, as in other parts of the world – are currently experiencing themselves as being disempowered, that is, as losing or having already lost the discursive power that traditionally came with being male and that required a specific, 'dominating' way of behaving. As a result, in an attempt to regain power, men are turning in divergent directions – some violent and/or reactionary, some progressive and salutary (like those trying to reconfigure their masculinity in novel, socially constructive ways), and some grotesquely, violently criminal, like that chosen by Du Toit and Kruger.

Appendix: The crime

An outline of the crime which constituted the event on which the ripper-rapist case was based would facilitate an understanding of the discourse-analysis pertaining to it. The woman named Alison was accosted by Frans Du Toit in her own car in front of her apartment in Port Elizabeth in the early morning hours of December 18, 1994, after she had taken a friend home. He forced his way into her car by threatening her with a knife, drove to a nightclub in the vicinity of which he picked up Theuns Kruger and then drove to a deserted spot called Noordhoek along the coast about 10 kilometres out of Port Elizabeth. There both of them raped her, then Du Toit strangled her and, in an effort to make sure that she was dead, they stabbed her in the abdomen multiple times before cutting her throat almost from ear to ear – in the process slicing her thyroid in two and severing all the main veins, but (fortunately for Alison) none of the main arteries. After they had left her lying on the ground (evidently believing she was dead) among the bushes, Du Toit and Kruger drove off in her car. Eventually she summoned up sufficient strength to drag herself to the road, where two cars eventually stopped, one of the passengers phoned the police and an ambulance, and she was finally taken to hospital, where an emergency operation was performed on her. The surgeon who performed the operation later testified in court that the severity of her injuries was such that he had doubted whether she would survive. But she did, miraculously, and testified in court during Du Toit and Kruger's trial. Two young women who had been raped by them before their attack on Alison also testified at the trial. The two men were both sentenced to life-imprisonment, without parole. For a fairly detailed account of this event, including the subsequent trial, see Thamm 1998.

References

Anderson,W.T. (ed.). 1996. 'Introduction: What's going on here?' *The Fontana postmodernism reader*. London: Fontana, pp. 1–11.

Baumer, F.L. 1977. *Modern European thought*. New York: MacMillan.

Bennington, G. 1993. *Derridabase*. In: Derrida, J., & Bennington, G. *Jacques Derrida*. Trans. Bennington, G. Chicago: The University of Chicago Press.

Benvenuto, B. & Kennedy, R. 1986. *The works of Jacques Lacan: An introduction*. London: Free Association Books.

Copjec, J. 1995. *Read my desire. Lacan against the historicists*. Cambridge, Mass.: The MIT Press.

Copjec, J. 1996. 'Introduction: Evil in the finite time of the world'. In: Copjec, J. (ed.) *Radical evil*. London: Verso, pp. vii–xxviii.

Cornwell, P. 2002. *Portrait of a killer*. London: Little, Brown.

Davidson, A.I. 1986. 'Archaeology, genealogy, ethics'. In: Hoy, D.C. *Foucault – A critical reader*. Oxford: Basil Blackwell, pp. 221–233.

Derrida, J. 1973. '*Differance*'. In: *Speech and phenomena and other essays on Husserl's theory of signs*. Evanston: Northwestern University Press, pp. 129–160.

'Du Toit se getuienis; Jonker se getuienis; Alison Jane Collier se getuienis; Meyer se getuienis' (Du Toit's, Jonker's, Collier's and Meyer's evidence). 1995. In: *Staat teen A. F. Du Toit en T. Kruger*. Port Elizabeth: Sneller Transkripsies.

Faludi, S. 1999. 'The betrayal of the American man'. *Newsweek*, September 13, pp. 48–58.

Faludi, S. 1999a. *Stiffed: The betrayal of the American man*. New York: William Morrow & Company, Inc.

Feyerabend, P. 1980. *Against method*. London: Verso.

Forrester, J. 1997. 'Foucault, power-knowledge and the individual'. In: Mouton, J. & Muller, J. (eds), *Knowledge, method and the public good*. Pretoria: HSRC Publishers, pp. 113–136.

Foucault, M. 1980. *The history of sexuality, Vol. 1: An introduction*. Trans. Hurley, R. New York: Vintage Books.

Foucault, M. (ed.). 1982. *I, Pierre Riviere, having slaughtered my mother, my sister, and my brother. A case of parricide in the 19th century*. Trans. Jellinek, F. London: Bison Books.

Foucault, M. 1982. 'Afterword: The subject and power'. In: Dreyfus, H.L. & Rabinow, P. *Michel Foucault: Beyond structuralism and hermeneutics*. Chicago: The University of Chicago Press, pp. 208–226.

Foucault, M. 1982. 'Tales of murder'. In: *I, Pierre Riviere, having slaughtered my mother, my sister, and my brother. A case of parricide in the 19th century*. Trans. Jellinek, F. London: Bison Books, pp. 199–212.

Foucault, M. 1984. 'Truth and power'. In: Rabinow, P., *The Foucault Reader*. New York: Pantheon Books, pp. 51–75.

Foucault, M. 1988. 'Questions of method: An interview with Michel Foucault'. In: Baynes, K. *et al.* (eds), *After philosophy – End or transformation*? Cambridge, Mass.: MIT Press, pp. 100–117.

Foucault, M. 1988a. *The care of the self. The history of sexuality, Vol. 3*. Trans. Hurley, R. New York: Vintage Books.

Foucault, M. 1990. 'Politics and reason'. In: Kritzman, L.D. (ed.), *Michel Foucault: Politics, philosophy, culture. Interviews and other writings 1977–1984*. New York: Routledge, pp. 57–85.

French, M. 1986. *Beyond power – On women, men & morals*. London: Abacus.

Gadamer, H.-G. 1982. *Truth and method*. Trans. & ed. Barden, G. & Cumming, J. New York: Crossroad.

Habermas, J. 1985. 'Modernity: An incomplete project'. In: Foster, H. (ed.), *The anti-aesthetic: Essays on postmodern culture*. Port Townsend: Bay Press, pp. 3–15.

Hardt, M., & Negri, A. 2001. *Empire*. Cambridge, Mass.: Harvard University Press.

Hurst, A. 2003. 'Killer in our midst: Part One'. *South African Journal of Philosophy*, 22 (4): pp. 291–307.

Hurst, A. 2003a. 'Killer in our midst: Part Two'. *South African Journal of Philosophy*, 22 (4): pp. 308–328. A shorter philosophical account and interpretation of the serial murder in question has appeared as Hurst, A. 2002. 'Self-formation and the speculative: Gadamer and

Lacan'. In: Commemorative Gadamer-edition of the *South African Journal of Philosophy*, 21 (4), pp. 258–273.
Jameson, F. 1993. *Postmodernism, or, the cultural logic of late capitalism*. London: Verso.
Kant, I. 1960. *Religion within the limits of reason alone.* Trans. Greene, T.M. & Hudson, H.H. New York: Harper Torchbooks.
Kant, I. 1983. 'Grounding for the metaphysics of morals'. In: *Immanuel Kant. Ethical philosophy*. Ellington, J.W. (tr.). Indianapolis: Hackett Publishing Company, pp. 1–69.
Lacan, J. 1977. 'The subversion of the subject and the dialectic of desire in the Freudian unconscious'. In: *Écrits: A selection*. Trans. A. Sheridan. New York: W.W. Norton & Co., pp. 292–325.
Laclau, E. 1990. *New reflections on the revolution of our time*. London: Verso.
Legendre, P. 1997. *Law and the unconscious. A Legendre reader*. Trans. Goodrich, P., Pottage, A., & Schütz, A. London: Macmillan.
Lemert, C.C. & Gillan, G. 1982. *Michel Foucault: Social theory and transgression*. New York: Columbia University Press.
Lyotard, J.-F. 1984. *The postmodern condition: A report on knowledge*. Trans. Bennington, G. & Massumi, B. Manchester: Manchester University Press.
Macey, D. 1994. *The lives of Michel Foucault*. London: Vintage.
Marsh, R. 1999. *With criminal intent. The changing face of crime in South Africa*. Kenilworth: Ampersand Press.
Miller, J. 1994. *The passion of Michel Foucault*. London: Flamingo.
Melchert, N. 1991. *The great conversation*. London: Mayfield Publishing Co.
Nietzsche, F. 1984. *Thus spoke Zarathustra. A book for all and none*. In: *The portable Nietzsche*. Trans. Kaufmann,W. Middlesex: Penguin Books, pp. 103–439.
Olivier, B. 1998. 'Freud and Lyotard on Civilization'. *South African Journal of Philosophy* 17 (2), pp. 126–141.
Olivier, B. 2000. 'Discourse, genealogy, social theory and a society in transition: The challenge facing the human sciences'. *Society in Transition (Journal of the SA Sociological Association),* Vol. 31 (1), pp. 45–57.

Olivier, B. 2001. 'Discourse, space and violence'. In: Von Maltzan, C., & Wilson, R. (eds), *Spaces and crossings: Essays on literature and culture in Africa and beyond.* Frankfurt am Main: Peter Lang, pp. 301–318.

Olivier, B. 2004. 'The logic of *noir* and the question of radical evil'. *Film and Philosophy*, Vol. 8 (US Journal of the Society for the Philosophic Study of the Contemporary Visual Arts.) Special interest edition: Ethical and existential themes in cinema; pp. 122–137.

Peter, J.-P. & Favret, J. 1982. 'The animal, the madman, and death'. In: Foucault, M. (ed.), *I, Pierre Riviere, having slaughtered my mother, my sister, and my brother. A case of parricide in the 19th century.* Trans. Jellinek, F. London: Bison Books, pp. 175–199.

Peters, T. 1994. *Sin. Radical evil in soul and society.* Grand Rapids, Michigan: W.B. Eerdmans Publishing Company.

Rajchman, J. 1985. *Michel Foucault: The freedom of philosophy.* New York: Columbia University Press.

Silverman, K. 1992. *Male subjectivity at the margins.* New York: Routledge.

Solomon, R.C. 1994. *The big questions.* Fort Worth: Harcourt Brace College Publishers.

Thamm, M. 1998. *I have life. Alison's journey.* London: Penguin Books.

Thompson, J.B. 1990. *Ideology and modern culture.* Stanford: Stanford University Press.

Windelband, W. 1958. *A history of philosophy, Vol. I: Greek, Roman, Medieval.* Trans. Tufts, J.H. New York: Harper Torchbooks.

CHAPTER 2

Lacan and narrative identity

A woman stands in the foyer of a concert building. People walk hurriedly past her up the stairs – the performance, in which she is supposed to play the piano, is about to begin. One of them – a handsome young man – tells her that he cannot wait to hear her play. When she seems to be alone, she opens her handbag, takes out a knife and stabs herself violently in the chest. With blood staining her evening dress she walks out of the building. This is the culminating moment in a film-narrative with puzzling, intermittent scenes of apparent masochistic or sadistic actions on the part of characters. What may seem incongruous at an intuitive, everyday level, however, turns out to be eminently comprehensible as part of the unfolding narrative with the aid of psychoanalytic theory – specifically that of Jacques Lacan.

What, if anything, does the psychoanalytical theory of the human subject, formulated by the poststructuralist thinker, Jacques Lacan, have to offer narratology? Plenty, as far as I can judge. The mere fact that Lacan's theory of the human subject is, like Freud's, a *developmental* theory, unlike the vast majority of philosophical theories[1] or models of the subject that have been formulated in the course of the history of (western) thought, already intimates such narratological fecundity. It is striking that, in the case of traditional philosophical anthropologies, the human subject is usually theorized as if it is born at once complete as a being, furnished with all the faculties that characterize the mature or adult human being, notably

1 Even those philosophical theories which do function by means of developmental principles – notably Hegel's and Marx's, as well as their derivatives – lack the all-important concept of the unconscious, which gives psychoanalytical theories their distinctive heuristic, hermeneutic value.

reason. It should be added, of course, that by and large, until Freud, this subject was assumed to be the *masculine* adult subject, in whose rational capacities women supposedly shared to a greater or lesser degree. It is also true that in the work of various philosophers are to be found scattered, largely undeveloped references[2] to children as beings who do not yet possess the full rational capacities of adult (male) humans, but it is only with Freud that an account – in narrative terms – of the emergence of the human subject is given with reference to developmental stages, and with Freud's successors (the ego-psychology school, for instance) his theories have been increasingly refined and revised or modified. Among those successors Jacques Lacan and the thinkers who have, in turn, developed his work further (Julia Kristeva, Slavoj Žižek and Joan Copjec, among others), occupy a distinctive place, given Lacan's claim to be 'returning to Freud' (via the structuralist linguistic theory of Saussure and the structuralist anthropology of Lévi-Strauss) in a resolute attempt to recuperate the radical implications of the place of the unconscious in the latter's theory of the subject – implications largely abandoned, if not perverted, according to Lacan, by the school of ego-psychology (Lee 1990: 32–34). It is on Lacan's theory of the subject – especially its narrative dimension – that I shall focus in this paper, with a view to drawing out its pertinence for narratology. In addition to unpacking Lacan's theory I shall attempt to demonstrate its structural-hermeneutic fecundity in relation to the film, *The Piano Teacher*[3] (based on the novel by Elfriede Jelinek), directed by Michael Haneke (2002).

2 There are exceptions to this rule, especially in educational-philosophical thought, although these differ from the psychoanalytical account concentrated on here as far as the role of repression and the unconscious in the development of the subject is concerned; these concepts are usually absent. The educational thought of Jean-Jacques Rousseau, as formulated in his *Émile* (see Copleston 1964: 92–95), is one such exception.

3 I could just as well have chosen Jane Campion's *The Piano* (1993) for this purpose – which makes one wonder whether this is a coincidence or if the phenomenon of music has something to do with its ostensible privileged function regarding the narrative history of human subjects. Schopenhauer would probably have affirmed this (see Olivier 1996). Or I could have selected – for a different reason – Haneke's

The Piano Teacher unfolds the narrative of Erika Kohut (Isabelle Huppert), a professor of music at a prestigious Vienna music conservatory, who is regarded as a 'Schubert expert', especially by her domineering mother (Annie Girardot), who tells her that Schubert is 'her department', and that she should not let her pupils 'surpass' her. From early on in the film the audience witnesses this professionally accomplished, but apparently lonely woman incongruously visiting sex shops to watch pornographic films (while sniffing spent tissues left there by other – masculine – customers, presumably for the smell of semen). Or one observes her going to a drive-in cinema, engaging in voyeurism and evidently getting (retrogressive, pre-genital) pleasure from urinating while regarding couples having sex in cars. She is also shown engaging in masochistic acts such as cutting herself between her legs with a razor blade (and with the aid of a mirror), causing such bleeding that her mother remarks scathingly on the blood running down her leg (despite Erika having used a sanitary towel to halt the flow), mistakenly attributing it to menstruation. Erika has a number of piano students, and also accompanies singers on the piano. In the course of an evening when she performs together with another pianist at a private home, she encounters a handsome young man called Walter Klemmer (Benoît Magimel), who is related to her hosts and who – despite not being an exclusively dedicated music student – gives a brilliant performance of a Schubert piece after her and her fellow-pianist's earlier recital, displaying precocious talent in the process. He shows a distinct interest in her, and as the narrative unfolds, it turns out to be an amorous one at that. Walter decides to audition for inclusion in Erika's master class for piano-recital, and so impresses her colleagues that he is admitted. In fact, she is the only one who votes against his admission.

One of Professor Kohut's students, Anna Schober, whose mother displays signs of being as domineering as the professor's own, is very unsure of herself when accompanying a singer on the piano. Erika does

---

Funny Games (1998), a film that addresses the issue of sadism in relation to ostensible, but spurious communication (at the level of the symbolic). In both these cases of serious cinema, Lacan's theory of the subject would function in an exemplary manner to elucidate narrative dynamics.

not treat her sympathetically, and while Anna is in the auditorium providing accompaniment for a singing performance of a Schubert piece, she stealthily goes to the dressing room, crushes a glass in a scarf and shakes the broken pieces into one of Anna's coat pockets. Later, while people are talking in small groups in the dressing room, a scream alerts one to the unsurprising discovery that Anna's hand has been horribly cut by the glass shards in her pocket.

Some time later Walter follows Erika into the cloakroom, and, having locked the door, starts kissing her passionately when she comes out of the toilet. She stops him, and – refusing to have sex with him in the 'conventional' way – insists on masturbating him by hand and by using her mouth. Except that ... she does not finish the job, so to speak, but stops, telling him she will send him her 'instructions'. Needless to say, the young man – who was evidently looking for a sexual fling with an older woman (whom he nevertheless professes to love) – is dumbfounded, disconcerted by Erika's unorthodox behaviour. She dominates him in the same way that her mother dominates her, telling him what he can and cannot do. At her apartment he insists on entering with her and accompanying her to her room, her mother's indignation notwithstanding. They barricade the door, but instead of making love, as Walter evidently hoped they would, he is persuaded to read the letter containing her masochistic instructions to him. Taken aback by her wish, that he should hurt her in various ways – she confesses that the 'urge to be beaten' has been in her 'for years', and shows him an assortment of torture instruments – he accuses her that she 'is sick', and that she 'repulses' him. After his departure Erika gets into bed next to her mother, as usual, and in response to her mother's complaints about all her own sacrifices, she suddenly gets on top of her mother and starts kissing her. The older woman accuses her of being 'mad', then switches to a different register and advises her to rest in order to be well prepared for the next day's performance. Incongruously, Erika tells her mother: 'I saw the hairs of your sex'.

Unexpectedly Erika arrives at Walter's ice-hockey club, wanting him to have sex with her and declaring her love for him, but when he finally agrees – after much reluctance, given their lack of privacy – she starts vomiting. Walter is clearly repulsed, and tells her that she 'stinks'. Later he arrives at her apartment and accuses her of wanting to make him a pervert too. After locking her mother, who tries to intervene, in her room, he starts slapping Erika. She wants him to stop, but he proceeds by kicking her. Her nose bleeds. Walter starts having sex with her, telling her that there are some things that a woman should not do to a man. Erika asks him to desist, but he ignores her.

The next day Erika, accompanied by her mother, goes to the concert hall to stand in for the injured Anna, that is, to accompany the singer on the piano, playing Schubert. As previously indicated, it is here where she waits in the foyer, looking at people arriving, some of whom greet and exchange a few words with her. Incongruously none of them remark on her black eye (or even show any awareness of it) – a reminder of the abuse that Walter inflicted on her the previous evening. It is here, too, that Walter, in the company of a group of other people, calls out to her that he 'can't wait' to hear her play, before she takes the knife from her handbag and stabs herself. In the final scene she is seen from outside, exiting the brightly lit building.

What is one to make of this strange narrative? As suggested earlier, Jacques Lacan's psychoanalytic, poststructuralist conception of the human subject proves invaluable when it comes to making sense of narratives – especially those involving subjects whose identities seem problematical, or in some way challenge conventional notions of identity. Clearly, the eponymous piano teacher of the film in question challenges 'normal' concepts of identity. Her behaviour seems pathological, to say the least. I also intimated earlier that Lacan's theory provides one with a 'structural hermeneutic'. It is the latter which bestows intelligibility on the incongruous actions of the professor of music concerned.

Of particular pertinence in this respect are Lacan's early papers on the family complexes (Lee 1990: 13–17), on aggressivity (Lacan 1977a), and on the so-called 'mirror stage' (Lacan 1977),[4] the latter of which provides a densely metaphorical account of an early phase in the subject's

4 Although the published, revised version of 'The mirror stage' (1949) succeeded that of the other papers mentioned here, its first version was actually written before Lacan wrote the latter, namely in 1936 (see Lee 1990: 13–17; 25).

development – one which is at once indispensable for a sense of self *and* simultaneously inimical to it in a certain sense. Briefly, he argues that at an early age (between 6 and 18 months) the infant finds or recognizes in its own mirror image the unity and wholeness that it lacks at a time when it is still largely physically uncoordinated. He stresses that, for this reason, it is a 'fiction' or a 'misrecognition', but one that nevertheless fulfills a necessary 'orthopaedic' or normative function – one that provides the basis for the subject's sense of self or identity in an 'irreducible' (that is, particularistic) manner, until such time that the subject acquires language. While the mirror-image inscribes the subject narcissistically in the register of what Lacan calls the 'imaginary', language enables it, at the level of the 'symbolic' register, via the universal (or concept), to attain its human 'destiny' *as* a subject – that is, as someone who, through language, finds his or her place in cultural (including kinship) relations, and is subject to the norms of this culture as embedded in language.[5]

Lacan puts it succinctly as follows (1977: 2):

> This jubilant assumption of his specular image by the child at the *infans* stage, still sunk in his motor incapacity and nursling dependence, would seem to exhibit in an exemplary situation the symbolic matrix in which the *I* is precipitated in a primordial form, before it is objectified in the dialectic of identification with the other, and before language restores to it, in the universal, its function as subject … the important point is that this form situates the agency of the ego, before its social determination, in a fictional direction, which will always remain irreducible for the individual alone, or rather, which will only rejoin the coming-into-being … of the subject asymptotically … this *Gestalt* … symbolizes the mental permanence of the *I*, at the same time as it prefigures its alienating destination …

It is further imperative to note in more detail how he conceives of the infant's passage from a state of imagined fragmentation to that of imagined wholeness, for this is crucial to be able to understand the narrative events in *The Piano Teacher* (Lacan 1977: 4):

5 It should be noted that, through the entry into the symbolic register of language, the subject is simultaneously 'castrated', to the extent that it becomes 'subject to' the laws of society (Lee 1990: 34–38; 46; Silverman 1983: 174–176).

> The *mirror stage* is a drama whose internal thrust is precipitated from insufficiency to anticipation – and which manufactures for the subject, caught up in the lure of spatial identification, the succession of phantasies that extends from a fragmented body-image to a form of its totality that I shall call orthopaedic – and, lastly, to the assumption of the armour of an alienating identity, which will mark with its rigid structure the subject's entire mental development.

The importance here of Lacan's claim that, in the development of a child, there is a passage from fantasized incoherence to one of fantasized coherence should already be obvious in so far as it makes Erika Kohut's behaviour intelligible. But first other relevant parts of Lacan's theoretical arsenal have to be adduced.

In the paper on aggressivity (1977a) Lacan had previously elaborated on the relation between what he refers to – in the preceding quotation – as 'a fragmented body-image' and the ostensibly unified mirror-image. Aggressivity is a human phenomenon whose provenance and elaboration as a structural psychoanalytical concept is to be found in Freud's *Beyond the pleasure principle* (1957) and *Civilization and its discontents* (1961). It is the one face of the death-instinct or -drive, the other being the tendency towards inertia or reconstitution of a previous state. For present purposes it is important to note that in the paper on aggressivity Lacan argued, on the basis of psychoanalytical evidence, that the lived-body experiences of the subject prior to the (spurious) 'unity' perceived in its own mirror image, assume the shape of fragmented body-images. These so-called *imagoes* represent aspects of (Lacan 1977a: 11):

> ... aggressive intentions ... the images of castration, mutilation, dismemberment, dislocation, evisceration, devouring, bursting open of the body, in short, the *imagos* that I have grouped together under the apparently structural term of *imagos of the fragmented body*.

In other words, aggressivity manifests itself in images of fragmentation and mutilation. Importantly, as Lee (1990: 25) remarks, for Lacan these images are the result of retrospective 'imaginary reconstructions' of recollected bodily experiences antedating the mirror stage and its 'unifying' function regarding the emergence of the ego or *moi*. Understanding this is not difficult if one keeps in mind that the infant who (mis-) recognizes its mirror image narcissistically as 'itself', experiences a profound disharmony between the 'fragmentation' of its own uncoordinated body, with its lack of motor control, and this mesmerizing, 'unitary' image with which it identifies. After all, as Lacan indicates in *The mirror stage*, this identification is simultaneously alienating. Following Lacan (1977a: 22), several commentators (see Benvenuto & Kennedy 1986: 57) have pointed out that this moment of alienation implies the 'otherness' of the mirror image, and imparts to the subject a structural rivalry with him- or herself; hence the aggressivity (see Bowie 1991: 34). Small wonder that the disharmony within the subject between the unitary visual *Gestalt* and a fragmented body is transferred to the infant subject's relations with others, insofar as she or he identifies with the iconic appearance (that is, body-images) of other human beings. As may be expected, rivalry – and concomitantly, 'aggressive competitiveness' (Lacan 1977a: 19) – is an integral thread of these relations.

It therefore comes as no surprise that Lacan posits a correlation (however unlikely it may seem at an intuitive level) between this aggressivity and the process of narcissistic identification, described earlier (Lacan 1977a: 16):

> Thesis IV: *Aggressivity is the correlative tendency of a mode of identification that we call narcissistic, and which determines the formal structure of man's ego and of the register of entities characteristic of his world.*

Lee (1990: 27; see also Lacan 1977a: 19) summarizes this state of affairs admirably:

> Thus, the disturbing realization of the gap between the child's lived experience of the still minimally competent and functionally fragmented body and his narcissistic identification with the unity of his visual reflection is displaced into various kinds of aggressive tendencies directed towards others. In other words, the discrepancy between the child's fragmented bodily experience and his unified, imaginary identity ... gives rise to a kind of primordial paranoia in the young *moi* ... In modeling oneself on another, one is also modeling one's desires on those of the other, and the inevitable consequence of this is an aggressive rivalry between the child and the other for the object desired by the other. In this way, aggression

> directed towards others is found at the very center of the *moi*'s structure, as it comes into being through the dialectic of the child's narcissistic identifications with various visual images.

It is important to keep in mind that this aggressivity towards others at the heart of the subject's structure as ego (*moi*) is in the first place, as pointed out earlier, aggressivity towards *oneself* – at least towards the image which is ambivalently experienced as being oneself *and* as being alien at one and the same time, and with which one enters into rivalry precisely because of it being experienced as 'other'. It is this 'otherness' which is transferred to other individuals when the child encounters them in various social relations, and which forms the basis for rivalry with, and aggression towards them. Working one's way further back, for the sake of uncovering the roots of Lacan's (structural) psychoanalytical account of the emergent constitution of the subject and its characteristic tendencies of narcissism and aggressivity, it is illuminating to note that his two early papers on 'family complexes' (written for Vol. 8 of the *Encyclopédie francaise* of 1938) not only further elucidate the formal conditions for narcissism and aggressivity, but actually provide the parameters for understanding the provenance of both psychosis (like that of the piano teacher in the film under discussion) and neurosis. Briefly, what Lacan outlined in the first of these two papers – 'The complex as a concrete factor of family psychology' – amounts to the fundamental structural or formal constituents of subjectivity. He distinguishes here among three so-called imagoes which, as basic family-structures, organize the behaviour of individuals (Lee 1990: 14). Each of these imagoes – the maternal, the fraternal and the paternal – is the unconscious embodiment or representation of a family complex that 'reproduces a certain reality of the environment' (quoted in Lee 1990: 14). The relevance of this for narratology consists in the manner that these unconscious imaginary representations (to be found in family relations) enduringly shape human responses to their environment in the form of actions or behaviour.

The significance of the 'maternal imago' consists in its connection with the child's 'weaning complex' and therefore its representation of the child's 'congenital deficiency', signalled by its dependence on the mother's breast as source of satisfaction for its bodily needs (Lee 1990: 14). It is not difficult to grasp the structuring function of this 'maternal' imago as being responsible for all those (fundamentally ideological) quests for a *plenum* of some kind, whether religious, 'philosophical' (that is, metaphysical) or political, insofar as it marks the interminable lack on the part of the subject in the face of whatever totality it desires (behind which the image of the maternal breast lurks; Lee 1990: 14). In Lacan's words (quoted in Lee 1990: 14):

> If it were necessary to define the most abstract form where it is refound, we might characterize it thus: a perfect assimilation of the totality of being. Under this formulation with a slightly philosophical aspect, we can recognize these nostalgias of humanity: the metaphysical mirage of universal harmony, the mystical abyss of affective fusion, the social utopia of a totalitarian guardianship, and every outburst of the obsession with a paradise lost before birth or of the most obscure aspiration toward death.

It should be clear that the 'orthopaedic' function that Lacan attributes to the mirror image in *The mirror stage* ultimately has its provenance in the 'maternal imago', and further that what Julia Kristeva (1997: 35) refers to as the semiotic *chora* of the maternal body (which provides the infant with its first experience of a quasi-wholeness) corresponds to this. Narratologically speaking, Lacan here focuses on a structural-dynamic motif which may be fruitfully implemented at a hermeneutic level to make sense of the actions of characters in fiction, as indeed in social life. The actions of the piano teacher in the film concerned are no exception in this regard, as I hope to show, although one should remember that actions on the part of characters can sometimes be assessed only in negative terms, that is, as being directed *against* the representation of wholeness rather than as being symptomatic of a striving towards a totality – even if these actions are ultimately to be construed as preliminary to the constitution of a new totality via the image.

The significance of the other two imagoes can be summed up as follows. The 'fraternal imago' corresponds to what Lacan calls the 'intrusion complex' (Lee 1990: 14), and underpins the envy that accompanies the child's discovery that her or his identity is inseparably conjoined with that of others. The envy or jealousy in question should, he argued, be understood in the first place as representing a 'mental identification', instead of 'a vital rivalry' (quoted in Lee 1990: 14). This claim is consonant with what Lacan argued in *The mirror stage* concerning the intimate connection between identification and aggressive behaviour, and appears here as the insight into the aggressive behaviour of siblings as the consequence of something more fundamental, namely their identification with one another (itself made possible by the prior identification with their own mirror image). In this way the 'fraternal imago may be seen as the unconscious foundation of human social behaviour, with the startling corollary that envy or jealousy appears to be 'the archetype of social feelings' (quoted in Lee 1990: 15). This imago, too, may be detected as playing a dynamically structuring role in the story of *The Piano Teacher*.

The 'paternal imago' is probably the most difficult to understand as a structuring factor in relation to the emerging subjectivity of the child. For Lacan this is what is behind the Freudian Oedipus complex (Lee 1990: 15), through which the child supposedly finds his or (more problematically) her place in kinship relations and society. Here Lacan draws attention to an ambiguity that, he claims, is usually overlooked in psychoanalytical theory, namely the parallel between the role of the father's 'threat of castration' in the repression of infantile (male) sexuality, on the one hand, and the process, on the other hand, by which the child's reality is sublimated (that is, transformed) by means of the paternal imago. The child is thus enabled to approach the world in an apparently 'desexualized' manner, while the flipside of this is inward-directed, narcissistic (sexual) self-interest – which again connects these insights with the 'mirror stage' as site of narcissistic identification. Lacan points to a 'subversive' tension (Lee 1990: 15) in the paternal imago, insofar as the very paternal authority responsible for the repression of the child's sexuality, *also* comprises the paradigm of sexual maturity for the narcissistic child.[6] As Lee (1990: 15) reminds one, this is nothing other than the ego ideal (or superego),

6 This is clearly a double function that can hardly be satisfactorily performed: as Lacan argued in the second of his papers on the family complexes ('The family complexes in pathology'), it is this inability to achieve both ends which makes the

at the basis of which the structuring function of the paternal imago can therefore be discerned. Lacan attributes the confusion and anxiety about sexuality – so noticeable in modern people (including the professor of music in the narrative under consideration) – to the above-mentioned tension (Lee 1990: 15). Lee further stresses that Lacan's main interest here is to show how human actions are structured by these unconscious imagoes in the shape of formal patterns for possible human behaviour – something with obvious resonances for narrative theory.

The part of the second of Lacan's papers on the family complexes ('The family complexes in pathology') that is especially relevant to my chosen theme of narrative identity on the part of a professor of music, is the one on psychosis (Lee 1990: 15–16). Here he argues again that these complexes, embodied in the different imagoes, play a formal role in relation to the psychoses insofar as they supply the basic 'themes' developed in different cases of psychotic delirium.[7] Such cases, Lacan argues, may be understood in terms of the parallel that exists between '*the evolution of* [a child's] *sexuality*', on the one hand, and the '*constitution of reality*' (quoted in Lee 1990: 16), that is, her or his understanding of their environment. The 'objects of psychotic delirium' therefore represent the '"stagnation" of sublimation [the transformation of libidinal or sexual energy into, for example, cognitive structures] at preliminary stages of the child's appreciation of the constitution of reality' (Lee 1990: 16), a process which may manifest itself in, for instance, a psychotic distancing from everyday reality. Perhaps here, too, one may find Lacanian clues for the understanding of the music professor's problematic narrative identity.

Right from the opening scene of the film – when the audience is privy to a physical struggle between Erika and her mother, which ends where she pulls a handful of hair from her mother's scalp – as the film-narrative progresses, more and more signs seep into the narrative that all is not

---

paternal imago the source of the different symptoms characteristic of the different neuroses (Lee 1990: 15–16).

7 Interestingly, Lacan claims that, in the case of the neuroses, the complexes (with which the imagoes correspond) do not merely play a formal role, but a causal one in the production of recognizable symptoms (Lee 1990: 16).

as it should be with the professor. After all, apart from the masochistic tendencies that one witnesses on Erika's part, she shares a bed with her mother, and when she becomes aware of Walter's designs on her, after initially ignoring his advances, she eventually switches to an apparently masochistic desire for him to hurt her in the course of making love to her – something that, as pointed out, disconcerts the young man thoroughly. When he finally yields to her masochistic demands, apparently more out of disgust than complicity, to his (and the audience's) surprise she is horrified instead of gratified. In the course of her involvement with music students she also commits what appears to be a cruel and sadistic act, by placing broken glass in a student's coat pocket, with the predictable effect of causing severe lacerations of the girl's hand when the latter reaches into her pocket, effectively preventing her from further participating in competitions for the foreseeable future. Having witnessed the student's domineering mother in action – reminiscent of Erika's own mother – and also knowing that Erika has reason to regard her as a rival as far as Schubert piano-interpretations are concerned, it is never unambiguously clear what her motives are with this ostensibly sadistic act. Does she set out to mutilate the young woman's hand to neutralize her as a rival (corresponding to the aggression that Lacan links with identification), or to rescue her from falling prey to the same fate as herself, under the tyrannical rule of an inexorably (and vicariously) ambitious mother?

I would propose that these disconcerting narrative events are made intelligible by Lacan's theoretical elaboration of the developmental conditions of the subject's 'identity', remembering that the latter is always to a greater or lesser extent 'fictional'. First, the scene where Erika literally pulls hair from her mother's head in the course of a mutual display of aggressivity, must be seen as an attempt to reverse the normal direction of identification, namely to break down the 'form of totality' assumed by her mother's body – that is, in so far as it symbolizes the 'maternal imago' – and return it to its primordial, fragmented state. Why? Because what her mother's body symbolizes, has become unacceptable to her – so much so that one witnesses an atavistic attempt to go back to what must necessarily precede any process of identification on her or her mother's part that would restore the situation between mother and daughter to 'normal'. After all, for Erika to be able to find a 'quasi-wholeness' in the 'semiotic *chora*' (Kristeva) of her mother's body, she has to experience it as protective, which is evidently not the case. But more drastic than her apparent aggressive wish to mutilate her mother's body in some or other way, is her desire to do so to her own body, as evinced in the way she cuts herself, as well as in her wish, that Walter beat her and inflict various injuries on her. Recall Lacan's words, quoted earlier, that '*imagos of the fragmented body*', including 'mutilation, dismemberment', and 'bursting open of the body', represent aggressive intentions.

The crucial question is why she should manifest such masochistic aggressivity towards herself, and to such a degree that it virtually drives the narrative events. The answer lies not only here, in the characteristic imagoes of the fragmented body as concretizations of aggressive intentions, but more fundamentally in the terms of the correlation that (as pointed out earlier) Lacan posits between the 'narcissistic mode of identification' and aggressivity via the rivalry that the subject enters into with the image – whether it is its 'own' or that of another person. If it is indeed 'normal' for the child to cling narcissistically to its own mirror-image as the 'orthopaedic' (if imaginary) corrective to the fragmentation it feels at the level of lived experience, then anyone as hell-bent as Erika on destroying her self-image by mutilating it the way she does, cannot be regarded as being narcissistic even in the minimal sense that every human subject may be said to be. On the contrary. Again, why? Recall that her domineering mother insists on her being the Schubert authority and urges her to guard against her pupils usurping that position. Clearly, a parent who wields that kind of power over a child even into adulthood, could be said to have engineered the child's identification-process in a direction that ultimately left the child – in this case Erika – dissatisfied, more than usually alienated from the self she has become. Lacan tells us that all of us are alienated from 'ourselves' to the extent that the image with which we originarily identify, is a fiction, albeit an orthopaedic one. But in Erika's case her self-image was evidently not of her own choosing – her mother selected it for her, in the same way that Anna Schober's mother seems to be doing it on behalf of her daughter (which seems to suggest that Erika's 'sadistic' act precipitating the mutilation of Anna's hand may indeed be intended as a rescue mission).

Add to this the element of rivalry with one's (alienating) self-image, linked as it is to the aggression accompanying identification, and more light is cast on Erika's actions: Lacan tells one that the aggressivity derives from the experience of sharing the desires of the image that one identifies with. But what if, as in Erika's case, those desires (belonging to a professor of music) have been imposed on one? It is unavoidable to share (that is, have) them, even if the identity to which they are attached has become intolerable to one. But this means that an unbearable conflict has to arise between the desires attributable to the intolerable identity and the desire to break down the latter, elevating aggression to the second degree, as it were. The structural role of the 'fraternal imago' may be discerned here, too, inseparable as it is from envy or jealousy – themselves feelings indissociable from rivalry and its accompanying aggression. Hence, Professor Kohut's psychotic acts of self-mutilation and desire for masochistic treatment at the hands of Walter are intelligible as desperate attempts to break down the unsolicited 'alienating armour' imposed on her by her mother. This also explains her taste for pornography and her spying on couples having sex in public – images diametrically opposed to that of a 'respectable' piano instructor at a prestigious institution, and therefore, in so far as they impart pleasure to her, directly subversive of the self-image that she carries like a curse. Small wonder – as Lacan observes regarding the role of the family complex-imagoes in the development of psychoses – Erika Kohut appears to be 'distanced' from everyday reality; to such an extent, apparently, that she seems to be oblivious of the dangers attendant upon her arrival at Walter's ice-hockey club with the intention of having sex with him in the locker-room.[8]

8 One should add that the role of the 'paternal imago' may be discerned here, too, in the 'confusion and anxiety' that Erika displays regarding her own sexuality, as well as in the fact that, being a woman, there was obviously no narcissistic inward turn in the face of a father's 'threat of castration' in her case. In the absence of the enduring salutary structuring role of the 'maternal imago', and of the related orthopaedic function of the mirror image – given Erika's self-loathing, for reasons

An obvious objection would be to point to Erika's resistance to Walter finally, ostensibly, rising to her expectations by hitting and kicking her. Isn't this what she wants, to enlist his help in breaking down her detestable 'identity' as professor of music? To see her plea, that he desist, as contradictory would be to misunderstand what is at stake for Erika in terms of power. When an infant identifies with its mirror-image and subsequently with the 'desirable' images of others in the social sphere, it wields a certain power over its own choices – to be sure, never an absolute power; witness the manner in which agencies of capital manipulate individuals', including children's, desire through 'desirable' advertising or branded images – but when a parent or some other influential person encourages certain identifications on the child's part, robbing her or him of its own capacity to choose, the foundation is laid for what one may call 'dis-identification'. Hence Erika's desire for Walter to abuse her – as usual, the masochist has to be in control. When Walter takes the initiative, power is once again wrested from her, exacerbating her self-hatred.

The film ends with the professor leaving a concert building where she was supposed to accompany a student singer. As intimated earlier, while standing in the foyer she takes out a knife and stabs herself in the chest (an apparently superficial wound, for it has no visible lethal effect). It is significant that this occurs directly after Walter had walked past her, telling her that he is looking forward to her piano-playing: the man on whom she depended for assisting her in breaking down her self-image – or at least for confirming the experience of not being at ease with that identity – once again reinforces precisely the image she is at pains to obliterate. Hence her act of stabbing herself in the chest. The last shot shows her from the outside, exiting the brightly lit building – in fact, it is conspicuously defined by neon and other lights. Iconically, the building may be seen as representing the well-defined contours of the ego as bastion

---

advanced here – one could therefore say that, instead of the paternal imago playing a positive role here, its role is negative. The fact that (as one learns from her) Erika's father became insane, implies that such negativity would be exacerbated in terms of 'confusion and anxiety'.

of the subject's putative 'identity', but here one that she wishes to destroy, and to leave behind in the same way that she leaves the building.

Although it cannot be pursued here, it is perhaps important to draw attention to the fact that Lacan also provides the theoretical terms for a re-inscription of one's identity, or perhaps rather, a re-narrativization of it at the level of the symbolic register as opposed to the imaginary – although one should remember that these two registers continually overlap each other as well as the register of the 'real'. The latter register also sheds light on the narrative events in question here, in so far as, for Lacan, it is that which resists symbolization, but nevertheless has 'effects' in the symbolic. It could be argued that what Erika is desperately seeking, are the symbolic means for the rearticulation of her symbolic identity, or what Lacan calls the 'I' (*je*) as opposed to the self or ego (*moi*). From this perspective, the instances where she mutilates herself are not only attempts to fragment her ego as a prerequisite for assuming a new or different one, but also psychotic manifestations of what Lacan calls 'foreclosure' which, in so far as it manifests itself in somatic guise, alludes to the 'real' (Lacan 1977b; Benvenuto & Kennedy 1986: 146–153; Olivier 1998, 2003 and 2004).

In conclusion it must be emphasized, once again, that – as I have tried to demonstrate in this article – Lacan's theory of the subject is a rich structural-hermeneutic source of pertinent concepts for the interpretation of diverse narratives, given the fact that it is a poststructuralist developmental theory. As such, its cardinal conceptual features enable the narratological interpreter to draw connections between the developmental stages in a character's life and the events that occur in the course of her or his unfolding personal life-story. What makes Lacan's theory poststructuralist (and not structuralist), is his employment of the logic typical of poststructuralism, according to which human beings cannot be adequately theorized as being (for example) *either* stable *or* unstable, but may be shown to be *both* stable *and* unstable at the same time, albeit at the level of different subject-registers or positions (Olivier 2004: 1–2). It is this characteristic ability of poststructuralist theory (whether that of Lacan, Derrida, Foucault, Lyotard, Kristeva or Deleuze) that enables one to come to grips with the complexity of the human condition.

And this condition is accessible to us, among other modes – but arguably in a privileged fashion – in the guise of personal narratives in the register of the everyday life-world as well as the registers of literary and cinematic art.

References

Benvenuto, B. & Kennedy, R. 1986. *The works of Jacques Lacan. An introduction*. London: Free Association Books.

Bowie, M. 1991. *Lacan*. London: Fontana Press.

Campion, J. (dir.). 1993. *The Piano*. Miramax Films.

Copleston, F. 1964. *A history of philosophy. Volume 6: Modern philosophy, Part one: The French Enlightenment to Kant*. New York: Image Books.

Haneke, M. (dir.). 1998. *Funny Games*. WEGA Film.

Haneke, M. (dir.). 2002. *The Piano Teacher*. WEGA Film.

Freud, S. 1957. 'Beyond the pleasure-principle'. In: Rickman, J. (ed.), *A general selection from the works of Sigmund Freud*. Garden City, New York: Doubleday Anchor Books, pp. 141–168.

Freud, S. 1961. *Civilization and its Discontents*. Strachey, J. (ed. and tr.). New York: W.W. Norton.

Kristeva, J. 1997. 'Revolution in poetic language'. In: *The portable Kristeva*. Ed. Oliver, K. New York: Columbia University Press, pp. 27–92.

Lacan, J. 1977. 'The mirror stage as formative of the function of the I as revealed in psychoanalytic experience'. In: *Écrits: A selection.* Trans. Sheridan, A. New York: W.W. Norton, pp. 1–7.

Lacan, J. 1977a. 'Aggressivity in psychoanalysis'. In: *Écrits: A selection.* Trans. Sheridan, A. New York: W.W. Norton, pp. 8–29.

Lacan, J. 1977b. 'The function and field of speech and language in psychoanalysis'. In: *Écrits: A selection.* Trans. Sheridan, A. New York: W.W. Norton, pp. 30–113.

Lee, J.S. 1990. *Jacques Lacan*. Amherst: The University of Massachusetts Press.
Olivier, B. 1996. 'Schopenhauer and Beckett: Towards a literature of the un(re)presentable'. *Journal of Literary Studies* 12 (3), pp. 338–353.
Olivier, B. 1998. 'Freud and Lyotard on Civilization'. *South African Journal of Philosophy*, 17 (2), pp. 126–141.
Olivier, B. 2003. 'Lacan: Problematisering van die filosofie'. *FRAGMENTE – Tydskrif vir Filosofie en Kultuurkritiek*, Nos 10 & 11, pp. 42–54.
Olivier, B. 2004. 'Lacan's subject: the imaginary, language, the real and philosophy'. *South African Journal of Philosophy*, Vol. 23 (1), pp. 1–19.
Silverman, K. 1983. *The subject of semiotics*. New York: Oxford University Press.

CHAPTER 3

Lacan and the question of the psychotherapist's ethical orientation[1]

Some time ago, during the final years of the apartheid era in South Africa, a psychologist I knew was required, as part of his postgraduate work, to offer psychotherapy to political prisoners in what was then a hospital for blacks in Port Elizabeth. He soon realized that he was faced with the invidious task of 'helping' these prisoners 'adapt' to a social and political situation that was as unacceptable to himself as to the prisoners. Paradoxically, he was expected to 'normalize' individuals in an obscenely 'abnormal' situation, something which confronted him graphically with his own values or ethics. The result was that he refused to carry out the required psychotherapeutic work and in the end opted out of the postgraduate programme concerned and left Port Elizabeth. In Lacanian terms, he 'assumed his desire' (a phrase that will be elucidated in due course). What became of him afterwards I do not know.

This would-be psychologist's situation highlights the dilemma experienced by therapists (as well as people like philosophers and theologians) in political situations which are unacceptable to them for moral or axiological reasons. The theologian Dietrich Bonnhoeffer, who was executed for his unwavering opposition to the Hitler regime is a case in point, as are all those scientists and intellectuals, such as Theodor Adorno, who had to flee Germany during that time. They all realized that German

1 In the course of preparing for the writing of this paper I benefited from the insightful contributions to various pertinent discussions on the part of Wim Kuit, a student of philosophy as well as postgraduate psychology student at the former University of Port Elizabeth (now NMMU). Needless to say, whatever inadequacies still remain in the written text are my own responsibility and not his.

society had become 'abnormal' or 'inhuman' in the sense of ethically unacceptable, as indeed did the young psychologist in question regarding apartheid South Africa. In these cases it may not seem to be such an insurmountable problem to know what to do – or perhaps what *not* to do; the problem may be to a greater extent having to gather the courage to act according to one's ethical insights in a situation claimed to be 'normal' by the political authorities of the day and subscribed to by many people around one, including family and friends.

The dilemma faced by psychotherapists is much more difficult to resolve when the social and political situation appears to be 'normal' in the sense of satisfying, for all intents and purposes, at least the politically and economically valorized principles of the day – in the contemporary era those of a constitutionally entrenched democracy, globally functioning, almost without exception, in conjunction with late capitalism. Here the difficulty manifests itself not in therapists having to help clients adjust to a distorted society, but in facing the task of assisting them in attaining psychical equilibrium or functionality without compromising their (the therapists') own ethical principles. This would entail, for instance, not condoning or encouraging murder on the part of the client while simultaneously not acting prescriptively either, for the sake of avoiding clients' dependence on them and, instead, cultivating a sense of responsibility on their part.

What would be the danger regarding ethical relativism here? The spectre of such an approach rears its paralysing Medusa-head precisely because the therapist eschews being prescriptive or judgemental – for ostensibly sound reasons concerning client-accountability, the goal of psychological independence on her or his part, as well as (the ethical requirement of) confidentiality. But this could entail having to ignore evidence of moral misdemeanours on the part of the client, with the result that the latter's *status quo*-situation is implicitly confirmed or reinforced. To be sure, given that psychotherapists' professional training usually imparts to them practical avenues to negotiate quandaries of a relativistic nature, through skilful questioning of the client they – especially 'critical' therapists – may well lead the latter to grasp the moral untenability of his or her situation. But this is unlikely to happen where therapists are exclusively intent on drawing from clients their own feelings about a situation, selectively described by them in the first place. (As I shall show, the case is significantly different with Lacanian psychoanalysis.)

The situation I am sketching here corresponds roughly to what Painter and Terre Blanche (2004: 520–521) characterize as mainstream psychology (here as elsewhere) being '... a product and producer of global capitalism', and as being largely in the service of '... neo-colonialism, racism, capitalist exploitation and neo-liberal market ideologies', with the result that '... an American-style, aggressively professional and market-orientated individual psychotherapy industry' flourishes. Small wonder, then, that in the kind of society that is, on the one hand, globally multicultural – differences on which market capitalism thrives, as Hardt and Negri (2001: 150–154) have pointed out – and on the other systematically constructed by market forces that promote and exacerbate all kinds of differences in needs and tastes on the part of consumers, one encounters a condition of postmodern fragmentation, where there is scant evidence of a common ethos or *Weltanschauung* in which people share. On the contrary, the prevailing global situation – one that psychotherapists ineluctably have to face in their consulting rooms – is one of pervasive relativism. Even if therapists are to some extent prepared, through training, for such a situation through the insistence on maintaining strict standards of professional ethics, the contemporary, multicultural or 'postmodern' era is no longer one where anyone can innocently believe in a unified world or worldview. As Lyotard (1984: xxiv) has famously put it: '... I define *postmodern* as incredulity toward metanarratives' – where 'metanarratives' entail distinct universalistic appeals to some metadiscourse or 'grand story' (such as Christianity or Marxism), which putatively provides a touchstone for the truth of everyday linguistic utterances.

This situation has been given fictional prominence in the popular award-winning television series, *The Sopranos*, where mafia boss Tony Soprano's therapist finds herself in the invidious position of realizing that those 'chapters' of her client's life that he routinely refuses to discuss with her involve murders, extortions and a host of other crimes that he ultimately has to take responsibility for. By not challenging him on these, and adopting the relativist position of refusing to judge the morality of his actions – concentrating only on the state of his own psyche, so to speak – she knows she is compromising her own ethical principles. By contrast, when his wife consults a psychotherapist because her conscience weighs on her unbearably, he (uncharacteristically) confronts her starkly with the obvious choice: either connive at your husband's crimes (and moral misdemeanours, like routinely cheating on her) and enjoy the material benefits of your life of luxury, or leave him and face a financially uncertain, but morally justified future. Which of these two therapists acted 'correctly', and on what grounds can one decide the matter? Are there such grounds at all which are available to the psychotherapist, or is every therapist unavoidably in the position of recognizing that no such grounds exist (especially in the contemporary, so-called 'postmodern' era of pervasive 'anything goes' sentiments in which one is faced with the utter arbitrariness of moral, ethical and axiological relativism)? After all, even a so-called rational, rule-based ethics, whether consequentialist or deontologically derived, does not invite or promote consensus in the present situation. On the contrary – it only seems to add to the proliferation of conflicting claims in the ethical arena, in this way exacerbating what already amounts to extreme relativism. In the present article I want to argue against such relativism.

To avoid confusion, it has to emphasized at the outset that the concept of 'the ethical' addressed in this paper has to be comprehended specifically as that which operates in the context of Lacanian psychoanalytic theory. As such (and as will become apparent), it is fundamentally different from, if not at odds with, 'ethics' as usually understood by the majority of South African psychotherapists, namely as a concept pertaining to a code of behaviour governing their professional training and eventual practice. Unless one were willing to go to the (sometimes very demanding) lengths of familiarizing oneself with Lacan's psychoanalytic theory, what it comprises as a distinct mode of thinking about the human subject, and therefore also what the place of the 'ethical' is within it, is bound to be elusive.

Lacan and ego-psychology

To be able to understand the value and pertinence of Lacan's psychoanalytical theory of the human subject for the problem of axiological arbitrariness raised above, one has to place it against the backdrop of his critique of the concept of the ego, and concomitantly of ego-psychology. Broadly speaking, Lacan's misgivings about the concept of the ego as it was developed in Freud's later structural theory (where the *id*, *ego* and *superego* are the components or agencies comprising the mind, psyche or human personality) (Mitchell & Black 1995: 19–21) hinge on his conviction that the subject's identity, which is inseparable from the putative unity and autonomy of the ego, is not something which emerges from contact with 'reality'.

It is well-known that 'ego-psychology' developed in the course of various theorists interpreting and revising or elaborating on Freud's structural theory of the id, ego and superego. These include the pioneer of this school of thought, namely his daughter, Anna Freud, as well as Ernst Kris, Heinz Hartmann, René Spitz, Margaret Mahler and Edith Jacobson, all of whom developed or refined certain aspects of ego-psychology (Mitchell & Black 1995: 23–59). As Mitchell and Black (p. 24) remark, ego-psychology is distinguished from other schools of thought that developed on the basis of Freud's theoretical and professional legacy by its 'careful preservation of Freud's drive theory'. More specifically, they point to the focus, on the part of ego psychologists, on the relationship between ego-defences and (libidinal as well as aggressive) drive impulses. It should become clear in the course of this paper that Lacan's objection to the work of ego psychologists issues from his critique of the ego or self which he sees as being grounded in the *fiction* or fantasy of the mirror-image, instead of being the supposed representative of 'reality' and the regulator of the drives in the face of this 'reality'.

Hence Lacan's (1977a: 42) advice to psychoanalysts, to 'suspend' the analysand's 'certainties' in the interest of liberating him or her from the mirages of imaginary identifications (which are essentially ego-constructs; the sense of this should become apparent in the course of this paper).

Mitchell and Black (1995: 196–197) illustrate the ease with which one could fall prey to imaginary constructs in their discussion of Lacan with reference to a specific case, and connect this with what Lacan took as the mistake on the part of ego-psychology, namely that of being a 'psychology of a social construction, a mirage mistaken for a reality' (p. 198).

In other words, the very same 'ego' that was the object of ego-psychologists' attempts, among other things, to strengthen and develop the subject's ego-capacities in the interest of psychic equilibrium, according to Lacan, was an entirely *fictional* construct, designed to give the subject a spurious sense of unity and coherence in the face of its experience of un-coordination, disunity and fragmentation. He formulates it as follows (Lacan 1977: 2):

> This jubilant assumption of his specular image by the child at the *infans* stage, still sunk in his motor incapacity and nursling dependence, would seem to exhibit in an exemplary situation the symbolic matrix in which the *I* is precipitated in a primordial form, before it is objectified in the dialectic of identification with the other, and before language restores to it, in the universal, its function as subject … the important point is that this form situates the agency of the ego, before its social determination, in a fictional direction, which will always remain irreducible for the individual alone, or rather, which will only rejoin the coming-into-being … of the subject asymptotically … this *Gestalt* … symbolizes the mental permanence of the *I*, at the same time as it prefigures its alienating destination …

What Lacan claims here, is that the infant's sense of identity is given a 'foundation' in its first experience of its own image, and – importantly – that this 'foundation' is an ambivalent one in so far as it is *fictional* and alienating while simultaneously, given its (misleading) appearance of wholeness and unity, being indispensable for the subject's further development. Moreover, because it is situated at the level of the imaginary, it is 'irreducible' regarding the uniqueness of the subject at this level, and it is only when the latter acquires language that the universalistic conceptual moment of being human is added to this imaginary aspect of its identity. Neither can the two registers ever coincide – the subject of the imaginary (ego) and the subject of the symbolic or language ('I' or '*je*') are irreducibly different subject-positions, and the subject is forever stretched between these (as well as a third position – the subject of the *real*, a register which will be addressed later in this article).

These startling insights were put forward in Lacan's well-known early paper known as *The mirror stage* (1977), where, in contrast to Freud's belief that the Oedipus complex (Bowie 1991: 30–32) marks the locus of the dramatic emergence of the subject's 'identity' in the context of rivalry with and eventual submission to the father by the boy-child (the Oedipal path of the girl-child being more complicated), he put forward a model which is more fundamental or 'prototypical' insofar as it involves a (largely narcissistic) relationship on the part of the subject with him- or herself. 'Lacan invites us,' says Malcolm Bowie (1991: 32), 'to look back beyond the play of rivalries and aliases that the Oedipal phase initiates, and to behold an anterior world in which the individual has only one object of desire and only one alias – himself'. This entails, according to Lacan (1977: 2–4), a simultaneous identification and alienation: the child (between 6 and 18 months) 'recognizes' itself in its own mirror-image, but simultaneously experiences alienation because the 'unified' image is false – it is really, according to Lacan, a 'misrecognition'. The child-subject does not experience the unity or coordination apparently exhibited by the mirror-image, which makes it (the image), in Lacan's words (1977: 4), 'orthopaedic'. In other words, it embodies something desired as a corrective to a given state of affairs, but not actualized at this (or at any later) stage in the subject's life. The subject is therefore split between what it is at this early stage – fragmented, incoherent, uncoordinated – and what it desires and mistakenly takes to be its 'identity', namely the fiction of a unitary image of itself, which is, in the final analysis, nothing more than 'imaginary'.

For Lacan this state of affairs does not (ever) make way for one where the adult subject can truly be said to be unified and 'coherent'. Human beings are irremediably torn between their desire for, and moments of spurious 'experience' of 'unity' (see Olivier 2003 in this regard). As Lee (1990: 47) points out:

> That the human subject is essentially a place of conflict between the *je* and the *moi*, between the symbolic and the imaginary, will remain one of Lacan's central theses throughout his career.

Indeed – as the above excerpt indicates – the human subject will, from this moment on, always be caught between the particular imaginary 'irreducibility' imparted to it by its specular image, and its symbolic or linguistic status as subject (articulated by means of universalistic concepts when language is acquired), and the two *will never coincide*. Bowie (1991: 21) captures the import of this short, but decisive text well:

> A hint that Lacan's 'ego' (*moi*) is to be a schismatic and not a stabilizing notion is detectable in the very title of his best-known early paper. The mirror stage (*stade du miroir*) is not a mere epoch in the history of the individual but a stadium (*stade*) in which the battle of the human subject is permanently being waged ... But the pun has large ambitions behind it: to find an early moment in the human life-cycle when the individual's humanity is already fully at stake, and to find a new beginning for the moral drama of psychoanalysis. Lacan's account of the 'specular' moment provides the ego with its creation myth and its Fall.

Not only is the reason for Lacan's resolute opposition to ego-psychology apparent in the last sentence of Bowie's commentary; given the theme of the present article, it is significant that he employs phrases like 'the battle of the human subject' and 'the moral drama of psychoanalysis' insofar as these clearly implicate the field of ethical responsibility and values. And while it is certainly the case that Lacan's focus in *The mirror stage* is on the provenance of the subject's (spurious) sense of identity, it is no less true that, in the same seminal paper, he already hints where one should expect to find an indication of the subject's capacity to transcend its potential imprisonment by the alienating straitjacket of its image-dependent 'identity', namely in the universalizing function of language. Why 'universalizing', and how is this connected to the question of ethical responsibility?

The symbolic register, the subject and narrative

It will be remembered that, in the above quotation, Lacan speaks about language 'restoring' to the subject its function in the 'universal'. This means that no one could be a *human* subject without language, because it is through language that one occupies, via the Oedipal relationship of submission to authority, one's place in kinship relations and society at large. As Jonathan Lee (1991: 20), commenting on Lacan's work, reminds one, it is through one's entry into language that one is able to situate oneself socially as an individual with a name and belonging to a specific family. It is no accident that this happens through language – language is not merely the bearer of meaning, but also of all the values and norms that pre-exist the individual and to which she or he submits her- or himself by entering into what Lacan calls the 'symbolic' sphere (that is, language in the encompassing sense of all those systems of meaning which constitute a culture, from a natural language like English or French to science, art, architecture, fashion and the like). To be a subject means to be 'subject to' all the relations of authority and value embodied in language in this wide sense – something that Lacan's friend, the structuralist anthropologist Lévi-Strauss, had demonstrated at length in his work (Lee 1990: 34–38; 62–63).

This explains why Lacan, to the bafflement of many readers, maintains that the unconscious 'is structured ... like a language' (1977c: 234) and refers to it as the 'discourse of the other' (Lee 1990: 59–60; Lacan 1977a: 55). After all, if one's entry into language amounts to the wholesale submission of the subject to the values of society, it stands to reason that no one is *conscious* of the whole complexity of all these interlinked values in the form of taboos, prescriptions, valorizations and so on, at any given time. Most of the time one is completely *unconscious* of them, and yet, they structure one's actions, choices and pronouncements in a thoroughgoing manner. Even murderers like fictional mafia boss Tony Soprano show every sign of being well aware of the egregious moral reprehensibility of their deeds, even as they continue perpetrating them. Tony's actions – such as his tell-tale avoidance, in the presence of his therapist, of the subject of those deeds that he knows would offend her, and which continue plaguing his conscience intermittently – are no less structured by the normativity embedded in language than are those of law-abiding citizens. To put it differently: individuals who have been socialized along the 'normal' trajectory of acquiring language, *know* when they 'do wrong' in terms of prevailing societal norms (which are embedded in language).

In this respect Lacan's 'unconscious' resembles Saussure's concept of the underlying system of language, *langue*, which comprises the unconscious, trans-individual repository of grammatical rules and social conventions on which a speaker draws when she or he articulates linguistic utterances, or what Saussure calls *parole* (Lee 1990: 35–36). Moreover, the 'otherness' of language (as 'discourse of the Other') is for Lacan a precondition of being a speaking subject – language as the symbolic order transcends and pre-exists the subject, who eventually finds her or his place in society through their entry into language.

How is all of this related to the question of the analyst's intervention regarding the analysand's pathology, specifically in so far as his or her ethical orientation and the direction of therapy are concerned? A brief examination of Lacan's stance on the function of speech and language in psychoanalysis (1977a) is required to answer this question.

It is well-known that psychoanalysis developed out of a reciprocal relationship between Freud's clinical practice (and initially Breuer's), on the one hand, and his theorization of various aspects of the subject's psyche, as well as appropriate techniques of addressing the latter's pathological needs, and that Freud, following Bertha Pappenheim or the so-called Anna O. (one of Breuer's early 'psychoanalytical' patients, if not their very first; Freud 1957: 5; Lacan 1977a: 46), referred to psychoanalysis as the 'talking cure'. To this extent, there is no quarrel between him and Lacan, but when it comes to what they understood by 'speech' or 'language' as the indispensable medium of psychoanalytic practice, it is evident that Lacan – who refers to language (or discourse) as the 'symbolic order' – has read Freud through the lenses of Saussurean structural linguistics and Lévi-Strauss's cultural-anthropological elaboration of it. 'Lacan's difference from Freud', observes Bowie (1991: 57–58),

> ... is nowhere more evident than in his talk of 'the Symbolic'. This category was important to Lacan precisely because it was versatile and inclusive and referred in a single gesture to an entire range of separate signifying practices. It linked, in what promised to be a coherent and durable fashion, the world of unconscious mental process to that of speech, and both of them to the larger worlds of social and kinship structure. 'The Symbolic', for Lacan in the mid-fifties, is a supra-personal structural order ...

How did Lacan arrive at this position, which depends heavily on the sense that Lévi-Strauss gave to the symbolic as a cultural system (Bowie 1991: 58–59; Lee 1990: 62–64)? To answer this question, one has to turn to the important paper, 'The function and field of speech and language in psychoanalysis' (Lacan 1977a).

Criticizing ego-psychologists and object-relations theorists (Lee, 1990, pp. 32–34), Lacan here claims that analysts have only the speech of the analysand to work with, and proceeds to show, via an analysis of the phenomenon of the 'free-associating' analysand's frustration in the face of the silently listening analyst, that the subject (as analysand) is led to the disconcerting discovery that his or her 'identity' is an illusion, that is, that it is the result of 'misrecognition' (as it was theorized in 'The mirror stage', where the infant mistakenly but understandably regards its mirror-image as itself) (Lacan 1977a: 41–42). He further argues that the subject comes to grasp that what had always been experienced as his or her 'desire', really belongs to an imaginary construct (p. 42), and that his or her speech had therefore in a certain sense been 'empty' – in Lee's (1990: 40) formulation, '... it has been emptied of the subject by being filled with his alienating *moi* identity'.

Essentially, this means that the analysand discovers, by way of the inescapable experience of frustration, that there is a chasm separating him or her from what was previously thought of as their 'identity', but is now uncovered as something alienating. As Lacan puts it (1977a: 42; see also Lee 1990: 39):

> ... he [the analysand] ends up by recognizing that this being [of his] has never been anything more than his construct in the imaginary and that this construct disappoints all his certainties ... For in this labour which he undertakes to reconstruct

> *for another*, he rediscovers the fundamental alienation that made him construct it *like another*, and which has always destined it to be taken from him *by another*.

Instead of indulging the subject's need for security supposedly attainable by strengthening the ego or *moi*, Lacan therefore recommends nothing less than the cultivation of *uncertainty* on the subject's part by 'suspending' her or his 'certainties until their last mirages have been consumed' (Lacan 1977a: 42). Simultaneously, the subject is led to the realization that there is a significant 'gap' between one's imaginary constructs of oneself (*moi*- or ego-identities as manifestations of the subject of *what is said*) in sentences such as 'I am a considerate husband' and the position from which one speaks about oneself (the *je* or 'I' as subject of the *speaking*) (Lee 1990: 40–41). This 'gap' between the two distinct subject-positions also indicates the crucial function of repression. This is easily demonstrated in so far as the 'I' or *je*, which designates the position from which one speaks (that is, the subject of language), cannot be confronted directly. The moment one focuses on it in thought or language, it has become a *moi* or 'me', and such focusing is always performed from an un-objectifiable 'I'-position.

Moreover, in opposition to ego-psychologists and object-relations theorists, Lacan's approach here is predicated on the claim that speech is all that the therapist has at his or her disposal – in fact, it would be downright detrimental to the analysand to have recourse to any form of unitary, but illusory, alienating and ultimately constricting imaginary construct, the dependence on which is precisely what the patient has to free him- or herself of. It is at this point where the crucial difference between psychoanalysis and other therapeutic models, which was alluded to earlier, becomes evident. The reason for Lacan's opposition to mainstream and ego psychology – which simultaneously signals psychoanalysis' distinctive position regarding the availability of a universalistic ethical framework to the psychotherapist – is succinctly formulated by Parker (2001: 68):

> Lacan objected to psychology. He objected, because psychology entails a profound misunderstanding of the discursive basis of psychoanalytic phenomena, and this error is compounded by ego psychology which pursued the aim of adaptation of

> the subject to society through the elaboration of a model of the 'individual' which is amenable to what he termed an 'orthopaedics' ...

What Parker is alluding to here, concerns the 'abyssal basis' of the difference between Lacan and adherents of other psychological models regarding the ethical – an oxymoron which beckons towards the universalistic (that is, constitutively human) discursive 'foundation' comprising the unconscious, as well as towards the disruptive relation of the third register, that of the 'real' (which still has to be taken into account). This 'discursive basis' is constituted by the 'abyss' of the unconscious in the specifically Lacanian sense of the concept, which – as will become apparent – is 'trans-individual', and hence not susceptible to pitfalls of relativism as in the case of 'individual'-centred psychologies (for reasons explained at the outset).

Unlike other psychological theories of the human subject, psychoanalysis – and here specifically the Lacanian variety – avails itself of a 'third term' (Lacan 1977a: 49) over and above the analyst and the analysand, namely the unconscious. In fact, were it not for the decisive function of the unconscious, one might get the impression in 'Function and field', that the dialogue between the therapist and the patient would be sufficient to render the latter 'completely' and unfailingly in charge of her or his life without further ado, as some varieties of 'pop'-psychology (of the 'Yes!' I love myself!'-type) claim to do – a promise, needless to say, that no psychological model is able to live up to. Moreover, as I shall show, it is this function of the unconscious as repository of cultural value-systems that enables the psychoanalyst to eschew the pitfalls of a relativistic ethical stance – something which ultimately substitutes relativistic amorality for morality.

How is this achieved? Briefly put, Lacan shows that the analyst's task, far from aiming for some putative experience of the 'reality' of the subject (Lacan, 1977a: 44) – which inevitably results in exploring imaginary relations – consists in assisting him or her to come to grasp the symbolic significance of their 'free association', a discourse ineluctably structured from the perspective of the *je-* or 'I'-position of the subject. Along this trajectory the 'empty speech' of the subject (which correlates with the imaginary *moi* or ego) will be transformed into the 'full speech' of the *je* or 'I' (corresponding, in turn, to interpretation at the level of the symbolic register; Lacan 1977a: 46).[2] One cannot overlook the irony, that the 'empty speech' marking the subject's alienated position within the imaginary, reflects a certain experience of 'fullness', albeit a spurious one deriving from the paradigmatic function of the mirror stage, while the 'full speech' of the psychoanalytically actualized subject at the level of the symbolic correlates with an *absence* of *imaginary* 'fullness' (that masks a more significant emptiness). What the analysand's attainment of 'full speech' instantiates, is her or his understanding of the 'hidden dynamic' according to which she or he is (at least potentially) the narrator of her or his own life-story (Lacan 1977a: 46–47; Lee 1990: 41–42). In a nutshell, what Lacan is at pains to demonstrate here is the itinerary for the construction of a temporal, that is, a narrative subject through psychoanalytical discourse: she or he who has been like this, and who has or anticipates a future – a future, moreover, that will bestow on past events in the subject's life-story their overall significance or 'truth' (Lacan 1977a: 47). In other words, the integrative narration on the part of the subject, which has the effect of rendering a 'coherent tale', constitutes the 'meaning' of his or her life, and is made possible by the intersubjective character of the psychoanalytical dialogue.

Lee reminds one that what is important in the narration of the subject's personal narrative is less the historical 'accuracy' – if such a thing is at all possible – of the events recollected by the analysand, but rather the intersubjectively comprehensible narrative reconstruction of these events in the form of a life-story. Lacan puts it as follows (1977a: 48):

> ... in psychoanalytical anamnesis, it is not a question of reality, but of truth, because the effect of full speech is to reorder past contingencies by conferring on them the sense of necessities to come, such as they are constituted by the little freedom through which the subject makes them present.

2 Lee (1990: 38–47) provides an admirably lucid interpretive account of the 'transformation' of the analysand's 'empty speech' into 'full speech', as outlined by Lacan in 'Function and field' (1977a). See also Olivier (2004) in this regard.

The 'little freedom' invoked here, is, of course, the subject's capacity for language or speech, without which there could be no question of truth or falsity. They are ineluctably a function of language, whether truth be defined in terms of correspondence, coherence, pragmatics or disclosure.

It will be remembered, however, that we referred earlier to the role of the unconscious as a 'third term' in the psychoanalytical situation, and that this mitigates the impression of 'too much' arbitrarily imposed (imaginary) coherence on the part of the analysand's narrative. One cannot simply construct *any* life-story one might choose, as the fancy strikes one. What is at stake here is what Lacan (1977a: 49) refers to as the 'transindividual reality of the subject' – '*trans*-individual' in so far as the 'third term' structuring the conversation, namely the unconscious, is not merely something peculiar to each individual in the form of particular 'tendencies', but (as pointed out earlier) the 'discourse of the other' (Lacan 1977a: 55), in the sense of the unconscious, but encompassing symbolic order as repository of (among other things) a culture's ethical values.

What access does the analyst have to the unconscious as a structuring force on the part of the analysand, though? Per definition it is not directly accessible. Lacan's answer is exemplarily Freudian, in so far as he acknowledges the significance of parapraxes or 'slips' of all kinds as meaningful signifiers – the 'language' of the unconscious is legible in, among other things, the subject's somatic symptoms, the memories of her or his childhood and in the very specific, 'idiosyncratic' diction or verbal expressions on his or her part (Lacan, 1977a: 50; Lee 1990: 44). In his elaboration on the significance of Freud's *The psychopathology of everyday life* (1901), Lacan (1977a: 58) clarifies the sense in which a so-called 'Freudian slip', despite being a 'mistake' or 'failure' in speech as far as conscious intention is concerned, may be understood as being 'successful' in a different sense, namely to the extent that it reveals, as a linguistic fragment of the 'discourse of the Other', what unconsciously determines the subject as conscious *moi*.

In fact, the 'gaps' in the subject's unavoidably fragmentary or 'incomplete' free-associative discourse are filled in through interaction with the analyst (who 'punctuates' the discourse) by drawing on these manifestations of the 'censored chapter' of the subject's life constituted by the unconscious. The importance of this insight cannot be emphasized too strongly, because it is the contributing role played by the unconscious (the 'discourse of the Other'),[3] as it appears in the range of manifestations mentioned above, which presents analysand and analyst alike with a transindividual repository of societal values that function to prevent – or, at least, militate against – any semblance of arbitrary ethical judgments by either party in the course of the unfolding discourse. This is why the 'subject' as he or she is actualized in the psychoanalytical situation – the *je*, 'I', or subject of the symbolic register – surpasses the so-called 'subjective experience' of the individual or ego/*moi* (Lacan 1977a: 55); it is the subject as it is positioned within the encompassing symbolic order which represents, in the sense that Lévi-Strauss gave to it, a cultural system akin to an unconscious 'background' language (Lee 1990: 63–64). Within this symbolic domain the subject is precisely a 'subject' in so far as she or he is 'subject' to the ethical norms that govern society. It is in this way that the subject as *je* is able to tell a life-story that goes beyond the imaginary constructions of the ego or *moi* – a narrative filled in, with the aid of the punctuating interventions of the analyst, through recourse to the signifiers representing the unconscious.

The unconscious as repository of ethical values

One may wonder, however, on what grounds it may be asserted that the unconscious, which is 'structured like a language', is also the repository of ethical norms. Why does Lacan (1981: 34), following Freud (see, for example, Freud 1957: 12–15), say explicitly that the status of the unconscious

3 Especially in his later work, Lacan tends to capitalize 'Other' in the phrase 'discourse of the Other' (referring to the unconscious). On the significance of this sometimes confusing term in Lacan's work, see Bowie 1991: 82–83.

is 'ethical'?[4] I have already referred to the encompassing 'background language' that constitutes the unconscious as trans-individual repository of social values. But it would not make sense if all the values which circulate in a society at any given time were on a par with one another – there has to be some organizing principle or 'anchoring point(s)' for organizing the system of values which structures social and cultural practices. Precisely such organizing principle(s) are singled out by Lacan. Referring to the structure of language as 'signifying chain', he says (1977b: 154):

> There is in effect no signifying chain that does not have, as if attached to the punctuation of each of its units, a whole articulation of relevant contexts suspended 'vertically', as it were, from that point.

This 'vertical' dimension involves the relation between language as a (metonymical) chain of signifiers and the network of signifieds (conceptual meanings) with which it is unavoidably connected (even if every

4 This question involves more than what can be addressed in the space of a mere paper. Here I shall concentrate on what is most directly connected with the theme of the paper, namely the positioning of the subject (*je*) as narrator of her/his life-story within the symbolic register, which – as 'discourse of the Other' – bears the ethical norms of society. But it is not only the two registers, namely the imaginary (instantiated by the mirror stage) and the symbolic, that affect the subject. The register of the 'real' – that which resists symbolization, and is in fact forever left behind when the subject enters language – is equally important, especially because it involves the subject's 'desire'. 'Desire' is, for Lacan, the *gap* that separates 'need' from its linguistically articulated 'demand' – such as when a child asks a parent for something to eat. The upshot is that, no matter how hard the parent tries to satisfy the child's demand, the need can never be met, in so far as the demand masks what it is a disguised expression of, namely a longing or desire for a 'filling' of the child's (commonly human) 'lack' or 'want' of being by way of recognition by the other (here, the parent). Needless to say, every person's 'desire' in this Lacanian sense (ultimately deriving from Plato's account of *eros* in *The Symposium*), is hidden from him or her by repression, in so far as (and this is the important point) their desire conflicts in some way or other with the *moral* demands of society. Žižek (1993: 206–207) adduces an exemplary instance from Freud's clinical practice of such a hidden desire (that conflicts with the moral norms of society) on the part of the subject. The final section of this paper addresses the difficulties involved here.

signified is again, in turn, a signifier referring to other signifieds). Language as a chain of signifiers is metonymical in the Saussurean sense of there being no positive terms (referring to some extra-linguistic 'reality', as the older referential model of language implied), but only differences among signifiers, so that the meanings of terms are determined with reference to all other signifiers (and their signifieds, which also function as signifiers), so that each signifier in the system of language functions as a metonymy, that is, as a part representing the whole. Derrida would say that every signifier bears the 'trace' of every other signifier.

One might say, then, that the linear chain of signifiers, manifested in the subject's discourse, is 'tied down', to use Lee's words (1990: 61), by the operation of metaphor, where metaphor functions as the replacement of 'repressed' signifiers by others, but also refers to the 'anchoring' or stabilizing signifieds or meanings of the subject's signifying discourse which fulfill a crucial axiological function. These anchoring points are themselves 'unsaid' in so far as they may not appear overtly in a particular discourse but nevertheless 'ground' or organize the other signifiers in a systematic axiological manner. In contemporary society, for instance, despite the apparent social changes in favour of women's emancipation that have occurred over the last hundred years, it is arguably the case that we still live in a largely patriarchal culture – one structured by and 'anchored' in the so-called 'name of the father' (Lacan 1977a: 67; 1977d: 199) as largely occulted but nevertheless pervasively grounding, authoritative signifier which imparts to all other signifiers their axiological 'place' in the cultural system. (The fact that the 'name of the father' is the repressed signifier that occupies the position of central authority in contemporary culture – hence the description of the patriarchal order as 'phallogocentric', that is, centred by the phallic *logos* or word – does not mean that its centrality cannot and has not been challenged, of course. It has indeed been challenged consistently and persistently by many thinkers, especially, for obvious reasons, feminist ones such as Luce Irigaray [1994], Julia Kristeva [1997] and others.)[5]

To use a more specific example: in the mafia discourse structuring the previously mentioned television series, *The Sopranos*, the authority of the mafia boss or leader, which sometimes appears *overtly* in the exchanges among members of the 'family', is itself *covertly* anchored in the patriarchal signifier of the 'name of the father' – a signifier which, of course, structures all patriarchal discourses from those of the Roman Catholic Church and Islamic religion to that of mainstream Hollywood cinema, but here functions with particular ferocity in so far as no resistance to the authority of the mafia 'boss' (that is, the particular incumbent of this symbolic position at any given time) is tolerated. The interesting thing in this case is that the functioning of the repressed signifier (the 'name of the father') is perverted so that, instead of it being the anchoring point of a 'benign' patriarchal order – where it supposedly (but debatably) guarantees ethical recourse to principles of justice for *all* cultural subjects – it grounds the *unquestionable* authority of the boss in the concept of a virtually untouchable, authoritarian and autocratic father-figure. Because Tony Soprano's psychologist knows this precisely through the symptomatic omissions and refusals on his part – 'signifiers' which point to the 'discourse of the Other' as repository of societal values as well as to repressed instances where this has been breached – she also knows that it would be useless to draw his attention to the incompatibility between his own moral depravity (in the guise of the perversion of patriarchal authority into unscrupulous and unquestionable autocracy within the organization) and the ethical responsibility implied and demanded by his symbolic identity as father and leader of a community of sorts. The audience witnesses her with a friend, lamenting her felt powerlessness to address Tony's obvious resistance and duplicity in his conversations with her. Needless to say, if he had felt free, in his sessions with his psychologist, to talk through the things that weigh on his conscience (including ines-

5 Besides, as Michel Foucault (1990: 84; see also Olivier 2000, 2001 & 2003a) has argued, the operation of a (dominant) discourse (in this case patriarchy) opens the way for a counter-discourse (such as feminism) to oppose it.

capable guilt in the face of being a murderer – indirectly, if not directly), she would have been in a position to invoke the ethical values which find their anchoring point in the 'name of the father', such as the prohibition of murder, theft (on a grand scale), extortion, and so on. (Arguably, given her role as interpreter of the analysand's position *vis-à-vis* the ethical as ineluctable dimension of language, she is in such a position anyway, regardless of whether he 'comes clean' with her or not. The psychologist consulted by Tony's wife, by contrast, does not hesitate to confront her starkly with the ethical choices facing her, given her unhappiness in the knowledge of her husband's criminal way of life.) Here is a clear indication of where the psychologist or psychoanalyst should turn for guidance regarding ethical values: they are right there, in the censored 'chapters' of the analysand's discourse – those that are omitted precisely because of their ethical charge and which, for that reason, are bound up with signs of guilt, even where this is negatively signified or expressed.[6]

In Lacan's work one could go even further than the 'name of the father' as pervasively grounding signifier which organizes the 'discourse of the Other' as unconscious linguistic-cultural system along axiological (if patriarchal), ethical lines. If there is a signifier more fundamental than this one, it is the signifier referred to as 'the phallus'[7] (which must be carefully distinguished from Freud's concept of the penis in his theory of castration) (Lee 1990: 66–67):

> In effect, the phallus is the ultimate *point de capiton*, the signifier that fixes the meaning of the signifying chains of every subject's discourse, by virtue of its being 'veiled' or repressed. The phallus is present beneath every signifier as the signifier that has been repressed, and as such every signifier in effect is a metaphor substituting for the phallus ... As such a signifier, the phallus is not anything that any man

6 Such a 'negative' expression of guilt could take the form of a *denial* of responsibility for certain states of affairs, or of too vehement a *refusal* to discuss certain topics with the psychologist.

7 Interestingly, the 'phallus' may be regarded as the symbolic counterpart, not only of the penis, but also of the clitoris (Sykes, *Concise Oxford English Dictionary*, 1983: 768). This would legitimize Lacan's use of the term as signifier of (unattainable) fullness for both men and women.

> or woman could possibly 'have' (hence, it must not be confused with the penis) ... Precisely because no one can *have* the phallus, it becomes that which all want to *be*. The phallus then serves to signify as well that fullness of being, that complete identity, the lack of which is the fact of our ineluctable want-of-being.

But if the 'name of the father' is the signifier that, according to Lacan (1977a: 67), instantiates a 'symbolic function' linked to the 'figure of the law' with its universalistic conceptual and ethical implications, it means that the 'name of the father' indicates precisely the human subject's separation, through language, from the (unattainable) 'fullness of being' represented by the phallus. In light of this it seems conceivable that another figure – possibly 'the name of the mother', or 'the human being in general' – could take the place of the centralizing axiological figure of the 'father' as representative of the moral 'law'. Whether or not the variety of critiques launched against patriarchy by, among others, feminists and poststructuralists, will eventually succeed in dislodging 'the name of the father' as symbolic figure of the law, however, it seems to me unavoidable that the repression of the phallus (or something else, such as 'the circle', rather than an apparently sex-specific concept like 'phallus' or 'womb') as symbol of unattainable fullness would have to correlate with a signifier 'anchoring' the cultural system of ethical values at present represented by the patriarchal signifier (the 'name of the father'). In so far as this cultural system is indirectly accessible to us – and to the psychoanalyst – at the level of the unconscious as 'discourse of the Other', it is noteworthy that, as Lacan (1977e: 288) indicates, it is the repression of the phallus as signifier (denoting the fullness of being that the subject loses increasingly through its separation from the mother's body, followed by its passing through the mirror stage and eventually its entry into language) which fundamentally functions to constitute the unconscious as discourse or 'a language'.

Without this, as argued in this article, the psychoanalyst would not have access (albeit indirectly) to a medium which serves as a touchstone for the relation of the subject as analysand to the ethical values in terms of which a culture functions, even if – as indicated – these values are not impervious to critique. Most importantly, for reasons advanced here, this medium or discourse provides an indispensable means to resist the ubiquitous pitfalls of relativistic moral stances that tend to render the psychologist helpless. One might say that the unconscious considered as 'structured like a language' constitutes the cultural system in its axiological 'structuredness', against the backcloth of which various identifiable 'conventional moralities' may be identified which deviate from (or pervert) the normative implications of the system as such. 'Conventional' morality does not simply coincide with the axiological articulation of the unconscious. The 'conventional morality' of the mafia (according to which the mafia boss has the right to eliminate members of the *cosa nostra* whose positions have become untenable within its operations), or of apartheid, or of Nazi-Germany of the Third Reich, would be such perversions. Normatively speaking, the unconscious, to the extent that it is structured as outlined above, and to the degree that (through psychoanalytically astute interpretation of the way) it manifests itself 'negatively' in the analysand's discourse, could therefore function as a basis of critique regarding so-called conventional morality.

The ethical import of the 'real' in psychoanalysis

It would be a mistake, however, to think that this is all there is to it – that all the therapist has to figure out is where the subject stands in relation to all those 'anchored' values which structure the unconscious as discourse of the Other. This would be to ignore the complicating function of the third Lacanian register, that of the 'real' (which should not be confused with 'reality'). What, precisely, is the 'real' in Lacan? The (impossible) 'real' in Lacan's work may appear to correspond roughly to what Kant understood by the *Ding-an-sich* or the noumenal realm, which is 'thinkable', but not 'knowable', as phenomena in space and time are. 'Reality' (or the phenomenal realm for Kant) would comprise the combined realms of the imaginary and the symbolic for Lacan (where the imaginary fills in the gaps in the symbolic through fantasy, as it were), while the 'real' is that which escapes or resists symbolization and imaginary representation. But Lacan's 'real' is not synonymous with Kant's *Ding-an-sich*. One could say that, instead of being that – the noumenon – which is somehow 'behind' Kantian phenomena, the 'real' is that which *remains* after the imaginary and the symbolic have been 'subtracted' from reality, albeit in an unrepresentable fashion.

The question regarding the 'real' is complicated (if not rendered absurd) by the consideration that, by definition, it is that which resists symbolization, which cannot be 'said'. Perhaps the distinction between what can be 'said' and what can be 'shown' is appropriate here, which would explain why arts like painting and cinema are capable of conjuring up a sense of the 'real' by 'showing' the inexpressible. (A case in point is Claire Denis's 1988 film, *Chocolat*, set in colonial and postcolonial Cameroon, where at various stages in the narrative the camera confronts the audience with the 'real' in its ineffable, yet powerful presence as that which, while escaping signification, has far-reaching effects in the symbolic sphere.) Although the matter cannot be further pursued here, I would argue that Lacan's 'real' is further related to what Derrida and Badiou call the 'event' (see Derrida 2003: 85–91; and Zupancic 2000: 235) and to that sense of 'nothingness' which evokes, for Nietzsche, either 'passive' or 'active' nihilism on the subject's part (see Olivier 2004b). 'Active' nihilism is an active, creative axiological response to the realization that all the value-systems that have ever existed, including the Platonic-Christian, rest on – or hang above – an abyss or nothingness. 'Passive' nihilism is what ensues on the horrified retreat from this abyss, in the (chosen) illusory belief that the old value system still retains its value: the subject continues acting as if nothing has changed. 'Active' nihilism is the active creation or generation of value (meaning, sense) in the realization that there is no pre-existing value (there is only the void of meaning, or Lacan's 'real': that which is left over after imaginary and symbolic constructions have been removed from 'reality'). This – the fact that there are no intrinsic values – would explain why one's own, actively generated values are as 'good' as any inherited axiological system, which has also been similarly generated, after all. It would also explain – as I will argue further – why what Lacan describes as 'assuming one's desire' (what Nietzsche calls 'active' nihilism) would always have to display the character of transgression of the social and axiological *status quo* or conventional morality, so that the crucial question is raised: can such a transgression function as a paradigm of ethical action which is worth emulating in a new, (perhaps impossible) society?

Another kind of example of the 'real' would be the body in its 'pure', (conclusively) unsymbolizable organic state, the *needs* of which one 'feels' without being able to articulate them *as* felt needs, but only as symbolized *demands* – for example: 'Mom, I am hungry', where the symbolization of hunger on the part of the child may manifest or *show* more than could ever be articulated or *said* in language, namely a need for the parent's love. Because there is always an unclosable gap between these needs and their articulation as demands, this gap is what constitutes *desire*, for Lacan (Lacan 1977c: 263; Lee 1990: 55–59). But the 'real' also alludes to the realm of excess – the noumenal, in Kantian terms – in a different sense, where, *if* humans could belong fully to it (as they cannot), they *could* act fully in accordance with the moral law or imperative that requires acting on the grounds of duty alone. It would therefore seem that, in terms of what was argued earlier in this article, ethical action according to culturally approved values, anchored in the phallus as transcendental signifier, would be possible – in fact, resides in the realm of the conventionally 'possible', even if (as indicated) decoding the logic of the unconscious is not easy – in a less problematic manner if human existence did not imbricate the 'impossible' real. The 'real' is 'impossible', just as acting consistently according to the moral law is impossible. In this sense, then, ethics is '... the dimension of desire, which circles around the real *qua* impossible' (Zupancic 2000: 3).

In *The ethics of psychoanalysis* (1997: 20) Lacan remarks:

> ... my thesis is that the moral law, the moral command, the presence of the moral agency in our activity, insofar as it is structured by the symbolic, is that through which the real is actualized – the real as such, the weight of the real ... (p. 21) ... Moral action is, in effect, grafted on to the real. It introduces something new into the real and thereby opens a path in which the point of our presence is legitimized.

Although Lacan here refers to the activity of psychoanalysts, it applies, I believe, to that of all people. It is notable that he appears to reverse his claim: the symbolically structured moral agency is that through which the real is actualized, but the former is also 'grafted' on to the real. This seems to suggest that the way to align the inescapable, albeit unsymbolizable real with the function of therapy as the 'talking cure' at the level of the symbolic register, is to take into account the effects that this real has in the symbolic, that a symbolically *disruptive* encounter with unpredictable and uncontrollable 'events' elicits in relation to the world of symbolically mediated moral action. This could occur in the guise of being brought face to face with one's own possible death, or with the possible death or permanent absence of a loved one, for instance. The 'ethical logic' of desire in relation to the 'real' here is as follows: human life does not have 'meaning' or 'make sense' by itself, but depends on something which 'surpasses' – or, for that matter, 'limits' – it in a double sense for such meaningfulness – that is, life is not self-justifying, but requires a moment of excess in more than one sense for its justification. On the one hand this 'excess' (or limit) refers to the 'real' as the brute, meaningless, symbolically resistant facticity of the 'given', while on the other it alludes to one's desire as that which 'is not' insofar as it is precisely what would be 'grafted on to the real' if the subject is able to 'take up' her or his desire (something that is not at all self-evidently the case).

An ethical act would hence be one where, for the sake of such justification, life itself could, paradoxically, be sacrificed (as in the case of Antigone [Lacan 1997: 243–287], or of Hamlet, for that matter), or one's happy relationship with a loved one is sacrificed, paradoxically, for the sake of the latter's happiness (as in the case of the woman in the film, *Welcome to Sarajevo*, who renounces her maternity to enable her daughter to be adopted by a British journalist) (Žižek 2000: xii). Or it could manifest itself in the guise of someone transgressing the symbolically mediated, moral code of her society by choosing to do something that conflicts with this code, and hence renders her guilty or 'criminal' in relation to the extant law, but simultaneously indicts this law as incapable of accommodating the desire of the individual, and hence as being in need of 're-invention' for the sake of a 'singular justice', as Derrida might put it

(Caputo 1997: 136–137). Hence Lacan's injunction (1997: 311–325), that the subject should 'act in conformity with' her or his 'desire'. Only by following the path of one's (usually hidden or repressed) desire is it possible to confront, in the form of an ethical act, the effects of the (impossible) real in human reality – effects which are likely to reconfigure one's world in surprising or decisive ways.

It is important not to misunderstand what this entails, as Judith Butler evidently does when she insists, in her debate with Žižek, on construing the 'real' as something completely 'outside' the symbolic (Žižek 2000a: 214): the 'real' must be understood, instead, '*... as the internal limit of the process of symbolization that sustains the space of historicity*' (Žižek 2000a: 214). In other words, contingent, symbolically meaningful (or, on the other hand, nonsensical) historical acts would be unthinkable if the symbolic sphere were somehow capable of semiotic saturation. The fact is that the latter cannot be self-sufficient; it always *fails* to attain a plenum or fullness of meaning – hence the constant need for ideologies as the false promise of such fulfillment. It is this failure of the symbolic to achieve totalization or completeness that is symptomatic of the 'real' as its inescapable (internal) limit. Joan Copjec articulates this insight in terms of the limits to signification (2002: 95–96):

> Lacan's definition of the real is precisely this: that which, in language or the symbolic, negates the possibility of any metadimension, any metalanguage. It is this undislodgeable negation, this rigid kernel in the heart of the symbolic, that forces the signifier to split off from and turn around on itself. For, in the absence of any metalanguage, the signifier can only signify by referring to another signifier ... Far from positing the existence of an elsewhere, the real as internal limit of the symbolic – that is, the very impotence of the signifier – is the obstacle that scotches the possibility of rising out of or above the symbolic.

By further characterizing it '... as a certain disturbance or dislocation in the order of historical being', Copjec (2002: 97) highlights what I am here arguing, namely that the 'experience' or impact of the real on one's life can reconfigure or overhaul its symbolic-historical parameters, down to its very foundation, for example what was referred to earlier as the 'name of the father', or alternatively, capital as major phallic signifier in the contemporary hegemonic economic system. An experience of the internal limits of capital – for instance via a wilderness-adventure which is both devastating and enriching – may indeed drive home the fact that capital does not instantiate the only possible symbolic universe. And such an awareness, with its concomitant desire, opens the way to ethical action.

What Žižek, referring to the traumatic effect of the Second World War, says about the 'real' as that which causes us to 'think', is also true of it as that which impels us to *act* ethically (2000a: 213):

> ... what provokes us to think is always a traumatic encounter with some external Real which brutally imposes itself on us, shattering our established ways of thinking. As such, a true thought is always decentred: one does not think spontaneously, one is *forced* to think.

One should remind oneself that what may seem to be transcendental logic here, in fact entails a quasi-transcendental twist: it is not simply a matter of life depending for its justification, or action for its ethical status, on something exceeding it or limiting its symbolic universe – this could, erroneously, be understood as some sort of 'guaranteed' justification. That which exceeds or limits it as the real should perhaps rather be understood as having a quasi-transcendental ethical function insofar as it justifies existence, but not in an unproblematical or 'pure' sense, so that existence, or motherhood for example, may *unproblematically* be sacrificed through an ethical act. The moral law to do one's 'duty' regardless of its consequences, for example, confronts one with the most difficult of choices. It justifies life ethically, but not in an uncomplicated, straightforward manner, just as 'living for one's child' (or for one's honour, as the Greek heroes did), does not dictate in clear, positive, algorithmic fashion exactly what one's course of ethical action should be, but reminds one through the experience of a bad conscience or guilt when one has violated it (see Copjec 1996: xiv–xv). Similarly, the 'real' may be claimed to have a quasi-transcendental function: given the assumption (or alternatively the voluntary sacrifice) of one's 'singular' desire (which radically individualizes the acting person), it is the condition of possibility of ethical action as well as of its 'impossibility' (that is, of un-ethical action from the perspective of the symbolic sphere of conventional values).

Žižek (1993: 206–207) draws one's attention to a paradigmatic instance, in Freud's work, of what is at stake here – one that simultaneously demonstrates the dependence of a non-relativistic psychotherapeutic stance on the symbolic sphere of societal values, as well as on the 'impossible real' as that which, by exceeding the symbolic, provides the (non-symbolizable) opportunity or event for an encounter with the radically singular nature of the subject's desire, which has to be seized if the normativity or law of the symbolic is to be mediated by the requirements for ethical fulfillment on the part of the individual subject. By this I mean that, insofar as the individual subject's 'desire' is hidden from her or him by repression or foreclosure,[8] it will always to a lesser or greater degree be incompatible with societal values (otherwise it would not be repressed or foreclosed). Hence, as the following case demonstrates, the psychotherapist is confronted by the value-system embedded in language, as well as by the analysand's desire as conflicting with, but simultaneously calling for a re-configuration of, the symbolic in such a way as to allow the realization of her or his desire. The pertinent example from Freud involves a woman married to a lawyer or 'Doctor of the Right', that is, a 'Doctor of Law' ('Doktor der Rechte'), who saw him on her wedding anniversary, and who had inadvertently nicked her left-hand ring finger while clipping her nails. In Austria wedding bands are worn on the right hand ring finger, and Freud realized the symptomatic relevance of her 'slip of the finger' when she informed him that the man she had been in love with was a medical doctor (colloquially called a 'Doktor der Linke' or 'Doctor of the Left'): her act of cutting her left ring finger on her wedding anniversary betrayed her unconscious – in fact, foreclosed (see note

8 'Foreclosure' denotes that which is so incompatible with the normative requirements of society that (in contrast to what is first traumatically experienced and then repressed), the socialized (Oedipalized) subject 'rejects' it from his or her consciousness. It is only to be perceived as a symptom on the body, for example as hallucination. See Benvenuto and Kennedy 1986: 146–153; Olivier 1998: 137–139.

8) – desire for this man from her past. Because such a desire on the part of a married woman conflicted with the values of Austrian society at the time, she was incapable of admitting to herself that it even existed in an unconscious, foreclosed state, but from the perspective of the wound on her finger (an instance of the *objet petit a*, as Lacan calls it, in which her desire is concentrated and can therefore become 'visible'), this desire was perceivable to the analyst (Freud). For her to 'assume her desire' and all it entailed would have appeared immoral, if not criminal in the symbolic terms of conventional morality, even if such an act would have been radically singular, and as such expressive of an implicit wish to re-invent extant society in a manner that would assimilate or accommodate her desire symbolically. Alternatively, were she able to face the 'real' which disrupts her symbolic universe via the little wound on her finger, one could say that a truly *ethical* act on her part might be precisely not to follow the path where the assumption of her desire would seem to lead (namely to divorce her husband, leave her family and seek out her long-denied love), but to sacrifice or 'give up' her desire for the sake of the happiness of her family (and perhaps another family too).

The most difficult question of all here is the following: what if the desire of the subject is such that it conflicts so drastically with the values of society that it does not so much offer a re-invention or renewal of the latter, but renders it null and void or excludes it conclusively? It is one thing to say that the Viennese woman who loved the medical doctor may have shocked her contemporaries by leaving her husband and seeking out her first love (but nothing more than that); and another to say that, by assuming her desire she would have pointed to the need for a re-invention of society, towards a future society where such hypocritical mores would not stand in the way of one's desire. But what about someone like Timothy McVeigh as a man who, in assuming his desire, inflicted death on hundreds of others (in Oklahoma City) who did not have a choice in the matter? Or Hitler as such a subject? Should one not perhaps say that radically singularizing, ethical actions of the Nietzschean type: 'Become who you are', subvert their own ethical status in Lacanian terms if they do not offer themselves as models to other subjects, that is, if they cannot function as a model for being 'repeated differently' by other, equally singularizing subjects (none of whom would be identical in terms of their own 'desire')?

As Derrida might put it, as far as the tension between law and justice is concerned: justice (here, the Viennese woman's desire) is impossible, because it conflicts with the (conventional) law; hence, the law has to be temporarily suspended and re-invented for this singular justice to prevail (Caputo 1997: 136–137). But the moment this has been done, or phenomenalized, justice is, again, lost because of the (unattainable) 'entry' into the symbolic of the 'real' of her singular desire, which would do other people in her life an 'injustice'. Hence the claim that Derridean justice, like the Lacanian real, is the 'impossible', and hence that the truly ethical thing to do on her part, once she has acknowledged her desire, may in fact be to 'give it up' – not because this accords with the conventional morality of being 'loyal to one's family', but precisely insofar as it (her singularizing desire) has been 'assumed', recognized, and yet been set aside for the sake of others. This seems to be what Lacan implies where he says (Lacan 1997: 21–22): '... the ethical limits of psychoanalysis coincide with the limits of its practice. Its practice is only a preliminary to moral action as such – the so-called action being the one through which we enter the real'. In other words, assuming one's desire is only a *preparation* for possible moral or ethical action, and a *condition* for it, because such taking up of one's desire – in accordance with it being radically and irreducibly singular for each person (Lacan 1997: 24) – would invariably have the character of a transgression of conventional (that is, conventionally sanctioned) morality. This is also why the unconscious as discourse of the Other plays an important role here as a kind of backcloth to such moral action – it is always in relation to this that the shattering experience or event of 'confronting the (impossible) real' happens, and against which *both* a transgressive acting according to one's desire *and* a sacrifice of this very (acknowledged) desire would attain ethical import. Hence, from a Lacanian point of view, neither of these possibilities can be regarded as the manifestation of mere whim, to be given utterly relativistic status: both possibilities are situated within an unconscious 'symbolic-cultural' network which is questioned via the subject's (transgressive, because utterly singular) desire, and whatever the course of action the subject embarks on (sacrifice of *or* acting in accordance with this desire), in ethical terms it is not arbitrary, but potentially transformative or reconfigurative of the very conventional morality it presupposes and questions. This implies further that, through such transgressive, transformative action, the ethical agent introduces a radical modification into the symbolic universe that she or he challenges via their action, and simultaneously reconfigures their very identity, in this way opening up the prospect of a differently configured symbolic universe – something that could assume the form of a radically new politics, even a new social order. Žižek (2000a: 220) clarifies what is at stake here:

> ... what the Lacanian notion of 'act' aims at is not a mere displacement/resignification of the symbolic coordinates that confer on the subject his or her identity, but the radical transformation of the very universal structuring 'principle' of the existing symbolic order.

What I have just outlined is one way of addressing the difficult question regarding the possibility of accommodating singularizing (if not criminalizing) 'ethical' action on the part of individual subjects in the universal domain of the symbolic as repository of cultural values. What would be the implications of this rather complex configuration between the real and the human reality of symbolically mediated choices and decisions for psychotherapy? And what is the connection between a person's encounter with the Lacanian real and ethical action? Two possibilities present themselves here: either the person concerned could have 'taken up her or his desire' prior to the devastating events in question, or, alternatively, the confrontation with the real, by putting the individual's symbolic-ethical horizon in question, functions powerfully to remind the person thus questioned that it is not the only such symbolic framework available – it is revealed in its constructedness, and hence its possible replaceability by another framework constructed by the radically questioned individual. As I see it, therefore, the therapist faces the difficult task of guiding the analysand to the point where she or he grasps the fact that ethical action requires the 'assumption of her or his desire' in the sense of figuring out what it is that 'justifies' his or her life, and acting accordingly when it is appropriate to do so.

In *The Sopranos*, referred to at the outset in this paper, Tony's wife is confronted with just this choice by her psychotherapist, when he points out to her that she could either connive at Tony's life of unmitigated crime and enjoy her life of luxury in a familiar symbolic universe (while enduring or ignoring the pangs of guilty conscience), or she could let the (silent) voice of conscience (silent, because it does not prescribe anything in positive terms) turn her symbolic universe on its head and 'take up' her desire. That is, she could choose to leave him – a desire implicitly communicated to the psychiatrist by consulting him – and live a 'morally good' life to the best of her (finite) ability, but without the conventional approbation of the *cosa nostra* community (which requires that a wife stand by her husband), or the material wealth that he provides. In other words, she has to discover and acknowledge what her 'real desire' is, in the face of the 'real' that impinges so powerfully on her life with its excessive, incalculable weight – in the guise of those occasions when life, denuded or devoid of value, asserts itself. Only when she has affirmed her desire in this sense, does an ethical act become possible in Lacanian terms.

In J.M. Coetzee's deeply disturbing novel, *Disgrace* (2000), one is afforded another pertinent fictional instance of how, through specific events, the 'real' may shatter or disrupt an individual's symbolic universe, and how this confronts the individual(s) concerned with an ethical choice – or rather, with the opportunity to act ethically. Soon after disgraced academic David Lurie moved in with his daughter, Lucy, on her Eastern Cape smallholding, they are subjected to a brutal assault by three men, and Lucy is raped by them. While David wants justice, and tries his best to persuade Lucy to want it, too, at least in the guise of laying a charge of rape against their assailants, Lucy refuses to do anything – even when it becomes apparent that the man who has bought part of her land from her, Petrus, may be implicated. It gradually becomes clear that, while David inhabits the 'western' symbolic (moral and legal) universe where certain acts (like rape) cannot be excused or accepted, Lucy has already reconfigured her own mindset to adapt (or switch) to a different, 'African' symbolic universe, where 'rape' may function to impress on a woman the fact that she is vulnerable and, as such, requires a man's (Petrus's?) protection. The fact that Lucy refuses counselling and that she even decides to keep the baby that results from the rape, is indicative, in my judgment, that she (having previously 'taken up her desire' by deciding to live in virtual subsistence economic terms on the land in close proximity to African people) is acting ethically in a Lacanian sense. Whatever residual attachment she may still have had to a typical western system of values, is decisively obliterated by the traumatic experience of the 'real' through the rape, and although some may argue that her subsequent decisions cannot be regarded as 'ethical' because they were forced by an act of terror (see Zupancic 2000: 213–221), in my view this is not the case: Lucy does have a choice, and she decides in favour of subjecting herself to what one may call an 'African' way of doing things – much to the understandable consternation of her father, who (with his love of the English romantics) is a European in cultural terms. In short: Lucy acts ethically in so far as she gives up her right to 'justice' in legal terms in order to be assimilated into a different symbolic universe where she believes she will be given a place to exist and survive.

In light of the theme of this paper the interesting question here is: What would a psychotherapist have advised Lucy if she had sought counselling? Any attempt to guide her in the direction of seeking 'justice' on her father's (and existing law's) terms would have elicited opposition from her (because she clearly thinks of such 'justice' as being irrelevant), as would any attempt to rationalize the rape as being 'just one of those things' in South African society. Although she accepts the rape stolidly, despite signs of trauma and repression on her part, this is not simply a matter of adapting to an 'abnormal society' (as was explained at the beginning of this paper regarding what was expected from my friend the psychologist). Rather, in Lacan's terms, she is taking an ethical stand in accordance with her desire, to be 'part of the land' in the Eastern Cape. And this ethical stance on her part requires of her to reconfigure her own mindset to be able to be part of an African symbolic universe. The child that she is carrying therefore becomes a powerful metaphor for a fusion of her and Africa's symbolic horizons, and the novel ends with her father symbolically 'giving her up' metonymically (something astutely observed by psychoanalytical theorist Andrea Hurst in conversation), when he 'gives up' the young dog (which has become attached to him) to death, in a profoundly moving act of soliciting a kind of redemption through sacrifice.

As pointed out earlier, in facing the difficulties discussed above the (Lacanian) psychotherapist has at his or her disposal the universalistic symbolic system of cultural values as it is embedded in the ('linguistic structure' of the) unconscious – something that is not vitiated by intercultural differences, given the fact that such differences are ineluctably articulated in conceptually negotiable language: a mother's or a woman's role may differ in various societies, but 'mother' and 'woman' are concepts which occupy specific positions in relation to anchoring signifiers (such as the phallus) in the signifying chain of language and therefore *imply* a universal meaning, which is thus interpretively negotiable. In addition, however, the psychotherapist must face the demands of the 'real' as that which shatters, limits or exceeds the symbolic universe of the subject in the form of the singularizing *event* that 'frames' the desire of the analysand. By implication the psychotherapist would fail in her or his ethical task if they neglect an opportunity to draw the analysand's attention to that something – what Lacan calls the *objet petit a* (Žižek 1993: 206–207) – from the perspective of which this singular desire can be seized. Only in doing this, is the way prepared for ethical action in a non-relativistic manner.

References

Benvenuto, B. and Kennedy, R. 1986. *The works of Jacques Lacan. An introduction*. London: Free Association Books.

Bowie, M. 1991. *Lacan*. London: Fontana Press.

Caputo, J.D. (ed.). 1997. *Deconstruction in a nutshell. A conversation with Jacques Derrida*. New York: Fordham University Press.

Coetzee, J.M. 2000. *Disgrace*. London: Vintage.

Copjec, J. 1996. 'Introduction: Evil in the finite time of the world'. In: Copjec, J. (ed.), *Radical evil*. London: Verso, pp. vii–xxviii.

Copjec, J. 2002. *Imagine there's no woman. Ethics and sublimation.* Cambridge, Mass.: The MIT Press.
Denis, C. (dir.). 1988. *Chocolat.* France/West Germany/Cameroon: World Films.
Derrida, J. 2003. 'Autoimmunity: Real and symbolic suicides – A dialogue with Jacques Derrida'. In: Borradori, G., *Philosophy in a time of terror. Dialogues with Jürgen Habermas and Jacques Derrida.* Chicago: The University of Chicago Press, pp. 85–136.
Foucault, M. 1990. 'Politics and reason'. In: Kritzman, L.D. (ed.), *Michel Foucault: Politics, philosophy, culture. Interviews and other writings 1977–1984.* New York: Routledge, pp. 57–85.
Freud, S. 1957. The origin and development of psychoanalysis. Trans. Chase, H.W. In *A general selection from the works of Sigmund Freud.* Rickman, J. (ed.). New York: Doubleday Anchor, pp. 3–36.
Hardt, M., and Negri, A. 2001. *Empire.* Cambridge, Mass.: Harvard University Press.
Irigaray, L. 1994. *Speculum of the other woman.* Trans. Gill, G.C. New York: Cornell University Press.
Kristeva, J. 1997. *The portable Kristeva.* Oliver, K. (ed.). New York: Columbia University Press.
Lacan, J. 1977. 'The mirror stage as formative of the function of the I as revealed in psychoanalytic experience'. In: *Écrits: A selection.* Trans. Sheridan, A. New York: W.W. Norton, pp. 1–7.
Lacan, J. 1977a. 'The function and field of speech and language in psychoanalysis'. In: *Écrits: A selection.* Trans. Sheridan, A. New York: W.W. Norton, pp. 30–113.
Lacan, J. 1977b. 'The agency of the letter in the unconscious or reason since Freud'. In: *Écrits: A selection.* Trans. Sheridan, A. New York: W.W. Norton, pp. 146–178.
Lacan, J. 1977c. 'The direction of the treatment and the principles of its power'. In: *Écrits: A selection.* Trans. Sheridan, A. New York: W.W. Norton, pp. 226–280.
Lacan, J. 1977d. 'On a question preliminary to any possible treatment of psychosis'. In: *Écrits: A selection.* Trans. Sheridan, A. New York: W.W. Norton, pp. 179–225.

Lacan, J. 1977e. 'The signification of the phallus'. In: *Écrits: A selection.* Trans. Sheridan, A. New York: W.W. Norton, pp. 281–291.
Lacan, J. 1981. *The four fundamental concepts of psycho-analysis.* (*Seminar XI.*) Trans. Sheridan, A. New York: W.W. Norton.
Lacan, J. 1997. *The seminar of Jacques Lacan – Book VII: The ethics of psychoanalysis 1959–1960.* Trans. Porter, D. New York: W.W. Norton.
Lee, J. 1990. *Jacques Lacan.* Amherst: The University of Massachusetts Press.
Lyotard, J.-F. 1984. *The postmodern condition.* Trans. Bennington, G. & Massumi, B. Manchester: The University of Manchester Press.
Mitchell, S.A. & Black, M.J. 1995. *Freud and beyond. A history of modern psychoanalytic thought.* New York: Basic Books.
Olivier, B. 1998. 'Freud and Lyotard on civilization'. *South African Journal of Philosophy*, 17 (2), pp. 126–141.
Olivier, B. 2000. 'Discourse, genealogy, social theory and a society in transition: The challenge facing the human sciences'. *Society in Transition (Journal of the SA Sociological Association),* 31 (1), pp. 45–57.
Olivier, B. 2001. 'Discourse, space and violence'. In: Von Maltzan, C., & Wilson, R. (eds), *Spaces and crossings: Essays on literature and culture in Africa and beyond.* Frankfurt am Main: Peter Lang, pp. 301–318.
Olivier, B. 2003. 'Lacan: Problematisering van die filosofie'. *Fragmente – Tydskrif vir filosofie en kultuurkritiek*, 10 & 11, pp. 42–54.
Olivier, B. 2003a. 'Discourse, agency and the question of evil'. *South African Journal of Philosophy*, 22 (4), pp. 329–348. Reprinted here, as Chapter 1 of this volume.
Olivier, B. 2004. 'Lacan's subject: the imaginary, language, the real and philosophy'. *South African Journal of Philosophy*, 23 (1), pp. 1–19.
Olivier, B. 2004b. '"Passive" nihilism in Clark's *Kids* and Hardwicke's *Thirteen*'. *South African Journal of Art History*, 19, pp. 97–108.
Painter, D. and Terre Blanche, M. 2004. 'Critical psychology in South Africa: Looking back and looking ahead'. *South African Journal of Psychology*, 34 (4), pp. 520–543.
Parker, I. 2001. 'Lacan, psychology and the discourse of the university'. *Psychoanalytic Studies*, 3 (1), pp. 67–77.

Sykes, J.B. (ed.). 1983. *Concise Oxford English Dictionary of Current English*. Oxford: Clarendon Press.

Žižek, S. 1993. '"The thing that thinks": The Kantian background of the *noir* subject'. In: *Shades of* Noir – *A reader*. Copjec, J. (ed.). London & New York: Verso, pp. 199–226.

Žižek, S. 2000. 'Foreword: Why is Kant worth fighting for?' In Zupancic, A. *Ethics of the real. Kant, Lacan*. New York: Verso, pp. vii–xiii.

Žižek, S. 2000a. 'Da capo senza fine'. In Butler, J., Laclau, E. & Žižek, S. *Contingency, hegemony, universality – Contemporary dialogues on the left*. New York: Verso, pp. 213–262.

Zupancic, A. 2000. *Ethics of the real. Kant, Lacan*. New York: Verso.

CHAPTER 4

The contemporary context of relativity and relativism

The signifying chain, relativity and relativism

In *The agency of the letter* (1977: 154), Jacques Lacan makes the following statement:

> There is indeed no signifying chain that does not have, as if attached to the punctuation of each of its units, a whole articulation of relevant contexts suspended 'vertically', as it were, from that point.

Commenting on Lacan's notion of a 'signifying chain' – something that forms part of his 'inventive' appropriation of Saussure's structural-linguistic conceptual arsenal – Malcolm Bowie (1991: 65–66) remarks:

> He needed a way of describing conjointly two features of language that mattered equally to psychoanalysis but that had not until then been brought into alignment. The first was its obdurate and impersonal systemic force, and the second its fecundity, the pluralizing semantic power that it enjoyed in the speech of individual persons. For these purposes the metaphor of the 'signifying chain' proves to be particularly versatile. It has a suitably penal and correctional air: the chain is what limits the speaker's freedom, and the concatenation of its links speaks of a rigid causal order in which he is powerless to intervene. Yet the chain is also mobile, sinuous and able to loop back upon itself; any one of its links can provide a point of attachment to other chains.

I shall return to the pertinence (for the present theme) of these references to the 'chain of signifiers' *á la* Lacan, but here I shall merely note that they provide a key to understanding the contemporary cultural and philosophical *context* within which an investigation regarding the meaning or implications of the concepts 'relativity' and 'relativism' could be (in my opinion profitably) conducted. This is the case, I believe, because what may be called the 'linguistic philosophical paradigm', or perhaps more broadly the philosophical framework of 'networks of signification' has decisively superseded the older one which took the centrality of consciousness as its point of departure (and the demise of which can be perceived in the desperate struggle of Husserl to ground the sciences in the endlessly re-animating conscious act of intuition). I am convinced that this frame of reference, in various guises, comprises the most encompassing context for the investigation of any and all phenomena today, including those under discussion here.

Suffice it to say at this point, then, that Lacan's Saussurean image of an endlessly extending and variously articulated 'signifying chain' enables one to conceive of an indefinite (if not infinite) number of signifying 'chainlets' comprising the signifying 'chain' in its entirety (something that raises the interesting question concerning the semiotic and epistemological status of the chain: is it closed or open, and if this [formally exhaustive] domain of meaning is closed, is it complete?[1]) The first important point is that *all the links and lengths of the chain that comprises language are interconnected and pre-exist individual subjects* – there is no link or length of the chain that can be said to be 'unconnected', and the subject acquires the ability to speak or write by 'entering' language. Even relatively useless or unused links are still somewhere 'connected' to the rest of the

1 This is a difficult question that cannot be exhaustively addressed at present. (See in this regard Sheridan, 1977: ix.) Another one of Lacan's metaphors for the signifying process is as revealing as that of the 'chain', namely his image of a train (Lacan, 1977: 152) moving through time and space. An additional advantage of this metaphor is that it allows one to grasp the positioning of the subject within the signifying chain/train, here envisaged as a boy and a girl sitting opposite each other in a compartment, and therefore 'seeing' things from their respective 'angles': the boy sees a sign at a station, 'Men', erroneously as naming the station, while the girl, making the opposite 'mistake', sees it as 'Ladies' and 'corrects' him accordingly. The moral of the story? We all understand things from the perspective of our position on or in the 'train' of language, or the symbolic register.

chain. Moreover, links or lengths of chain can be detached from specific points and re-attached elsewhere. The human subject, who her- or himself occupies a 'position' in the signifying chain, is capable of situating her- or himself differently within language from time to time.

Here I want to argue that every distinguishable length of the signifying chain may be compared to what is today commonly referred to as a 'context', and that one could also think of it as a 'frame of reference', in Heideggerian (1978: 116) terms as a (relational) 'totality of involvements', or in Einsteinian (or Galileian) terms as an 'inertial frame' (of reference) relative to which pertinent judgements regarding motion can be made (Coles, 2000: 10–12; Shlain, 1991: 60, 121). One would not have much difficulty either, I believe, to show that, today, there are other suggestive ways of representing Lacan's 'signifying chain' – ways that model the interconnectedness of contexts of meaning with the purpose of highlighting different features of this all-encompassing signifying medium. So, for example, Deleuze and Guattari's (1987: 3–25) botanical metaphor of the 'rhizome' and therefore of a processual, ever-reconfiguring 'subterranean' rhizomatic network of meanings (at different levels) is a fecund metaphor for expanding, largely invisible semiotic processes happening at multiple (social, economic, political, scientific, artistic, literary) levels at the same time. So, too, Hardt and Negri's (2001: 298–300) conception of two intersecting axes by means of which the functioning of contemporary information- or communication-systems can be understood, namely the horizontal, democratic level, exemplified by the internet, and the vertical, 'oligopolistic' level, exemplified by radio-broadcasting networks, enables one to come to terms with the fact that (as Lacan's train-metaphor also suggests; see note 1), wherever meaning operates, one encounters countervailing tendencies of power.

The second important point is that, regardless of the frame of reference or meaning-context within which one finds oneself at any given time – that of the (Husserlian) lifeworld or of everyday experience, that of a specific culture or religion, that of a (natural or social-) scientific discipline, of an institution, and so on – and regardless of the tacit assumptions that govern such a frame of reference or relational totality (for example the 'referential' metaphysical assumption of an independently pre-existing, concrete, material world governing the structure of everyday experience as well as the 'empirical' or positivistic approach in the natural and the social sciences), *Lacan's metaphor of the 'signifying chain'* (and its derivatives, such as 'text') *applies to all these contexts without exception*. There is nothing that exempts even the conceit of the ontological independence of the 'concrete world' from its conceptualization in terms of the signifying chain, or the 'symbolic order'. This is not to say there *is* nothing outside of the signifying chain or what Derrida has metaphorically called the 'text';[2] only that what is not available in terms of signification, or what is not symbolizable remains, by that token, unintelligible[3] – this comprises what Lacan terms the 'real', as opposed to 'reality', which is constituted as an amalgam of the orders of the symbolic or language, and the 'imaginary' order or realm of images.

2 In this regard it is instructive to note that Derrida's (1980: 158) famous (or notorious) remark, often translated as 'There is nothing outside of the text' is misleading in this formulation. An alternative translation, namely 'There is no outside-text' renders his position more accurately, namely that anything 'outside' the field of possible signification or symbolization is not approachable as a 'text' (in the metaphorical sense of a 'signifying complex'). See also note 3, below.

3 This insight has been variously articulated by thinkers from Kant through Wittgenstein and Gadamer to Lacan and Derrida. Gadamer (1982: 432), for instance, says that: 'Being, insofar as it can be understood, is language'. The qualification, 'can be understood', is all-important. Similarly, Lacan's order of the 'real' denotes that which resists symbolization (cf. Bowie, 1991: 94). To claim that the 'real' in this sense (which corresponds with the Kantian 'thing-in-itself') can be *known* in terms of its specifiable properties, is to overlook the significance of Kant's transcendental turn (or 'Copernican Revolution') as well as that of the later 'linguistic turn' (for which it paved the way) on the part of thinkers such as Wittgenstein, Heidegger, Gadamer, Lacan and Derrida, namely that conceptually or linguistically articulated experience is *constitutive* of 'reality' (as opposed to the Lacanian 'real'). John Caputo (1993: 78) elaborates in an illuminating manner on the paradox concerning the 'ineffable' (the Lacanian 'real'), namely that one is able to symbolize it at least minimally *as unsymbolizable*, or as he puts it (borrowing a term from T.S. Eliot), as 'effanineffable'. In other words, we can talk about it *as* that which we cannot talk about. (Needless to say, in all of this, the term 'language' and its equivalents are used in an encompassing sense which includes all signifiers or bearers of conceptual meaning, such as gestures, written and spoken language.)

Against the backdrop of what I have said so far I would like to argue that Lacan's metaphor of the 'signifying chain' provides one with a model that resists charges or suspicions of unavoidable epistemological and semiotic *relativism* while simultaneously illuminating the ineluctable *relativity* (contextuality, relationality) of meaning and of knowledge-claims. As I shall attempt to show, it presents one with the formal means to negotiate all and any process of meaning-generation and therefore, in a sense, provides a 'constant' by means of which divergent situations can be assessed or judged, analogous to the way in which the speed of light provides a constant (in an expanding universe) by means of which specific, situational space-time relations can be understood in Einstein's theory of special relativity. Moreover – and this is the upshot of the present inquiry – the notion of the signifying chain, with all it entails, enables one to negotiate the immensely complex 'relativity' (of context-based knowledge, for instance) by which contemporary culture is characterized, and which many intellectuals mistakenly seem to regard as good reason to affirm an inescapable cultural relativism. How is this possible?

First of all I should explain that by 'relativity' I do not primarily have in mind the very specialized sense that the concept bears in Einsteinian relativity physics, although I shall draw certain connections between my use of the term and its meaning in physics. As suggested earlier, my deployment of the term concerns the 'relativity' of meaning or of knowledge-claims that invariably and ineluctably are context- or frame-of-reference bound, even if such claims can be and continually are – *not* without semiotic or epistemic consequences – reinscribed in new contexts (as I shall show by means of examples which concern Einstein): no one has access to an 'absolute' frame of reference or conclusively 'true' perspective (Bodanis, 2001: 82).[4] By 'relativism' I mean the belief that nothing which

4 That this is a suitably humbling thought, which serves as a *caveat* against all manner of fanatical appeals to absolutes – usually of a religious or political-ideological kind – should be obvious. But lest anyone needs an informed reminder of the kind of destruction, terror and persecution that such an ideological invocation of absolutes has all too often given rise to in the history of the human race, Leonard Shlain (1998: 292–377) recounts some such instances vividly in his gripping account of

has 'meaning' is really worthy of the name in any intersubjective sense, much less of the status of 'knowledge', mostly because such functioning of meaning fleetingly (and arbitrarily) operates for individuals or communities of various stripes in ephemeral situations, and are at best only 'valid' in a situation for as long as it lasts.[5] One could say that supporters of a relativist position believe that all human experience, language or interpretation is subject to a kind of tetherless 'freeplay', and not merely to the 'play' of meaning – the latter position being the one that Lacan and Derrida represent, where there is a 'play' between stability and instability, being and becoming, systematicity and flexibility. Moreover, the kind of claims on the part of those who fiercely insist on the legitimacy of their 'cultural knowledge' or, for that matter, their own value-judgments, ultimately mistake personal or communal preferences or 'meaning' and affective, gut-level biases for genuine 'knowledge' in the sense of intersubjectively 'justifiable' chains of signification.[6] By contrast, I want to argue

---

the frenzy of internecine religious conflicts during the sixteenth-century European Reformation.

5 See in this regard Brimer's (1992) relativistic argument that the interpretation of a Shakespearian passage by a multicultural group of students is not subject to 'correction' of any kind in so far as every student's inscription of this passage in her or his own cultural situation has to be accepted as being legitimate. As I shall show, this relativistic conclusion may be avoided by re-inscribing each of these interpretations in the model of 'context-relativity' outlined here.

6 A chilling example of this kind of relativistic claim was afforded by the television spectacle, a few years ago, of a spectator, fortuitously caught on camera during the broadcast of a soccer match, kicking a black cat to death in full view of spectators. Because of the outcry that ensued, the man was tracked down and when confronted about his (to many, if not most viewers repulsively horrific) deed, claimed that it was justified in light of the belief (knowledge?) in his culture, that unless one kills a black cat that has crossed one's path, one would experience bad luck for the rest of one's life. The argument I am putting forward here enables one to understand this man's claims as being relativistic, given the possibility of re-inscribing his cultural beliefs in a wider context or signifying chain where the meaning of 'black cat' emerges in a different light when linked to distinctions between 'superstition', 'knowledge' and 'rationality' (or, in Barthesian terms, between 'primary signification' and 'secondary signification' or 'myth'). 'Black cat' may therefore be seen as

that the context-relativity (or -relationality) of meaning or signification and of knowledge-claims does not vitiate their semiotic decipherability but may well affect their (epistemic) status as far as intersubjective justifiability is concerned. To be able to do this, a more detailed discussion of the full implications of the 'signifying chain' as well as of 'context' and 'relativity' is required.

The concept of the 'signifying chain' can only be understood adequately in light of the Saussurean concept of the 'sign', which introduced a versatile means of conceptualizing the generation of meaning, compared with the traditional, metaphysically burdened referential model of meaning. According to the latter, meaning is a function of a sign (a word or a picture, for example) 'referring' to an individual thing, or alternatively, to a concept or idea. Depending on which of the latter two alternatives is affirmed, meaning is given a materialistic (and usually nominalistic) or an idealistic ontological underpinning, which cannot account referentially for the 'surplus' abstract and flexible character of language as a system of meaning (not every word or phrase in language can be referentially accommodated). By contrast, the Saussurian 'sign' has proved to be capable of accommodating every conceivable system of meaning. It is well-known that Saussure divided the sign into two inseparable components, namely the 'signifier' (a spoken or written word, a gesture, a picture or image: anything that 'signifies') and the 'signified' (the abstract concept which is the flip-side of any signifier). Language as a system therefore consists of a chain of signs (signifiers with their signifieds), regardless of the metaphysical or ontological value that anyone may attribute to these, and instead of retaining a referential relationship of meaning, Saussure showed that meaning is a function of differences: in language there are no positive terms, only differences ('cat' differs in meaning from 'rat', 'sat' and 'mat', not because of what it refers to, but because of the transposition of phonemes or graphemes [r, s, m and c]; depending on whether these

functioning differently relative to different frames of reference or contexts, and this difference is not innocent. It has concrete, lethal consequences in some of these contexts which include those of sixteenth-century European beliefs in witchcraft and similar African beliefs persisting in the twentieth and twenty-first centuries.

are spoken or written signifiers) that affect the functioning of signifiers as symbols. For Saussure (Olivier, 1993: 247) the volatile signifier (the word for 'lion' differs as signifier from language to language) was anchored in the stable signified (the concept of a lion remained the same, in his view), in this way subjecting the signifier to the authority of the signified or concept. This is, despite the revolutionary consequences of his structuralist linguistics, a conservative gesture on Saussure's part, as Derrida (1978: 281) indicates where he says that the traditional tendency to annihilate the (revolutionary) distinction between the signifier and the signified 'consists in reducing or deriving the signifier, that is to say, ultimately in *submitting* the sign to thought ...' Needless to say, this means re-affirming the primacy of consciousness, with all the anomalies and metaphysical commitments it entails.

Lacan's prioritization of the signifier and Derrida's deconstruction of context

It is hard to overestimate the full intellectual significance and revolutionary consequences of what may be thought of as the post-structuralist liberation of the signifier, as wrought in the work of Lacan and Derrida, among others. In Lacan's thought, instead of yielding to the temptation of characterizing the realm of the 'repressed' as that of the signified – a temptation all the harder to resist, given the ease with which psychoanalytical thinkers could think of repressed materials as constituting the 'meaning' of the subject's 'symptoms', speech and actions (Bowie, 1991: 72–73) – the signifier is prioritized instead, in this way ensuring the systematicity and decipherability of the signifying chain (see note 12 concerning similarities between Lacan and Derrida in this regard). For Lacan the unconscious is not, as Freud sometimes tended to think of it in topographical terms, a 'deep, dark chamber' – the sole access one has to the unconscious is via the signifier: the unconscious is inscribed in language, albeit negatively in the guise of omissions, negations and parapraxes of al kinds. Bowie (1991: 73) explains Lacan's prioritization of the signifier as a determination to avoid occult qualities:

> The whole drift of Lacan's thinking in this area has to do with protecting the right of systems to remain systematic. Whereas certain linguistic categories – metaphor and metonymy, for instance – maintain and enhance those rights in respect of the signifier, others infringe them grievously. The signified is the most dangerous member of the second group. Metaphor and metonymy are modes of connection in the signifying chain, principles of structure and cohesion, but the signified is an undercover agent for vagueness and pathos.

Besides, what Lacan is resisting here is the lingering influence of the obsolete philosophical paradigm of consciousness, still active in Saussure's attempt to use the signified as conceptual anchor of stable meaning, and as exemplified in the conceptual claims of the Cartesian *Cogito ergo sum* – in the place of which Lacan (1977: 166) remarked famously in an obvious reference to the unconscious: 'I think where I am not, therefore I am where I do not think'. In other words, if one adds to this his contention that the unconscious is 'structured like a language' (Lacan, 1977a: 55), it should be clear that the priority of the signifier enables Lacan to sweep aside the traditional tendency to think of the subject in substantialist terms as *essentially* a thinking substance, or for that matter as an epiphenomenon of material processes. Instead the subject is in a sense 'thin' or 'empty' – it is, in Bowie's (1991: 76) terms, 'a series of events within language', and can therefore be understood in terms of the various ways in which the signifier 'human subject' or 'human being' is articulated with axiologically burdened signifieds (which, in their turn, again function as signifiers). A case in point is the signifier 'man' as putatively representative of the human species, a claim easily debunked as ideologically and asymmetrically privileging the masculine sex when the path of the signifier is followed where it leads. To put it differently: the linguistic paradigm of the signifying chain (of signifiers) enables one to think in terms of contexts of signification, or frameworks of meaning, none of which have any grounds for claiming absolute, inherently permanent meaning, while at the same time not representing complete semantic or epistemic flux either – every relational context or framework of 'relative signification' lends itself to being understood, and even when signifiers are removed from certain contexts and re-inscribed in others, they do not thereby lose meaning, but become enriched (or impoverished) by means of new connections in the signifying chain – eventualities that sometimes give rise to ironic twists in the signifying history of words.[7] Despite the unstoppable, diversifying and yet systematically coherent unfolding of the traceable historical path of the signifier, that which

7 So, for example, the history of the word 'snob' evinces a strange itinerary: initially, in the years leading up to the French Revolution, revolutionary writers parodied the custom of members of the nobility – to add to their signatures on letters the abbreviation 'nob' to indicate their status – by adding to their own signatures the abbreviation 's'nob', signifying '*sans nobilitas*' or 'without nobility', in this way making a virtue of what had been regarded as a vice, so to speak. The word 'snob' in contemporary English, indicating someone who puts on airs, implicitly claiming a certain status which he or she does not, somehow, deserve, preserves and enriches the initial meaning of the term in its present context of application. Other words, such as 'gay' or 'amateur' seem to undergo a virtual reversal of meaning in new contexts, although every context within which they, and other words have functioned, can be tracked down (at least in literary cultures). In the case of 'amateur' its present meaning tends towards the pejorative, especially when contrasted with 'professional', and yet, at its inception 'amateur' meant more or less the same as 'professional' today, namely 'someone who does something well', but with a rider lacking in 'professional', signifying that the skill or knowledge on the part of the person described as an 'amateur' derives from her or his *love* of the activity in question. One last example: it may come as a surprise to most people living in today's technophiliac culture that the word 'computer' once referred to a human being, specifically to the undervalued, underpaid, patriarchally exploited but nevertheless efficient, capable women (mostly spinsters) whose sole job was to carry out laborious computations (without the 'benefit' of computers in the current sense of the word). These included the women dedicated to the measurement of star locations at the Harvard Observatory in the early 1920s (Bodanis, 2001: 178). The paths followed by the signifier in these examples are attached to signifying chains that comprise a complex web of meanings – sometimes mutually reinforcing, sometimes mutually contradictory. It is the ability to follow these (sometimes tortuously tensional, problematic and aporetic) paths that enables someone like Derrida to carry out 'deconstructions' of concepts such as speech and writing, forgiveness, law and justice, the gift, hospitality and the like.

remains 'constant' (but flexible) is the signifying model of signifier/signified as related to the 'chain of signification'. Meanings change, but are nevertheless decipherable, understandable, because of their accessibility along this chain – albeit never with any guarantee that they will stay the 'same'; that is, they are in(de)finitely revisable, and a certain degree of semiotic 'entropy' inevitably occurs, especially as far as writers' or speakers' 'intended' meanings are concerned.

If anything, Derrida's treatment of the signifier is even more radical than Lacan's. Here I do not want to concentrate so much on the implications of his neologism or 'non-concept', *différance*, but on his rethinking of 'context' in relation to communication, signs and what he calls 'writing' (Derrida, 1982). Suffice it to say that the term *différance* indicates the process that is productive of meaning along a 'spatial' as well as a 'temporal' axis – hence the oft-repeated clarification according to which it indicates 'difference' (spatial) as well as 'deferral' (temporal): in short, meaning is only possible because of signifying differences *á la* Saussure as well as temporal deferrals of decoding or interpretation of signifiers (Derrida, 1982a: 19). At the same time, however – and this is no less part and parcel of *différance* – these differences and deferrals also ensure that there is *no guarantee* that meaning *will* occur (or recur as it once has); *différance* is therefore *also* the 'basis', if not 'abyss', of the 'failure of meaning', or of its 'impossibility'[8] (as manifested, for example, in those phenomena that give rise to relativistic claims). In his analysis of the manner in which signifiers or 'marks' function in given contexts this 'quasi-transcendental' function of *différance* is presupposed throughout.

In 'Signature event context' (1982), to my mind one of Derrida's most seminal essays (*and* 'disseminative' ones, given the persistent interpretation of his work as 'relativist', if not 'irrationalist'!), he raises the question

8 It is an example of what has become known as a 'quasi-transcendental' – something that functions simultaneously as the condition of the possibility and the 'impossibility' of something else (in a 'pure' state; see Bennington, 1993: 276–277). There are many examples in Derrida's work of 'quasi-transcendentals' – *différance* is one; for another, concerning the ambivalent conditions regarding the 'effects' of signatures, see Derrida, 1982: 328–329.

(among many other interrelated ones) and provides a provisional answer (1982: 310):

> ... are the prerequisites of a context ever absolutely determinable? ... Is there a rigorous and scientific concept of the *context*? Does not the notion of context harbor, behind a certain confusion, very determined philosophical presuppositions?
>
> To state it now in the most summary fashion, I would like to demonstrate why a context is never absolutely determinable, or rather in what way its determination is never certain or saturated.

It is important to note that Derrida is here employing the notion of '*structural* nonsaturation', which immediately touches upon something that is crucial in his essay and for my present purposes: it is not because of any 'empirical' or factual impossibility to 'determine' or 'saturate' a context – in the sense of setting up the prerequisites for *full* discursive, mutual understanding and 'consensus' to be attained in a given context such as the present one of a conference on relativity and relativism – but because of the very (structural) conditions of possibility of communication, understanding or interpretation within any and all contexts, that 'saturation' of meaning is unattainable. The point is that the currently fashionable appeal to 'contexts' hides the very traditional, metaphysical prejudice, that implicitly, if individuals can agree on a context of some kind, agreement or mutual communication is believed to be possible along the trajectory of the simplistic notion of communication involving a sender, a message (meaning) and a recipient. In brief, what Derrida demonstrates in complex but persuasive detail, is that the very conditions that make 'communication' (of meaning) or mutual understanding within any context possible, also make it 'impossible'.[9]

It is also impossible to render an adequate account of the complexity and richness of his argument in this regard, save by repeating it verbatim, so I shall restrict my remarks to what seems pertinent to my present purpose. Turning to the customary notion of 'writing' as

9 See in this regard my paper, 'The (im-)possibility of communication' (Olivier 2004). See also note 8, because one is here once again confronting a 'quasi-transcendental'.

a 'means of communication', Derrida (1982: 311) reminds one that it is usually regarded as an extension of 'oral or gestural' communication, something that, in turn, presupposes a kind of homogeneous communicational space. Writing seems only to extend the field of locutionary communication to a much wider range. This is 'banally self-evident', he says. But we know that philosophers are recognizable by their Socratic questioning of the 'gods of the city' – we ought to suspect the 'bread-thinkers' (Schopenhauer) who routinely set out to use their wits in the service of the commonsensically self-evident, the powers that be, or of conventional/customary/politically correct, 'normalising' assumptions – they are *not* philosophers. But Derrida decidedly *is*, in an exemplary fashion. Turning to a paradigmatic traditional-philosophical interpretation of writing in the work of Condillac (1982: 311–312), he uncovers all the 'normal' gestures on Condillac's part, including the belief that writing is a species of communication, that picturing is a proto-writing that leads to properly graphic, written communication, which is but the expression of ideas (so that writing essentially serves thought), that *absence* is what motivates the invention of writing and that Condillac thinks of writing as a 'mechanical' and 'restricted' economy of meaning where the most space-and-time-efficient graphic investment of the writer is recouped in the reader's decoding of the writing.

But the notion of 'absence' (all-too-obviously of the addressee) casually introduced by Condillac is not as innocent as it seems. For, Derrida points out, this is a structural determinant of all writing (in fact, of all language), and not merely something empirical which is remedied through graphic representation (writing) as modification of communicational presence. What does he mean? Simply that, instead of characterizing writing as a *break* in the supposed presence of oral communication, Condillac presents it as a continuous reparation and sustaining of this putatively indispensable presence. But, as something that *supplements* communicational 'presence', writing not only ruptures it but paradoxically ensures communicability or decipherability in the *absence* of the writer as well as the (any) addressee through its *iterability* or repeatability. 'A writing that was not structurally legible – iterable – beyond the death of the addressee would not be writing', Derrida (1982: 315) remarks. He continues (pp. 315–316):

> This implies that there is no code – an organon of iterability – that is structurally secret. [Wittgenstein's familiar denial of the possibility of a 'private language' comes to mind; B.O.] The possibility of repeating, and therefore of identifying, marks is implied in every code, making of it a communicable, transmittable, decipherable grid that is iterable for a third party, and thus for any possible user in general. All writing, therefore, in order to be what it is, must be able to function in the radical absence of every empirically determined addressee in general. And this absence is not a continuous modification of presence; it is a break in presence, 'death' or the possibility of the 'death' of the addressee, inscribed in the structure of the mark ...

These words go to the heart of the matter concerning the structural nonsaturation or indeterminability of 'contexts'. They imply nothing less than the 'radical destruction ... of every context as a protocol of a code' (p. 316). What does this mean? Simply that, if supplied with a code for deciphering a message – whether it is the tacit conventions governing ordinary, everyday language, a key to decoding an encrypted message or, say, the theoretical concepts underpinning a scientific terminology – one is not uniquely privileged in being able to decode or understand it. The *specific* context is therefore not a prerequisite for understanding the sign-sequence constituting the 'message' – because all signs or marks as 'writing' are by their very nature iterable or repeatable, the context of their articulation is not essential for them to be deciphered or understood by a third party. To be sure, the latter could use various strategies for or approaches to decoding the sign-sequence or -configuration, such as reconstructing the historical circumstances and/or theoretical framework of its articulation, or the phenomenological approach aimed at systematically denuding the sign-configuration as phenomenon by jettisoning all layers of prejudicial assumptions. Whatever the case may be, though, the 'message', having been removed from the context of its provenance, is ineluctably inscribed in or 'grafted' onto a new context within which it will generate meaning which will either be consonant with and enrich its 'earlier' meaning, or conflict with it (see note 5 in this regard). In either case, meaning is generated, in this way giving credibility to Derrida's notion of 'dissemination'(as opposed to the milder 'polysemy' which is still reconcilable with semiotic 'insemination'), with its implication of uncontrollable 'scattering of seeds' (of meaning).[10]

Hence, when Derrida (1982: 317) claims that '... a written sign carries with it a force of breaking with its context ...', and that: 'This force of breaking is not an accidental predicate, but the very structure of the written ...', he is preparing the way for the insight, that signs are 'abandoned' to an 'essential drifting' the moment they have been produced by a so-called 'author', which insight affirms the legibility of the sign in the absence of this author. Moreover, apart from this context of its production, there is the 'internal' semiotic context – such as a theory, a novel or a painting – from which a sign can be removed at any time to be re-inscribed elsewhere (Derrida, 1982: 317):

> ... there is no less a force of breaking by virtue of its essential iterability; one can always lift a written syntagma from the interlocking chain [the same metaphor Lacan uses; B.O.] in which it is caught or given without making it lose every possibility of functioning, if not every possibility of 'communicating', precisely. Eventually, one may recognize other such possibilities in it by inscribing or *grafting* it into other chains.[11] No context can enclose it. Nor can any code, the code being here both the possibility and impossibility of writing, of its essential iterability (repetition/alterity).

As can be expected, it is easy for Derrida to expand these features of the relation between signs, writing and contexts to *all* language in the broadest sense, including that traditional bastion or touchstone of the

10 Needless to say, it is precisely the 'control' of meaning, knowledge, truth and related concepts that has always been central to western metaphysics, hence the sometimes violent (and reactionary!) reaction against Derrida's scrupulously argued, radical thinking.

11 The present context, receiving as it does its character from the selected theme of 'relativity and relativism' constitutes just such a new context onto which these signifiers are grafted, and within which older meanings may be enriched or impoverished by adding or juxtaposing new ones to them; but in any event this new context opens up other possibilities of signification and understanding.

immediacy and reliability of 'present' meaning, namely speech. After all, for anything to be decipherable – whether it is written, spoken, painted, filmed, 'built' (as in architecture) or even given in experience (such as the illuminating example of hoofmarks, footprints and broken branches so deftly decoded by Brother William in Eco's *The name of the rose*; 1984: 23–25) – it has to display the structure of a chain of signifiers of some kind. This is the 'constant' in question, presented to writers, philosophers and scientists by this new (linguistic or semiological) paradigm of thinking – a paradigm which comprises the 'mobile context' within which even something as ostensibly far removed from it as 'relativity' or 'relativism' may be inscribed, or which could alternatively function as a key giving access to realms of meaning engendered by grafting these two signifiers onto new contexts (such as the present one). The elements of this 'constant', but flexible paradigm or model, it bears repeating, are those of the sign, namely signifier and signified, and related to them, 'signifying chain', 'context' and 'writing' (in the Derridean sense).[12] But why do these enable

12 In 'Structure sign and play …' (1978: 280–281) Derrida formulates what may be regarded as a succinct account of the argument that I have put forward here. In brief, he shows that the structure of the sign as comprising (sensible) signifier and (intelligible) signified allows for an endless, unstoppable proliferation of meaning(s) – essentially what I have tried to show here by scrutinizing his critique of context – but that, paradoxically, this is only possible on condition that the signifier 'sign' has a determinate meaning, namely the arbitrary relation between signifier and signified. In other words, for any meaning whatsoever to be generated, and for the *impossibility* of restricting, limiting or 'saturating' the meaning of any concept (term, word, sign, etc.) to become apparent, the *possibility* of momentarily stabilizing the meaning of a concept – in this case that of the very concept that has made this thought-revolution possible, namely 'sign' – has to be affirmed. In a nutshell, what this means is that meaning *is and is not* determinable. It is nothing unusual in the history of thought to reduce the sensible signifier to its intelligible signified, thus submitting sense to thought. Or one could, like Derrida (and Lacan: recall what was said earlier about his reasons for being suspicious of the signified; reasons which are similar to Derrida's) use the distinction in question to destabilize the metaphysical system of which it forms part – but not by jettisoning the 'signified' or conceptuality in the process, even if every signified could be shown to function as signifier in its turn. (Andrea Hurst reminded me of this account

one to come to an enriched understanding of relativity and relativism? A little closer attention to relativity is called for at this point.

Relativity and the subversion of absolutes

The following observation by Leonard Shlain (1991: 132) highlights the pertinence of a comparison between the effect and implications of the (post-) structuralist model of signification, outlined above, and the implications of Einstein's theory of special relativity:

> In his 1905 article Einstein nullified the concept of absolute rest as meaningless since the immovable ether does not exist – the laws of physics are the same in all inertial frames. Since everything of substance is moving relative to everything else, there is no physical location that is motionless in the universe

---

by Derrida when I was setting out my own argument concerning the structural parallel between Lacan's model of the signifier and the signifying chain, Derrida's radicalization of the notion of context, and the role of the constancy of light-speed in Einstein's special theory of relativity. For this, and more generally regarding my benefitting from her thorough knowledge of especially Derrida's work, I owe her thanks.) Unless one is able to discern the path where a given sign, concept or term leads, its ineluctable inscription in new contexts or horizons, totalities, or frameworks (and therefore the unavoidable proliferation of meanings) would be unthinkable. Conversely, unless this multiplication of meanings could, in principle, occur – given the arbitrary connection between signifier and signified – one would be unable to trace (some of) them back to 'relatively' determinate, (but non-saturable) context-dependent meanings, the exemplary case being that of the concept 'sign'. Epistemologically speaking – and I realize that the field of epistemology is fraught with metaphysical pitfalls of all kinds – it means that we are not the involuntary heirs of relativism, but neither are we the proud and deluded possessors of an epistemic algorithm that guarantees absolute, unshakeable, permanent knowledge. We know and we don't know: our knowledge is limited to contexts that are but 'weakly' (or conditionally) determinable.

By analogy, there is no subject-position in the human cultural universe that is interpretively 'motionless', that is, where interpretation does not happen. If there is one thing that humans do incessantly (at least in waking life), it is to interpret or decode their surroundings. Moreover, just as, in the realm of human experience, no one can extricate her- or himself from their spatiotemporal, linguistically inserted perspective, thus attaining a perspectiveless, absolute, 'view from nowhere', so, in the realm of physics, the only conceivable Einsteinian 'ideal', namely light itself, cannot be used as a vantage point or platform for observation (as the ether had earlier been thought to offer an ideal, motionless platform; Shlain, 1991: 121) because its speed is unattainable (Shlain, 1991: 132). To appreciate the novelty of these insights when they were first formulated by Einstein one has to remind oneself that, in Newtonian physics, space and time were absolute – space being regarded as homogeneous, static and flat (not curved), and time as constant or invariant, unidirectional and consciousness-independent (Shlain, 1991: 120–121). According to this model, light was accorded more or less the same place that Hermes had in ancient Greek mythology, namely that of messenger – bearing information between various spatial locations at a certain speed, that is, in a specific amount of time.[13] These conceptions of space, time and light are consonant with perceptual common sense. However, Shlain (1991: 121) points out that:

> Einstein turned everything upside down by declaring that space and time are relative and only the speed of light is constant. Einstein based his entire special theory upon two deceptively simple postulates. The first is that the laws of physics take the same form in all inertial frames of reference[14] (that is, there is not one privileged

13 The speed of light, 186000 miles per second, was measured by Fresnel in the early 1900s on the assumption of the ether as a place of absolute rest (Shlain, 1991: 121).

14 This useful notion of an 'inertial frame of reference' was formulated by Galileo in the seventeenth century and forms part of what is known as the 'Galilean theory of relativity' (Shlain, 1991: 60–62). All this means is that, in order to ascertain if something is moving, it has to be related to a frame of reference (for instance a room within which one is sitting, or walking to and fro). To judge if the room,

inertial frame – or place in the ether – that is at absolute rest). The second is that the speed of light is constant for all observers regardless of how fast and in which direction they are moving.

Similarly – one is now in a position to assert – in the linguistic-conceptual realm of meaning there are no absolutes either. While there is a theoretical constant comparable to *c* or the speed of light in Einstein's theory – the model of the signifier/signified, or the signifying chain – meaning is spatiotemporally (i.e. historico-culturally or perspectivally) relative. All meaning (and therefore any knowledge-claim) is generated (or is to be assessed) within and has to be understood relative to the counterparts of 'inertial frames of reference', namely specific linguistic chains, semantic or conceptual frames or contexts; contexts, moreover, which cannot be 'saturated' or stabilized in a privileged manner, but the constituent elements (or chain of signifiers) of which are continually re-inscribed in new contexts, just as light is continually powering away from every observer, regardless of the speed at which she or he is moving. Analogically speaking, just as space and time were shown by Einstein to be relative instead of 'absolute', meaning, 'reality' and knowledge, instead of being absolute, depend on how and where a perceiving or interpreting subject is situated relative to ('open') contexts or signifying chains. By means of the model of the signifying chain, meaning may be traced along the defiles and rhizomatic networks of signifiers, in this way enabling one to assess the status of meaning- and 'knowledge'-claims.[15] This means that it is impossible to

---

in turn, is moving, one has to relate it to another, more encompassing inertial frame of reference which is, again, assumed to be at rest. If this room were to be a cabin aboard a ship (an example of Galileo's), its motion could be ascertained in relation to the 'stationary' land, and so on. Hence, one can speak of movements *within each frame*, which is itself taken to be at rest for the purpose of measuring movements.

15 I deliberately put 'knowledge' in scare-quotes, because I'm not so sure whether it would not be better to think in terms of '*potentially* intersubjective or *shareable* (not necessarily *shared*) meaning' rather than 'knowledge', given the unfortunate connotations of 'permanence' and unshakeability that attach to the term 'knowledge'. All too often what is claimed to be knowledge in this sense is later unmasked as

proscribe or preclude the continual generation of meaning in relational contexts where knowledge-claims turn out, on closer inspection, to be relativistic (such as those on the part of the cat-killer referred to in note 6). At the same time, however, such claims can be re-inscribed in new, more encompassing relational contexts which enable one to discern their contextual relativity (and concomitantly, in some cases, their relativism) while tracing their connectivity with perspicuous, if not explanatory signifying chains. We are not in a position where one can choose between these two types of framework within which meaning is generated and knowledge-claims are made – we have to continue relating them to one another, not neglecting either lest understanding of the 'freeplay' of relativistic claims be sacrificed on the altar of foundationalist epistemologies, or alternatively, lest *temporarily* stabilizing theoretical frameworks[16] and the re-contextualizing interpretations they allow be irrevocably exposed to the disintegrative decay of communicationally prohibitive, relativistic claims invoking complete incommensurability.

These parallels between the implications of the signifying chain-model and Einstein's special theory of relativity are further reinforced by considering the shift in thinking of which the concept of 'field' is symptomatic across a wide range of intellectual activities, from physics through visual art to the human sciences. In a nutshell: just as in physics the 'field' was shown to be more important than – in fact, to be a pre-

---

beliefs or 'meaning(s)' operating quite satisfactorily within a specific context until a better, more inclusive or explanatory theory (which gives rise to new beliefs) is formulated, usually to address incongruities or anomalies that have arisen in the light of new evidence (of the kind that Kuhn refers to; see Kuhn, 1970). Einstein's theories are cases in point, and so is the very 'rational' belief in the flatness of the earth (which I refer to further on) during a time when evidence to the contrary was not persuasively available.

16 See in this regard Andrea Hurst's (2002) illuminating study of the contradictions, in Heidegger's Rectoral Address, between a philosophy of science that instantiates precisely the salutary model (of 'taking a stand' or establishing a 'relational frame', combined with the recognition that time will eventually *ruin* this 'stand') I am talking about here, and an ideology predicated on the (im-)possibility of a totally 'unified' people.

requisite for – the existence of 'particles',[17] so too in painting as well as in structuralist linguistics the 'field' was shown to be inseparably conjoined with, if not presupposed by the functioning of entities, things, objects, words, sentences, and so on within the field demarcated by the canvas or by the chain of signifiers comprising the system of language. Shlain (1991: 248–249) shows, for example, that one's initial disconcertment in the face of Jackson Pollock's abstract swirls makes way for understanding when, instead of searching for objects represented there, his canvases are understood as instantiating an energy-field without any centre or hierarchical spatial coordinates.[18] In physics this is matched by the concept of a 'field' within which things in the form of particles can first take shape, while the Saussurean concept of language or Lacan's symbolic order (the chain of signifiers), within which meaningful configurations first become possible, is equally consonant with this sense of the 'field'. Without the field constituted by the chain of signifiers, no signifier, taken by itself, would or could signify anything – there are no positive terms in language, only differences, and these comprise the 'field' in question.

17 See in this regard Shlain's observation (1991: 245):

> As a result of insights garnered from both relativity and quantum mechanics, the field more than the particle came to be recognized as the true nexus of reality ... In Einstein's formulation of the special theory it was the field of light itself that determined the structure of space and time. Quantum physicists discovered that 'things' constructed out of matter originated in fluctuations of insubstantial fields of energy.

18 Shlain (1991: 248) captures the remarkable parallel between the concept of the 'field' in physics and the revolutionary abstract expressionism of Pollock in formulations such as the following:

> Pollock's work reiterates a profound truth the physicist discovered: The field is more important than the particle, the process supersedes the object ... Pollock's vision, like the field in physics, is an invisible tension, made out of nothing, that cannot be captured and placed under the microscope for scrutiny. Pollock's painting is not a res. In physics, the field becomes manifest only by its effects on the behavior of things within it. Pollock found a way to express the same notion with paint ... In Pollock's most famous paintings there are no things, merely the expression of energy and tension ... They have no center or hierarchy of interest but instead give all areas of the picture equal importance ... His works approximate the principle of the field as conceived in physics.

A more accurate formulation of the relation between field and the entities that manifest themselves within it, in poststructuralist terms, would be to say that the field and the entities – whether these are particles, signifiers or discernible swirls of paint (or images) – are inextricably intertwined: to recognize a signifier as such, for example 'cat', or 'woman', not only presupposes the 'field' or chain of language, but the latter only makes sense as an insubstantial 'something' which, in its turn, presupposes signifiers and processes of signification which first alert one to the functioning of the encompassing field. Without these, one could not speak of language, as one would not, in physics, postulate the supposed 'primacy' of the 'field', were it not for the *res* or physical things which are said to be its effects. It is merely the persistent tendency to think in oppositional or binary terms that impels even astonishingly insightful thinkers to accord primacy to the one or the other, instead of – like poststructuralist thinkers – thinking them together.[19]

Grafting relativity onto new contexts

The manner in which newly established, but 'unsaturable' contexts are continually re-inscribed in new, equally unsaturable contexts where their initial meaning is *both* preserved and changed in the manner of a quasi-Hegelian *Aufhebung* ('quasi-', because there is never any question

19 These considerations raise the interesting and important question: Why is it the case that people seem to have an irresistible tendency to think *exclusively* in binary terms, instead of accepting what seems to me – and here I am following thinkers such as Heidegger, Merleau-Ponty, Lacan, Derrida, Foucault, Lyotard, Deleuze, Kristeva, Zizek, Caputo and Copjec – the ineluctable ambivalence of the human world and its implications for meaning, knowledge and moral action? The answer to this question, which obviously has to do with the binary structure of language, would throw light on many phenomena regarding human behaviour, not least of which is the persistence of ideological mystification (racism, patriarchy, capitalism, socialism, etc.) on the part of large numbers of people.

of teleological progress towards any final, all-encompassing synthesis; cf. Derrida, 1982a: 19–20) is strikingly demonstrated by events in the subsequent theoretical history of Einstein's famous equation at the heart of his special theory, namely $E=mc^2$.

Einstein had already upset the theoretical physics-applecart by positing an equivalence between energy and mass multiplied by the colossal figure of the speed of light squared (Bodanis, 2001: 6–8; 48–54; 68–69; 73–85; 184–219). But not long afterwards, he himself was led to re-inscribe this formula in a more encompassing field – that of 'general' relativity – as a result, it seems to me, of some further lateral thinking on his part concerning the implications of his formula regarding gravity and the behaviour of light. It had been well-known in physics that light has no mass or weight (Coles, 2000: 29, 71), but consists of photons (conceived of as 'pure' energy), in the language of physics. But if there is an equivalence between energy and mass (multiplied by c squared), then one might expect to find that light, too, behaved like ordinary, 'massive' bodies in fields of gravity. This thought is linked to the insight, in Bodanis's words (2001: 205), '... that the more mass or energy there was at any one spot, the more that space and time would be curved tight around it'. In Newton's physics, and even in Einstein's special theory, light was thought of as proceeding along straight lines, but if space and time were to curve under the influence of mass or energy (these being equivalent), then light could be expected to curve as well. These considerations resulted in Einstein's formulation of his more complex general theory of relativity in 1915, in which $E=mc^2$ was inscribed in relation to other components. Bodanis explains (2001: 205–206):

> The equation that summarizes this has great simplicity, curiously reminiscent of the simplicity of $E=mc^2$. In $E=mc^2$, there's an energy realm on one side, a mass realm on the other, and the bridge of the '=' linking them. $E=mc^2$ is, at heart, the assertion that Energy = mass. In Einstein's new, wider theory, the points that are covered deal with the way that all of 'energy–mass' in an area is associated with all of 'space–time' nearby, or, symbolically, the way that Energy–mass = space–time. The 'E' and the 'm' of $E=mc^2$ are now just items to go on one side of this deeper equation.

What one witnesses here is the curious 'logic' of lifting a signifier (in this case a composite one, namely $E=mc^2$) from one context and 'grafting' it onto another: it remains the same *and* simultaneously changes through being inscribed in a new context. Without retaining the meaning that it has in the special theory, it could not be fruitfully transposed to the wider context of the general theory of relativity, but at the same time, by being related to space–time, as well as the gravity and acceleration of the 'real' physical world (instead of the conditions of pure theory and thought of the special theory), it also changes by being enriched by and enriching those concepts together with which it has been woven into a new, more complex chain of meanings.

Needless to say, like all scientific theories, Einstein's new, general theory required confirmation through testing – it had to be 'falsifiable', in Popper's terms, even if it were confirmed in the end. (It would take longer, ironically, for $E=mc^2$ to be 'experimentally' confirmed in a truly devastating manner – I shall presently turn to this.) How this happened, and who was involved, is fairly well-known;[20] suffice it to say that it entailed testing the theory in terms of the prediction that light would be curved by passing close to a massive body such as the sun – something that could only be done by measuring the deviation, if any, of the light indicating the positions of distant stars in relation to the sun (which could, for obvious reasons, only be done during a solar eclipse), from their positions at night, when light from them does not appear in the vicinity of the sun. But Einstein's theory was, and has since been confirmed on many occasions; the important point for my present purposes being that this inscribed the signifier 'Einstein', as well as that of 'relativity' and of $E=mc^2$ yet *again*

20 A wonderfully informative and humorous account of these events, involving Einstein's disastrous Jonah of an assistant, Freundlich (!), as well as Arthur Eddington, is given by Bodanis (2001: 204–219; see also Coles, 2000: 33–61). Both these authors highlight the manner in which Einstein, who might otherwise have remained an obscure, if scientifically acclaimed physicist, attained the status of an icon because of world-attention being focused on him through the media at the time of the eclipse-expeditions. This is a 'context' very different from a narrowly scientific one, although it depended on Einstein's prowess in the latter.

in a new context, because, as Bodanis (2001: 213–217) and Coles (2000: 56–61) both show, without the spectacular media-communication of the confirmation of his theory's 'prediction' that light would be found to 'curve' around the sun, Einstein's name, as well as the term 'relativity', would not have become household words. Again, grafting these signifiers onto new (historical) contexts, their meanings have been amplified by paradoxically remaining the 'same' *and* changing.

Moreover, the 'sliding of the signifier', $E=mc^2$, along various chains of signification did not end there, nor does one have any reason to suspect that it will ever stop its historical and/or theoretical sliding or drifting. I shall mention only five more such instances of grafting $E=mc^2$ onto new contexts. First, Cecilia Payne's 'discovery', through her reflections on $E=mc^2$ in the 1920s, that (contrary to what physicists believed until then), the sun does not consist largely of iron, but its colossal energy-output is due to its predominant hydrogen mass (Bodanis, 2001: 173–183); second, Subrahmanyan Chandrasekhar's discovery, through similar reflections, that about 6 billion years from now, the sun and all the planets in our solar system, will end – as Robert Frost has so perspicaciously foreseen in his poetry – in fire and ice when the final energy-outbursts of our sun will occur (Bodanis, 2001: 195–203); and third, Fred Hoyle's lateral use of $E=mc^2$, together with the notion of implosion, in the 1940s to solve the tantalizing riddle of the origin of life through the creation of carbon, oxygen, iron, and so on by imploding and exploding stars (Bodanis, 2001: 184–191). Ironically – and this is the fourth instance of re-contextualizing Einstein's fecund formula – Hoyle's creative reflections on the link between $E=mc^2$ and the origin of *life* had as their point of departure his awareness of the formula's integral importance in the development of an atom bomb (a source of *death* on unprecedented scale: the antithesis of life) in America's so-called Manhattan Project. Without the theoretical implications of $E=mc^2$ the atom bomb would be unthinkable. It is not possible to recount all the stages and dramatic events of the race between Germany – with none other than Werner Heisenberg leading the Nazi project – and America here (Bodanis, 2001: 93–169); the point is that $E=mc^2$ has been inscribed in meaning-preserving and meaning-modifying contexts of the most diverse kinds imaginable, on the spectrum stretching from life to mega-death.

But one could go even further with the theoretical-historical reinscription in new contexts of Einstein's theory by including a fifth, of a philosophical-aesthetic kind. The unlikely manner in which revolutionary artists anticipated Einstein's similarly revolutionary theories in physics constitutes a splendid example of how the 'path of the signifier' sometimes leads, by way of novel connections and what Derrida calls 'grafting', to startling insights concerning connections between contexts of meaning (or frames of reference) previously thought to be incompatible – just as Einstein's own work that resulted in his special theory of relativity in 1905 was the outcome of such novel conceptual juxtapositions in physics that, as Foucault would say (1972: 224), his fellow-physicists initially did not recognize that it was even 'within the true', that is, that it belonged recognizably to a legitimate field of research within the discipline (Bodanis, 2001: 73; 77–78).

In his startlingly innovative study, *Art & physics: Parallel visions in space, time, and light* (1991), Leonard Shlain (to whom I have already referred in my discussion of the concept of 'field') constructs a conceptual framework or context that demonstrates admirably the claims of post-structuralists like Lacan and Derrida, that signifiers can be detached from the chain of signification and attached elsewhere – that is, that they may be removed from their 'home'-context (which is therefore 'unsaturable') and grafted onto different ones in a manner that amplifies their meaning while retaining the meaning with which they were initially invested. Shlain's book covers the immense field from Ancient Greece until today with a view to drawing a parallel between iconic artistic representations of reality and abstract, alternately analytical and synthetic theoretical approximations of its physical structure. His central thesis is that artists may be shown as having uncannily anticipated fundamental changes or shifts in the understanding of reality only later articulated in physics, and he fleshes this out by way of a detailed study of pertinent artists and physicists, (including Einstein).

The implications of Einstein's theories were anticipated, Shlain shows (1991: 101–137), in the art of Manet, Monet and Cézanne. From 1863

Manet's painting violated the (since the Renaissance) taken-for-granted laws of perspective in various ways – including his use of multi-directional lighting, his elimination of the 'middle ground' in the representational space of a painting, 'camouflaging' and curving the horizon line, and obscuring the 'guiding' verticals – in this way leaving viewers visually rudderless. As Shlain (1991: 104) reminds one, Manet's unconventional constructions subverted Aristotelian logic as well as Euclidean (and Newtonian) space, and with these the entire thought-framework which had governed the modern epoch since the Renaissance.[21] What's more, in addition to introducing the idea of curved space (which is an important part of Einstein's general theory), the kind of foreshortening of perspective and flattening of shapes that a thought-experiment involving the visual effects of travelling at the speed of light conjures up, were anticipated by Manet in his *Le Déjeuner sur l'herbe* (Shlain, 1991: 130). Monet, in turn, anticipated a corollary of Einstein's theories of relativity through his implicit treatment of time in his different 'series' of paintings (for instance of Rouen Cathedral), namely that time comprises a fourth dimension, that of duration or sequentiality, without the addition of which things' location in space is inadequately indicated (Shlain, 1991: 108). In other words, he intuited what Minkowski would later, in 1908, call the 'spacetime continuum'. It is therefore not surprising that, as in the case of Einstein's work, light is of central importance in Monet's work, and that his determination to catch the light-suffused moment in paint resulted in his smudging of boundary lines in a manner consistent with the predicted '*sfumato*' (instead of traditional *chiaruscuro*) visual effects of lightspeed-travel (Shlain, 1991: 112, 130). Moreover, Monet's preoccupation with capturing the fleeting impression of the moment or 'now' in a series of successive moments – something uncannily reminiscent of Husserl's phenomenological analysis of time-consciousness as well –

21 The fact that the historical context within which Manet was working had undergone a major shift, is also evident in the way that he (like his contemporary Degas) eventually omitted the horizon line completely from his paintings, capturing the kind of random, candid, non-composed moments that a contemporary invention, the camera, had made commonplace (Shlain, 1991: 107).

through his style of 'Instantaneity', corresponds to the predicted effect of moving at lightspeed, namely the dilation of the present moment to the point where past and future merge with or are 'contained' in it (Shlain, 1991: 110, 131). In the case of Cézanne, the manner in which time seemed to 'slow down' and eventually 'stopped' or froze into a 'motionless *everlasting now*' in the development of his painting (Shlain, 1991: 113; 131–132), bears a striking similarity to Einstein's suggestion that, 'objectively' speaking, '... the distinction between past, present and future is only an illusion, however persistent' (quoted in Shlain, 1991: 132). Further similarities with Einstein's work are apparent from Cézanne's treatment of light (which abandoned the traditional angle of declination) as well as his use of multiple perspectives in a single painting (which questioned the notion of a privileged place in space) and, concomitantly, his subversion of the 'integrity of the straight line' (Shlain, 1991: 114–117).[22]

It does not seem to me to be an exaggeration to say that few people would have anticipated this grafting onto a novel context – that of art-history – of Einstein's theories by Shlain. In the process one witnesses

22 Shlain (1991: 117–118) summarizes these artists' achievements as follows:

> Manet first curved the straight line of the horizon, Monet blurred his straight boundaries, and Cézanne splintered the straight edge of his tables. What we see at the focusing point of vision are clean-edged objects arranged around the vanishing point intersection of the upright vertical and rectilinear horizontal. The view from the periphery of vision – that is, the wider, more encompassing one – is unfocused and curved and has more than one point of view. These three artists presented just such a view. Their revolutionary assaults upon the conventions of perspective and the integrity of the straight line forced upon their viewers the idea that the organization of space along the lines of projective geometry was not the only way it can be envisioned. Once people began to see space in non-Euclidean ways, then they could begin to think about it in new ways too.
>
> If the questions these three artists raised were misunderstood by their contemporaries it was only because no one at that time could know that the whole conceptual framework of reality was soon to be supplanted. It would take the elegant calculations of an Einstein years later to provide the proof in black and white of what had been stunningly accurate artistic hunches expressed in form and color.

again the strange ambivalence of meaning: in order to be amplified in relation to art-history, his concept of relativity had to remain what it was/is, but once having been inscribed in novel chains of signification, it will never be exactly the same as before. It has been enriched and further complexified. Only someone with a referential, and ultimately untenable 'atomistic' theory of meaning could argue against this.

Each of these books that I have referred to in connection with Einstein's theories and their relevance to a divergent array of issues instantiates, of course, in their turn, a unique combination of signifiers, comprising novel frameworks of signification or meaning within which Einstein's $E=mc^2$ is inscribed in a complex, different and – given the diversity of personal, literary, scientific, philosophical or conceptual pre-understanding(s) that each reader brings with her or him to these texts – completely non-saturable manner.

Solomon (1994: 165) affords one insight into something else that is at stake here where he points out that, to be 'rational' often entails making certain judgments that may be proved 'wrong' by subsequent generations with different kinds of information (and therefore frames of reference) available to them, although at the time, given the information or 'knowledge' at their disposal, these judgments may have seemed to be perfectly 'rational' on the part of people of the era in question. To illustrate his point, he adduces the example of the ancient belief that the earth was flat which, given the evidence available at the time, was the most 'rational' belief to hold; to believe in a spherical earth, although 'true' from a later perspective, simply did not seem rational within the astronomical context of the era. One could also say that, in the context of ancient Greece, given all the elements of meaning (or 'knowledge') available at the time, it made sense to believe that the earth was flat. According to this approach, which rejects any possibility of ever being in a position to claim incontrovertible or *absolute* 'knowledge' (cf. note 15), the latter (knowledge) amounts to iterable or repeatable structures of meaning which are generated by articulating specific signifying chains which, in turn, may be grafted anew onto historically novel contexts, a process that could repeat itself indefinitely. Even the 'reconstruction' of what might be called a 'past context of discovery' (for instance the historical-scientific situation within and *despite* which Einstein formulated his own theories) is undertaken within an historically novel situation, where different factors come into play when the reconstruction is carried out. The same may be said of the 'context of justification' – it may indeed follow what appears to be the 'same' logical and scientific path, but each reader, writer or student of science (or scientist) who 'repeats' the trajectory of signification along which the 'justification' is carried out, does so within a historically new situation, where the signifying process is at least potentially complexified by their awareness of new developments in the field in question (apart from those [more numerous?] cases where lack of awareness or insight may prevent the 'reader' from doing justice to the theory in first place, and where relativistic claims are more likely to occur; see note 5 in this regard).

I believe that, just as Einstein's inscription of $E=mc^2$ in his general theory resulted in a theory that was more encompassing (involving as it does gravity and acceleration, and conceiving of space-time as dynamic) and therefore had more explanatory power than the special theory, one could formulate a general theory of cultural practice (or cultural dynamics), which would incorporate the theory of meaning that the model of the signifying chain offers.[23] This model of signification, aligned with diverse, spatiotemporally (historically) changing cultural practices would enable the philosopher, anthropologist, semiotician or cultural theorist to map patterns of change in space and time (that is, in history) according to the sometimes surprising, mostly unpredictable signifying paths followed by the signifier. In this way an encompassing '*Critique of cultural reason*' could be written (with acknowledgement to Kant).

23 Needless to say, one could cite several thinkers – among them Roland Barthes, Lacan, Derrida, Lyotard, Foucault, Joan Copjec, Slavoj Žižek and Kaja Silverman – who have already commenced, in diverse ways, with the formulation of such a theory of cultural practice.

References

Bennington, G. 1993. *Derridabase*. In: Derrida, J. & Bennington, G. *Jacques Derrida*. Trans. Bennington, G. Chicago: The University of Chicago Press.

Bodanis, D. 2001. *E = mc²: A biography of the world's most famous equation*. London: Pan Books.

Bowie, M. 1991. *Lacan*. London: Fontana Press.

Brimer, A. 1992. 'Reception: A South African experience.' In: Lategan, B. (ed.), *The reader and beyond. Theory and practice in South African reception studies*. Pretoria: Human Sciences Research Council, pp. 29–39.

Caputo, J. 1993. *Against ethics. Contributions to a poetics of obligation with constant reference to deconstruction*. Bloomington: Indiana University Press.

Coles, P. 2000. *Einstein and the birth of big science*. Cambridge: Icon Books.

Deleuze, G. & Guattari, F. 1987. *A thousand plateaus. Capitalism and schizophrenia*. Trans. Massumi, B. Minneapolis: University of Minnesota Press.

Derrida, J. 1978. Structure, sign and play in the discourse of the human sciences. Trans. Bass, A. In: *Writing and difference*. Chicago: The University of Chicago Press, pp. 278–293.

Derrida, J. 1980. *Of grammatology*. Trans. Spivak, G.C. Baltimore: The Johns Hopkins University Press.

Derrida, J. 1982. 'Signature event context'. In: *Margins of philosophy*. Trans. Bass, A. Chicago: University of Chicago Press, pp. 307–330.

Derrida, J. 1982a. 'Différance'. In: *Margins of philosophy*. Trans. Bass, A. Chicago: University of Chicago Press, pp. 1–27.

Eco, U. 1984. *The name of the rose*. Trans. Weaver, W. London: Picador.

Foucault, M. 1972. *The discourse on language*. In: *The archaeology of knowledge*. Trans. Smith, A.M.S. New York: Pantheon Books, pp. 215–237.

Gadamer, H.-G. 1982. *Truth and method.* Trans. and ed. Cumming, J. & Barden, G. New York: Crossroad.

Hardt, M. & Negri, A. 2001. *Empire.* Cambridge, Mass.: Harvard University Press.

Heidegger, M. 1978. *Being and time.* Trans. Macquarrie, J. & Robinson, E. Oxford: Basil Blackwell.

Hurst, A. 2002. 'To know and not to do is not to know': Heidegger's Rectoral Address. *South African Journal of Philosophy* 21 (1), pp. 18–34.

Kuhn, T.S. 1970. *The structure of scientific revolutions.* Second, enlarged edition. Chicago: The University of Chicago Press.

Lacan, J. 1977. 'The agency of the letter in the unconscious or reason since Freud'. In: *Écrits: A selection.* Trans. Sheridan, A. New York: W.W. Norton, pp. 146–178.

Lacan, J. 1977a. 'The function and field of speech and language in psychoanalysis'. In: *Écrits: A selection.* Trans. Sheridan, A. New York: W.W. Norton, pp. 30–113.

Olivier, B. 1993. 'Deconstruction'. In: *Conceptions of social inquiry.* Ed. Snyman, J. Pretoria: Human Sciences Research Council, pp. 241–267.

Olivier, B. 2004. 'The (im-)possibility of communication'. *Communicare,* Journal for Communication Sciences in Southern Africa, Vol. 23, (1), pp. 79–91.

Sheridan, A. 1977. 'Translator's note'. In: Lacan, J. *Écrits: A selection.* Trans. Sheridan, A. New York: W.W. Norton, pp. vii–xii.

Shlain, L. 1991. *Art & physics. Parallel visions in space, time and light.* New York: Perennial, Harper Collins.

Shlain, L. 1998. *The alphabet versus the goddess. The conflict between word and image.* New York: Penguin Arkana.

Solomon, R.C. 1994. *The big questions.* 4th edn. New York: Harcourt Brace.

CHAPTER 5

The question of an appropriate philosophical response to 'global' terrorism: Derrida and Habermas

How to respond philosophically to 'terror' and 'terrorism'? This has been for some time an increasingly unavoidable question on a planet where space has shrunk, not only for international travellers in the multicultural world of postmodernity, but for those intent on exporting 'terror' as well.[1] The 'terrorist' attacks on the twin towers of the World Trade Center and the Pentagon in the United States on September 11, 2001, have triggered such responses in various quarters (see Sorkin & Zukin 2002, for a collection of diverse responses; Olivier 2002, 2003), but in my judgement few could be as philosophically significant as those on the part of Jacques Derrida and Jürgen Habermas – until the time of Derrida's

1 There is a strange ambivalence about the fact that a figure such as Osama bin Laden, who represents an extremist Islamic group (Al Qaeda) with *premodern* beliefs (that is, religious beliefs which are characteristic of a pre-Enlightenment world – one where reason has not yet manifested itself as the agreed-upon means to understand the world in conjunction with experience [science], or to organize human society according to secular values such as equality and justice) uses electronic means of communication, such as television and internet websites, which represent what Hardt and Negri (2001: 280–300) describe as the hallmark of *postmodernity*, namely, 'informatization'. It is further well-known that television footage broadcast soon after *9/11* shows bin Laden wearing what appears to be a technologically advanced Timex sports watch – somewhat ironic for someone who opposes everything that the (post-)modern world of rapid technological progress stands for. Steger's 'deconstructive' analysis of this phenomenon brings many of these ambivalences to light, especially in relation to globalization (Steger 2003: 2–7)

death in October 2004 arguably the world's two most important living thinkers – brought together by Giovanna Borradori (2003) in exemplary manner. Here I shall concentrate more on Derrida's contribution than on Habermas's because I believe – for reasons that I shall adduce in due course – that it is significant and far-reaching in a more multidimensional manner than the German philosopher's.

Why should it be the case that the question of a philosophical response to terrorism is ineluctable? A possible answer to this question is that 'terrorism' appears, at first blush, to challenge the very notion of reason, or rationality, especially in its Enlightenment guise. After all, to invoke the historical Enlightenment (or enlightenment as a process or attitude) amounts to a reminder that there once was a collective trust, even 'faith' in reason as an 'enlightening' power, that is, as a force to combat the 'darkness' of superstition, fanaticism and barbarism at various levels, including the scientific, the social, the political and the artistic. Both Habermas and Derrida are what one may describe as 'philosophers of enlightenment', and of what may be called a 'new' Enlightenment, even if their philosophical 'styles', approaches, preoccupations, and focus areas are as different as can be. While they seem to be in agreement that there is a chasm separating justice and power (Habermas 2003: 39; Borradori [on Derrida] 2003b: 168), for instance, their ways of approaching this issue diverge fundamentally – as should become apparent in this article – with Habermas putting his trust in the normative power of constitutional democracy, and Derrida deconstructing the complex relationship between justice and law. It is therefore not surprising to find that important 'Enlightenment' themes are addressed – but very differently – in their respective responses to this, the most devastating terrorist attack in history, as I shall try to show.

It is by no means easy to convince some philosophers that Derrida is a champion of enlightenment (see Caputo 1997: 36–44) – Habermas himself, in his *The philosophical discourse of modernity* (1987) resisted this idea strenuously, arguing that Derrida is guilty of erasing the 'genre difference' between philosophy and literature in favour of 'universal textuality', in this way vitiating philosophy's capacity for 'solving problems' by fatally assimilating it to the 'world-disclosing' function of art and literature (Habermas 1987: 190; 205–207; Olivier 1998: 167–172). But the persistence with which Derrida has addressed questions of undeniably 'enlightenment'-provenance, such as those concerning truth and justice (to mention but two; see Caputo 1997: 125–155; Norris 1996: 50–57), seems to have convinced even Habermas – by the time that Borradori approached him and Derrida with a view to including interviews with both in a philosophical book on *September 11* – that, notwithstanding his criticism of Derrida's specific philosophical approach, he is, after all, on the side of reason and enlightenment (Borradori 2003: xi; 1; 14–18).

One pertinent manifestation of Derrida's affiliation with the movement of enlightenment, as well as the historical Enlightenment, is his response to a question by Richard Kearney about a month after *9/11* (Derrida 2004: 7–8), namely, how he (Derrida) understood the 'dialectic' between the American nation and the 'other out there', as well as (more disturbingly) the 'other within' the nation. Derrida's 'short' answer alludes to the (ironic) consequences of the Cold War, in the course of which America had surrounded itself with nondemocratic allies (bin Laden was trained along 'American lines' for these purposes), some of whom have since turned against it. The 'longest' way to understand this dialectic, however (Derrida 2004: 8):

> ... will be the study of the history and embodiment of Islam. How can one explain that this religion – one that is now in terms of demography the most powerful – and those nations which embody its beliefs, have missed something in history, something that is not shared with Europe – namely, Enlightenment, science, economy, development? ... it took some centuries, during which Christianity and Judaism succeeded in associating with the techno-scientific-capitalistic development while the Arabic-Islamic world did not. They remained poor, attached to old models, repressive, even more phallocentric than the Europeans (which is already something).[2]

2 In the interview with Borradori, Derrida (2003: 122–123) also elaborates on related aspects of the history and present socio-economic conditions of Islamic cultures.

In this interview with Kearney, Derrida therefore implicates an 'other' that already features prominently in the earlier interview – during the same period immediately following *September 11* – with Borradori (Derrida 2003: 95, 98). It is significant to note that, later in the Kearney interview, he explicitly refers to the importance of the political as a sphere that requires restructuring, for enlightenment to be effective even in an Islam within which there are different, countervailing stances regarding violence (Derrida 2004: 9):

> These differences, however, within Islam, cannot be developed efficiently without a development of the institution of the political, of the transformation of the *structures* of the society.

This is a clear indication of where Derrida stands on questions of 'enlightenment': the political manifestation of the failure of Islam, historically, to adopt reason, as the West did, in its Enlightenment guise as fundamental principle for the transformation of an erstwhile autocratic, hierarchically authoritarian society, politics, culture and rules governing cognition, is the contemporary persistence, in Islamic countries, of repressive, hierarchically theocratic rule. This, despite the ironic fact that, until the late Middle Ages, Islam was the equal, if not the superior, of Western Europe in philosophy, 'science' and the technology of the time. The important point Derrida is making, above, is that unless Islamic states were to create the conditions where they do not simply use the technology developed in the course of a long history – albeit a problematic one – by the West (see note 1), but allow their political and social structures to become subject to the transformative power of broadly rational political principles (in their contemporary guise embodied in a constitutional democracy), one would hope in vain for the establishment of a foundation for dialogue between the West and these states which would ameliorate the perception on the part of the West (particularly America) of Islamic peoples as 'the other'.

Clearly Habermas (2003: 31), too, finds it impossible to avoid the question concerning the chasm that seems to separate the West and Islam (which was, to be sure, also 'Western' at its inception during the Middle

Ages). In answer to a question by Borradori (Habermas 2003: 30) on his conception of fundamentalism as a modern phenomenon, he states that (Habermas 2003: 31–32):

> When a contemporary regime like Iran refuses to carry out this separation [between state and church] or when movements inspired by religion strive for the reestablishment of an Islamic form of theocracy, we consider that to be fundamentalism. I would explain the frozen features of such a mentality in terms of the repression of striking cognitive dissonances. This repression occurs when the innocence of the epistemological situation of an all-encompassing world perspective is lost and when, under the cognitive conditions of scientific knowledge and of religious pluralism, a return to the exclusivity of premodern belief attitudes is propagated.

What makes this kind of fundamentalism specifically modern, according to Habermas (2003: 32), is therefore its (pre-modern) insistence that its particular religious doctrine, as well as the accompanying political consequences, be regarded as universally compelling, while obstinately ignoring the fact that it exists in a modern (or post-Enlightenment), techno-scientifically structured, pluralistic social situation where 'the same respect is demanded for everybody' who still adheres to a religion (whether it be Muslim, Christian or Judaic, Hindu, Buddhist, or even something adhered to by quasi-religious 'unbelievers'). Such an anomaly could only be, for Habermas, a modern phenomenon. When perpetrators of 'terror attacks' (such as *September 11*) in various parts of the 'global' world are identified – by their own insistence – as belonging to such fundamentalist groups, it therefore makes the situation all the more intractable for would-be mediators: individuals whose actions are orchestrated by principles dogmatically regarded as binding on everyone, regardless of the fact that the contemporary situation is one of epistemic pluralism, are not open to rational (or, evidently, any other kind of) persuasion. This explains why Habermas (2003: 40–41) contends that non-paternalistic, mutual tolerance is only possible in a situation where political or religious opponents operate within a social space politically regulated by a commonly accepted, democratic constitution (more on this later).

It is interesting to note that Hardt and Negri (2001: 147–150) cast religious fundamentalism in the light of the 'failure of modernization', but unlike Habermas, they insist that it is properly understood as a postmodern phenomenon. The reasons for this are complex, but simplifying somewhat, one could say that, according to them, (Islamic) fundamentalism's postmodernity consists in its 'refusal of modernity as a weapon of Euro-American hegemony' (Hardt & Negri 2001: 149). This is a stance they detect in the work of contemporary Islamic scholars such as Akbar Ahmed, who contrasts Islamic modernism, recognizable by its '... pursuit of Western education, technology and industrialization', with its postmodern counterpart, characterized by '... a reversion to traditional Muslim values and a rejection of modernism' (quoted in Hardt & Negri 2001: 149). In brief, Hardt and Negri view the current 'resurgence' of fundamentalism as a 'refusal' of the contemporary global alliance of dominant western powers at an economic, political, cultural and military level.

The question that poses itself here concerns the relevance of the link between (especially Islamic) fundamentalism and the question guiding this article, namely that of a philosophically appropriate response to 'global' terror or terrorism. One possible answer, I believe, is that – as Derrida points out (above) – one would not understand the connection between such terrorism and Islam unless one painstakingly traced the historical circumstances (perhaps in the form of a Foucaultian genealogy of sorts[3]) surrounding the parting of the ways between the West and Islam around the time of the emergence of modernity during the Enlightenment. Part of a philosophical response to global terrorism would be to understand the historical – but also the conceptual and the religious – conditions of its justification by Islamic extremists. Add to this Habermas's contention

3 One of Foucault's writings that would be extremely helpful in such a project is his 'The discourse on language' (1972), where he articulates, in succinct and programmatically suggestive manner, the principles governing the control *and* the production of discourse in society. These would illuminate the conditions under which Islamic 'discourse' emerged – in the Foucaultian sense of 'language, where meaning and power converge' – which was alternately hostile and emulating regarding Western culture. For an elaboration on discourse in this Foucaultian sense (in relation to criminal actions on the part of discursively constituted subjects), see Olivier 2003a.

that, unless Islam allowed rational principles to transform it socially and politically in the direction of a constitutional democracy, it would remain intractable regarding any attempt to enter into constructive dialogue with it. Perhaps one could retort – implicitly endorsing Derrida's stance on the prerequisites for understanding Islam's historical imperviousness to the Enlightenment – that this presupposes an understanding of the grounds for Islam's resistance to the adoption of such rationally transformative principles. That is, why should it resist the embodiments of reason in science, politics and the like, if Islam – even Osama bin Laden (see note 1) – readily makes use of Western technology, which would be unthinkable without preceding developments in Western philosophy, science and the political and economic restructuring of society?

On the issues discussed so far there does not seem to be significant philosophical differences of judgement between Derrida and Habermas, even if the particulars of their respective stances may differ. And indeed, there are several other things that they agree on, by and large – the 'uncertainty' that appears to be inseparable from 'global' terrorism of the kind in question here, the need to grasp its significance in relation to the broad movement of globalization, the necessity to address the issue of internationalism versus cosmopolitanism (or what Hardt and Negri call the emergence of 'a supra-national order'; 2001: 3–8) regarding the appropriate institutional response to such terror – too many to discuss in detail here (see Borradori 2003: xi–xiv). Are there any 'significant' differences in their respective responses to *September 11*? In my judgement there are. Probably the most significant of these – and one towards which the others gravitate – concerns what one may refer to as Habermas's (modern) reliance on *transcendental* philosophical strategies, in contrast to which Derrida, as poststructuralist, avails himself of a *quasi-transcendental* logic (see Hurst 2004).[4]

4 This, to my mind decisive, difference between these two philosophers is behind the following remarks by Borradori on their respective responses to *9/11* (2003: xii):

> Habermas's dialogue is dense, very compact, and elegantly traditional. His rather Spartan use of language allows his thinking to progress from concept to concept,

A pertinent demonstration of this kind of thinking on Habermas's part occurs in the dialogue with Borradori when he admits (2003: 40–41) that tolerance has usually been practised with a certain paternalism, that is, that it is practised 'within a boundary beyond which it would cease ...'. This means, as he then points out in a startling deconstructive 'move', that it '... possesses itself a kernel of intolerance'. But instead of proceeding further along the deconstructive route (as Derrida would), demonstrating that the impossibility of avoiding the *aporia* that opens up around 'tolerance' has significant practical-ethical possibilities (not least because of the quasi-transcendental functioning of the 'impossible' in the very concept of tolerance), Habermas dismisses deconstruction of the concept because it 'falls into a trap' (2003: 41). Instead, he appeals to the 'constitutional [democratic] state' in so far as it undermines the paternalism attaching to the concept of 'tolerance' – the reciprocal granting of equal rights to one another by citizens precludes, for Habermas, the possibility of anyone arbitrarily 'setting the boundaries of tolerance' (2003: 41).

This is a good example of 'normative critique' on Habermas's part,[5] which is easily recognizable as an extension of a neo-Enlightenment, transcendental way of thinking in so far as it consistently 'asks back' (*zurückfragen*) to the conditions of possibility of something, that is, to what must be presupposed by that something. In this case, the condition of the possibility of overcoming the paralysis induced by the ostensibly inescapable 'intolerance at the heart of tolerance' (the fact that it is prac-

with the steady and lucid pace that has made classical German philosophy so distinctive.

By contrast, Derrida's dialogue takes the reader on a longer and winding road that opens unpredictably onto large vistas and narrow canyons, some so deep that the bottom remains out of sight. His extreme sensitivity for subtle facts of language makes Derrida's thought virtually inseparable from the words in which it is expressed. The magic of this dialogue is to present, in an accessible and concentrated manner, his unmatched ability to combine inventiveness and rigor, circumvention and affirmation.

5 Habermas's 'normative' approach, which differs radically from that of poststructuralists generally, is brought to light very clearly by Borradori (see especially 2003c: 45–48) in her discussion of terrorism in relation to his philosophical project.

tised within certain boundaries only) is, for Habermas, the democratic constitution which enshrines citizens' rights. This constitution is the guarantee, he believes, that tolerance of the paternalistic variety cannot – or rather, *should not* – flourish. The emphasis that Habermas places on norms that putatively regulate human actions in such a way that every citizen in a democratic state would enjoy the same rights, is precisely what differentiates between him and Derrida.

Not that Derrida would not endorse such constitutionally enshrined rights; on the contrary. But instead of regarding it as guarantee that tolerance will necessarily be practised reciprocally, without undermining itself, his thinking proceeds, not along a transcendental avenue, but in a more paradoxical, *quasi*-transcendental manner. Such thinking would acknowledge the strange tendency at the heart of tolerance to limit itself, lest advantage be taken of the tolerant party, but Derrida would – analogous to his analysis of the concept of hospitality (see Caputo 1997: 109–113) – show that, as with many other interhuman phenomena, tolerance is inescapably subject to two countervailing 'economies' (even when it is practised in a constitutional democracy). The first of these, the 'economic', displays a structural dynamic of 'investment and return', that is, it is conditional upon certain expectations (this is the 'paternalistic' notion of tolerance). On the other hand, however, there is the 'aneconomic' moment of excess or transgression, an 'impossible' structural dynamic which limits, and is limited by its economic counterpart (see Hurst 2004: 251–257). Although 'impossible' in any pure, unadulterated sense, this possibility of an 'excessive' tolerance – as in the case of hospitality – is what first allows tolerance to happen, even if it is constrained and held in check by its economic counterpart. Conversely, the economic dynamic of tolerance – the functioning of a limit to its practice – is what gives rise to the transgressive gesture of an 'unbounded', aneconomic tolerance (which is 'impossible' because it is always restrained by its economic counterpart). This mode of reasoning is *quasi*-transcendental: it takes transcendental logic or reasoning a step further because it does not simply articulate the conditions of *possibility* of a phenomenon, but demonstrates (as the above example shows) that these are simultaneously the conditions of *impossibility* of the phenomenon in question. Admittedly, this is just a formula for the claim that the very conditions that make something possible, ensure that it is not possible in a 'pure' state, or that the phenomenon is 'ruined' by the very conditions of its own provenance. Hence, 'pure' paternalistic tolerance (or 'purely hostile' hospitality) is not possible because nothing would be tolerated by it (it is 'ruined' by its counterpart, the aneconomic); similarly, 'pure' excessive tolerance (or unbounded hospitality) is impossible because it would undermine the very possibility of it being extended (it is 'ruined' by its counterpart, the economic).[6]

From this example it is apparent that Derrida, instead of (like Habermas) extending a 'normative critique', articulates a quasi-transcendental analysis of phenomena or of events. To put it differently, he does not deal with counterfactuals as Habermas does, but uncovers the complex, paradoxical or aporetic logic underpinning some of the most common experiences on the part of individuals. And the point is: he does it in such a way as to show that one is *not* paralyzed, as Habermas thinks, by the interwoven logic of the economic and the aneconomic, but is precisely galvanized into action by the necessity to *act*: as Caputo (1997: 110–111) explains regarding Derrida's logic, no one would be able to extend hospitality to a potential guest unless spurred on by a wish to *open* one's home to the other in an unlimited fashion (hospitality accompanied by all manner of limitations and prohibitions is not hospitality), but hospitality would be equally impossible if this impulse to be unconditionally hospitable were not limited by a smidgen of '*hostility*', if not possessiveness, on the part of the hosts (one has to allow for implicit limits, otherwise the host might soon not be in a position to offer any hospitality).

To return to these two philosophers' respective responses to *September 11*, the quasi-transcendental pattern of Derrida's thinking is immediately apparent in his analysis of this 'event' at various levels, not least of which is that of the very notion of it being a 'major event'. To anyone familiar with Heidegger's work – and with the fact that Heidegger is one of Derrida's important precursors – it would be immediately apparent that

6 See Andrea Hurst's (2004) exemplary exposition, by way of a discussion of a number of telling instantiations – such as justice and the gift – of this quasi-transcendental pattern of Derrida's thinking.

the concept of the 'event' touches on one of the Heideggerian roots of deconstruction (as Mark Ralkowski has reminded me, and) as Derrida acknowledges in the Borradori interview. What is important to note, as he points out (2003: 90), is that Heidegger's notion of *Ereignis* ('event'), which bears on the '... *appropriation* of the proper (*eigen*)', is inseparable from the countervailing movement of '... a certain *expropriation* that Heidegger himself names (*Enteignis*)'. He then adds (2003: 90): 'The undergoing of the event, that which in the undergoing or in the ordeal *at once opens itself up to and resists experience*, is, it seems to me, a certain *unappropriability* of what comes or happens'. This goes to the heart of Derrida's understanding of the 'event', as will become clearer in what follows here.

While Habermas (2003: 26), in response to Borradori's question, whether he considers *September 11* 'an unprecedented event', seems content to leave the very notion of the 'event' itself unquestioned – although he grants that the 'monstrous act itself was new' in terms of its 'symbolic force' (2003: 28) – Derrida (2003: 86–94), by contrast, immediately closes in on this notion, problematizing it to the hilt. He concedes that it is 'at least *felt*', with ostensible immediacy, to be an event of an 'unprecedented' kind, but questions the authenticity of such a feeling of immediacy, reminding one that (2003: 86):

> ... this 'feeling' is actually less spontaneous than it appears: it is to a large extent conditioned, constituted, if not actually constructed, circulated at any rate through the media by means of a prodigious techno-socio-political machine.

This, despite, or perhaps because of the fact that one does not 'yet really know how to identify' this event, which would perhaps explain why the 'minimal deictic' of the date is resorted to as a way of naming this ineffaceable, (but also ineffable – 'like an intuition without concept') 'thing' that has happened (2003: 86). After all, he points out, describing it as an act of 'international terrorism' is hardly what one might call a 'rigorous concept' that would capture the utter 'singularity' of what occurred. The impotence of language to assign this event a horizon of signification, Derrida insists (2003: 86), reveals itself in the 'mechanical repetition' of the date – an observation which marks another cardinal difference between himself and Habermas, in so far as it reveals his intimate knowledge and efficacious interpretive use of psychoanalytic theory. Who could fail to notice the similarity of Derrida's remark concerning the 'powerlessness' of language to grasp the singularity of *September 11*, to Jacques Lacan's contention that the register of the so-called 'real' announces itself precisely there, where language comes up 'against its own limits'?[7] He drives home the pertinence of this psychoanalytical insight when he elaborates on the necessity of repeating the date like a mantra (Derrida 2003: 87):

> ... on the one hand, to conjure away, as if by magic, the 'thing' itself, the fear or the terror it inspires (for repetition always protects by neutralizing, deadening, distancing a traumatism, and this is true for the repetition of the televised images we will speak of later), and, on the other hand, to deny, as close as possible to this act of language and this enunciation, our powerlessness to name in an appropriate fashion, to characterize, to think the thing in question, to get beyond the mere deictic of the date: something terrible took place on September 11, and in the end we don't know what.

No one should fool themselves into believing that reason in the guise of clear, distinct conceptual language is adequate to grasp what happened that day; Derrida is here reminding latter-day rationalists like Habermas that, what is known in psychoanalysis as the 'repetition compulsion' (which he explicitly names later in the interview), has precisely the function to make the unbearable bearable, *but* at the cost of falsifying the 'thing' which one tries repeatedly to nail, to pin down in language and

7 Joan Copjec explains Lacan's notion of the 'real' as follows – effectively prohibiting the inclination to equate it with the Kantian *Ding-an-sich* (2002: 95–96):

> Lacan's definition of the real is precisely this: that which, in language or the symbolic, negates the possibility of any metadimension, any metalanguage. It is this undislodgeable negation, this rigid kernel in the heart of the symbolic, that forces the signifier to split off from and turn around on itself. For, in the absence of any metalanguage, the signifier can only signify by referring to another signifier ... Far from positing the existence of an elsewhere, the real as internal limit of the symbolic – that is, the very impotence of the signifier – is the obstacle that scotches the possibility of rising out of or above the symbolic.

image-replay. For no matter how apparently efficaciously one succeeds in inscribing it in the dominant discourses of the time – and even if one articulates it in terms of esoteric ones – or how familiar the sequence of images depicting the mesmerizing implosion of the twin towers, one after the other, becomes, the 'event' itself will always prove to be elusive. The function of the repetition is precisely to weave a web of iconic and symbolic familiarity around the 'event', within which it will be (or has perhaps already been) archived 'historically' (problematic as this last term may be). But in so far as it has the status of the 'real', it eludes one the moment you think you have managed to 'name' or describe it. This does not mean that one should avoid articulating it in language – on the contrary, as Derrida insists (2003: 87–88):

> I believe always in the necessity of being attentive first of all to this phenomenon of language, naming, and dating, to this repetition compulsion (at once rhetorical, magical, and poetic). To what this compulsion signifies, translates, or betrays. Not in order to isolate ourselves in language, as people in too much of a rush would like us to believe, but on the contrary, in order to try to understand what is going on precisely *beyond* language and what is pushing us to repeat endlessly and without knowing what we are talking about, precisely there where language and the concept come up against their limits: 'September 11, September 11, *le 11 septembre, 9/11*'.[8]

But Derrida wishes to push this analysis even further, to the point where he problematizes the very question, whether *September 11* 'really' constitutes an 'event' in this sense of something, some 'thing', which tantalizes our ingenuity in naming, in fabricating conceptually adequate appellations, by means of which we can, once and for all, inscribe it in the archive of a presumably shared, social and political, human history. Thus, in contrast to Habermas's (2003: 26–28) willingness to abide by the conventional or consensual efficacy of subsuming *9/11* under the rubric of the 'event' – conceding, incongruously, its symbolic novelty, while refraining from

8 Here, again, it is clear that Derrida's remark is perfectly consonant with Lacan's articulation of the register of 'the impossible real'. Compare Copjec on this in note 7, above.

probing its putative signal singularity – he unravels the aporetic logic of 'eventspeak'. Resorting to a quasi-Humean terminology, Derrida (2003: 88) agrees with Borradori, that one could speak of an 'impression' of a '*major event*' here, reminding her at the same time that the 'menacing injunction' to repeat the name, *September 11*, comes from a constellation of dominant powers, themselves dominated by 'the Anglo-American idiom', from which, in its interpretive, rhetorical, globalized guise, this impression cannot be divorced. However, to distinguish rigorously between the 'impression' as a putatively 'brute fact', and the interpretation pertaining to it is, Derrida believes (2003: 89), a philosophical and political duty. 'We could say', he remarks (2003: 89):

> ... that the impression is 'informed', in both senses of the word: a predominant system gave it form, and this form then gets run through an organized information machine (language, communication, rhetoric, image, media, and so on). This informational apparatus is from the very outset political, technical, economic.

There is therefore a 'resemblance' between the 'impression' as a global effect and the 'thing' that produced it by means of or through a whole web of mutually reinforcing agencies (the media, technoscience, as well as military, economic and diplomatic institutions), although neither the 'thing' nor the event is reducible to this impression (Derrida 2003: 88–89).

This somewhat cryptic observation becomes more intelligible in light of his subsequent explanation (2003: 89), that the '*event*' comprises the '*thing*' itself as that which 'happens' ('event' is in a sense 'advent' or 'arrival'), together with the '*impression*' (that is simultaneously 'spontaneous' and 'controlled') created by it. From this it seems to me that, although one is not entitled to say that the ineffable 'thing' *is* in any meaningful sense 'outside' the agencies which produce the 'impression', one might say it is refracted through these agencies as through a prism, so that it first becomes visible as 'event' in its constituent 'colours' when it has 'passed through' the prism of language, dominant discourses, images, media and communication channels. Here one comes up against the limits of language – a sure sign that one has encountered the Lacanian 'real' – for even the prism-metaphor falls short of capturing the relation between the 'thing' and the 'impression'. Perhaps that of a crystal ball, in which amorphous phantasms swim into intelligible shapes, is more accurate: at first there is 'nothing' there, and then, out of the not-present, something perceivable 'morphs' into visible being, like James Cameron's T–1000 terminator (see Olivier 2002) assuming its terrifying shape from out of a 'liquid metal' matrix of pure possibilities. Importantly, whatever it is that thus becomes 'visible' must of necessity do so in terms of the spectrum of humanly visible colours, which here represents language and iconicity in their widest sense.

Further – and here one witnesses deconstructive thinking delineating the 'other side' of the 'constructedness' of the 'event' – with every successive linguistic or iconic appropriation of the 'event' one witnesses a cumulative process in action: with each appropriation (iteration, description, discussion, analysis, framing) something is added to it, complexifying it, enhancing it, constituting it *as* 'event', with the paradoxical corollary that it increasingly assumes the character of something 'sublime' in the aesthetic sense of being, strictly speaking, 'unpresentable'.[9] In this way it highlights the paradox, that the more is said or written about it, the more it recedes from humans' attempts to incarcerate it, as it were, in the 'prison-house' of language in the widest sense, and the more it asserts its irreducibility. Importantly, at the same time as the symbolic network progressively appears to assimilate or appropriate the event (*Ereignis*), the countervailing process of withdrawal or 'expropriation' (*Enteignis*), referred to earlier, occurs in a corresponding manner, announcing – however imperceptibly – that 'something' escapes it. And it is this traumatically experienced 'something' which continually, *repeatedly*, returns, challenging and exhorting one to appropriate it interpretively in an attempt to exorcise its effects.

Even these finer distinctions are difficult to sustain, as Derrida (2003: 89) acknowledges, for it is virtually impossible to distinguish between the 'impression' as 'brute fact' and as 'interpretation' made possible by

9 For an extended discussion of the sublime as 'unpresentable', specifically in the context of postmodern culture, see Olivier 1998a.

the system of representations of and information about it. If this were not the case, *other* 'events', in the course of which thousands of people also died – the Rwandan genocide comes to mind – might also have given the 'impression' of having been 'major events'. To understand why this is the case, he suggests (2003: 89) that a distinction should be made between two kinds of 'impression': on the one hand, unconditional compassion and sadness for the victims of such events and condemnation of their death – a response that touches the kernel of the 'event' beyond all simulation; on the other hand, the 'informed' or already 'interpreted' impression, conducive to persuading one to 'believe' that *9/11* is a 'major event'. Derrida puts special emphasis on '*belief*' here – 'the phenomenon of *credit* and of *accreditation*' (2003: 89) in so far as it is inseparable from evaluation (which results in the 'inflated' significance attributed to the dating). Indeed, he suggests, perhaps the questions concerning the nature of an 'impression' and a 'belief' (in the language of British empiricism), but especially of an *event* in the true sense are 'opening up' again here in a novel manner (2003: 90):

> For could an event that still conforms to an essence, to a law or to a truth, indeed to a concept of the event, ever be a major event? A major event should be so unforeseeable and irruptive that it disturbs even the horizon of the concept or essence on the basis of which we believe we recognize an event *as such*. That is why all the 'philosophical' questions remain open, perhaps even beyond philosophy itself, as soon as it is a matter of thinking the event.

Here Derrida forces one to confront the limits of Husserlian phenomenology in relation to history: if one is able to delineate the universal essence of a phenomenon (such as the 'event'), all instances that conform to this essence should be recognizable on the basis of this known essence. But historically *novel* phenomena which might be subsumed under the rubric of especially names like 'event' or 'innovation' would then be paradoxical. They would conform to *and* transgress their own character simultaneously, that is, they would 'disturb' their own 'horizon' of 'anticipatability'. A 'major event' would therefore be 'unforeseeable', as Derrida insists, even if, once having occurred, it unavoidably demands to be recognized, comprehended and appropriated as a 'major event'. But (2003: 90–91),

> ... there is no event worthy of its name except insofar as this appropriation *falters* at some border or frontier. A frontier, however, with neither front nor confrontation, one that incomprehension does not run into head on since it does not take the form of a solid front: it escapes, remains evasive, open, undecided, indeterminable. Whence the unappropriability, the unforeseeability, absolute surprise, incomprehension, the risk of misunderstanding, unanticipatable novelty, pure singularity, the absence of horizon.

In short, Derrida's radicalization of phenomenological reasoning has the disconcerting effect of uncovering the *aporia*, that 9/11 *is and is not* an 'event'. In so far as one is able to affirm that, as manifestation of an irreducible 'thing', it has shaken the framework by means of which we have been accustomed to recognize 'events', it *is* an 'event', but paradoxically, to the degree that the 'impression' within which it has been couched is a production by and of a vast, powerful, globally dominant machinery of information and discursive-interpretive construction, it is certainly *not* an event. In fact, he argues, from the latter perspective, far from being an 'unforeseeable event', it was quite possible to anticipate such an attack on American territory. (In fact, as early as 1994 this was foreseen by certain architects; see Derrida 2003: 186–187; note 6.)

Against the backdrop of this cautionary note Derrida (2003: 91) grants that one could nevertheless proceed by speaking of *9/11* as an 'event'. In the final analysis, even the most insignificant or 'banal' quotidian occurrence in human experience, he reminds us, has something unforeseeable and event-like about it. If this seems like a strange claim to pragmatically-minded, common sense-adherents, they merely have to remember that, *strictly speaking*, no particular future occurrence is predictable with absolute certainty, even if one could anticipate, with good reason (whether on Humean or, alternatively, Kantian grounds), that such occurrences would, in all probability, conform to causal patterns that one is accustomed to. This is what Derrida calls the 'messianic' structure of experience (see Derrida in Caputo 1997: 22–25, as well as Caputo's elaboration on this; 1997: 156–180) – the quality of experience that reveals an abiding receptivity, if not a veritable exigency for the 'advent of an event', the tacit possibility that the 'other' (or otherness) may surprise one. Hence, it should teach one that one should always be open to the 'incoming other', that the very structure of experience exhibits this unforeseeability, even if unforeseeability itself is, paradoxically, 'foreseeable'. And, as the advent of *9/11* shows, 'expecting the unexpected' does not necessarily bear on something pleasantly surprising.

To persuade his audience that he is not engaged in an idealist pursuit by invoking a 'horizon of nonknowledge' (2003: 94) or of unforeseeability, Derrida's exemplary analysis goes even further, along the trajectory suggested by the preceding reflections, towards the 'more concrete'. And again he employs the same aporetic or 'quasi-transcendental' logic, which here assumes the form of the 'law' governing what he terms an '*autoimmunitary process*' (2003: 94):

> ... an autoimmunitary process is that strange behavior where a living being, in quasi-*suicidal* fashion, 'itself' works to destroy its own protection, to immunize itself *against* its 'own' immunity.[10]

The logic of this autoimmunity unfolds in what Derrida describes as '*three moments*' of 'autoimmunity', of 'reflex and reflection'. The first: '*The Cold War in the head*' (2003: 94), or to summarize brutally, autoimmunity as the fear of terrorism that spawns terror and defence at the same time – the fear of terror(-ism) 'in the head' (that is, psychologically in the individual's head, politically in the figure of the Capitol and the White House, and economically in the figure of the Twin Towers as the 'head' of capital) terrorizes most, and it engenders a 'double suicide' (of the 'terrorists' and of those hosts who trained them). The second: '*Worse than*

10 The metaphor of 'immunity' or 'autoimmunity' clearly derives from medical-immunological discourse, in conjunction with those of zoology, biology and genetics. And indeed, Derrida has written elsewhere on such 'autoimmunity' as the (paradoxical) process, on the part of a living organism, '... of protecting itself against its self-protection by destroying its own immune-system' (quoted in Derrida 2003: 187–188, note 7). An allergic reaction to certain toxins, venoms, natural or industrial materials would be an example of such a process, and as will become clearer, in the case under discussion one could also perhaps speak metaphorically of an 'allergic reaction'. See also what Derrida says about this *aporia* as an example of the *pharmakon*, something that is remedy and poison at the same time (2003; 124).

the Cold War' (2003: 96), or, again mercilessly condensed, the 'event' as trauma displays the paradoxical temporality of proceeding neither from the present, nor the past, but from 'an im-presentable to come'[11] (2003: 97): traumatism (with no possibility of a suffering-alleviating 'work of mourning') is produced by the future, by 'the threat of the worst *to come*' (2003: 97). And the third: '*The vicious circle of repression*' (2003: 100), or the paradox, that even if this worst of all terrors 'touches the geopolitical unconscious (inscrutable as it may be) of every living being and leaves there indelible traces' (2003: 99),[12] it can 'simultaneously appear insubstantial, fleeting, light, and so seem to be denied, repressed, indeed forgotten, relegated to being just one event among others ...' (2003: 99). Yet, the effect of these attempts to deny, disarm or repress the traumatic impact of the 'event' amount to nothing less than the autoimmunitary process according to which 'the very monstrosity they claim to overcome' is generated or invented, produced, 'fed' (2003: 99). This is how repression in both its psychoanalytical and its political senses works.

The question ineluctably arises (somewhat incongruously, given the fact that he has 'performed' the answer to it from the outset in the dialogue in question!) – as Borradori intimates to Derrida (2003: 100) – what the role of philosophy is in the face of the 'event' of *September 11*. It should be apparent from the preceding discussion that this performance of philosophy's task on Derrida's part has assumed the form of a deconstruction of the 'event' of *September 11*, not merely regarding its ambivalent status, but also by delineating the strange 'autoimmunitary' logic within which it is embedded. It is with this in mind that his answer

11 See in this regard Olivier (1998a: 204–205), for a discussion of what is implicated here, namely what I there termed the terrible or 'bad' sublime as a species (often ignored) of the figure of the sublime.

12 It may seem somewhat strange to readers familiar with Borradori's book (2003) that I refer here to the page *before* the one on which the third moment of 'autoimmunity' is announced, which ostensibly still comprises part of the discussion devoted by Derrida to the second moment. Despite this incongruity I cannot ignore the fact that this part of his elaboration on page 99 (Derrida 2003) pertains thematically to the third moment, regardless of it only being articulated explicitly on page 100.

to Borradori's question concerning the function of philosophy should be understood (2003: 100):

> Such an 'event' surely calls for a philosophical response. Better, a response that calls into question, at their most fundamental level, the most deep-seated conceptual presuppositions in philosophical discourse. The concepts with which this 'event' has most often been described, named, categorized, are the products of a 'dogmatic slumber' from which only a new philosophical reflection can awaken us, a reflection *on* philosophy, most notably on political philosophy and its heritage. The prevailing discourse, that of the media and of the official rhetoric, relies too readily on received concepts like 'war' or 'terrorism' (national or international).

This, after already having demonstrated the short-sightedness of attributing too quickly to *9/11* the status of a 'major event' – an attribution that obscures more than it reveals. One could easily forget what a salutary reminder Derrida's Kantian observation is: so-called philosophers are prone to forgetting that 'dogmatic slumbers' do not pertain to the same concepts in every era. Kant had Hume to thank for awakening him from his dependence on certain received notions concerning experience and reason; today, philosophers ought to ask themselves precisely which concepts are too taken-for-granted, and hence most in need of critical scrutiny (including perhaps the contemporary counterparts of 'experience' and 'reason', which are by no means easy to determine, given the way that these concepts have their paradigmatic embodiments in every era). Here Derrida mentions (in addition to those he has already examined) 'war' and 'terrorism' – concepts which he proceeds to unravel in the succeeding pages, in the process making a number of important points. These pertain to (among others) the impossibility of identifying the 'enemy' against which the Bush administration has declared 'war' in any clear-cut manner, as under conditions of conventional warfare; the deterritorialization of the 'technologies of aggression' (2003: 101); the ambivalence of the concept of 'terrorism' which – most people forget – is largely derived from the Reign of (state) Terror during the French Revolution (2003: 102–103), thus making the oft-rejected notion of 'state terrorism' appear decidedly less absurd; the dogmatic use and obscurity of the concept of 'international terrorism', coupled with the need for subjecting it to a philosophical debate; and the importance of recognizing the 'dominant power' behind the imposition, the legitimation and, indeed, the legalization of a certain terminology which already calls for a certain interpretation of 'events' (2003: 105).

On an earlier occasion Derrida had expounded on precisely this process in which events are 'artifactually created' by powers which monopolize the 'actuality effect' (2002: 3–5), in relation to the question of philosophy's role or responsibility. Derrida understands 'actuality' as something which is, contrary to conventional assumptions, 'precisely, *made*' (2002: 3–4):

> It is not given but actively produced, sifted, invested, performatively interpreted by numerous apparatuses which are *factitious* or *artificial*, hierarchizing and selective, always in the service of forces and interests to which 'subjects' and agents (producers and consumers of actuality – sometimes they are 'philosophers' and always interpreters, too) are never sensitive enough. No matter how singular, irreducible, stubborn, distressing or tragic the 'reality' to which it refers, 'actuality' comes to us by way of a fictional fashioning. [Uncannily, this remark seems to adumbrate *September 11*! B.O.] It can be analysed only at the cost of a labor of resistance, of vigilant counter-interpretation, etc. Hegel was right to remind the philosopher of his time to read the papers daily. Today the same responsibility obliges him to learn how the dailies, the weeklies, the television news programs are *made*, and *by whom*.[13]

In our time, therefore, the philosopher's duty is first and foremost to render a vigilant critique – Derrida would say 'deconstruction' – not only of those events (like the Gulf War, or *September 11*) that are crucial for the understanding of cultural and historical transformations, but also (perhaps especially) of those processes at work, mostly imperceptibly – given the extent to which they are taken for granted – in the production or generation of a certain 'reality effect'. Inseparable from this is the cratological-political question of the power, force, or relations of

13 It is important to note which terms are placed 'under erasure' by Derrida in this quotation by the use of inverted commas – these are the concepts that he pointedly wishes to question and problematize most severely.

domination[14] underpinning the operation of the processes in question – processes which, it will be remembered, were shown by Derrida to have been at play throughout the emergence of *September 11* as a 'major event', although the latter could not be reduced to these processes either. This – Derrida's rigorous logic of *aporia*, which uncovers a phenomenon as being 'impure', or constituted by elements which cannot conveniently (and misleadingly) be reduced to each other – is what distinguishes him from Baudrillard, who would arguably have us believe that we live in an all-encompassing 'hyperreality' of simulacra (see Baudrillard 1996) which hides the fact that it is all there is, that contemporary technologies generate this realm so pervasively that everything is a matter of 'cultural construction'. Such a pseudo-ontological stance all too easily lets the philosopher – and everybody else, too – off the hook. By contrast, Derrida insists that (2002: 5–6):

14 In his formidable *Specters of Marx* (1994: 81–84) Derrida provides a list of 'plagues' of the present world order, which are intimately connected to these questions of power, and all of which require close philosophical scrutiny. These include unemployment; the exclusion of homeless citizens from participation in democratic processes; the 'ruthless economic war' among nations worldwide; the insurmountability of the contradictions inherent to the concept of the 'free market'; the connection between the worsening of foreign debt and economic hardship on the part of many millions of people; the apparently irreversible integration of the 'arms industry' with economic activity worldwide; the spread of nuclear weapons; the global proliferation of inter-ethnic wars; the virtually invisible or seamless infiltration of states and economies by 'phantom-States' (like the mafia and the Japanese Yakuza) as a strictly capitalist phenomenon; and the present condition of international law and its institutions, in so far as it suffers from certain historical and state-specific cratological limitations. Anyone – so-called 'philosophers' included – who believes that, by and large, all is well with the globalized, 'liberal-democratic', technophiliac, capitalist world, should look carefully at this list, together with Derrida's comments on the enumerated 'plagues' (which are inseparable from social and economic suffering), to realize that all of them are intimately connected to capitalist economic power.

> ... the requisite deconstruction of this *artifactuality* should not be used as an alibi. It should not give way to an inflation ... of the simulacrum and neutralize every threat in what might be called the delusion of the delusion, the denial of the event: 'Everything', people would then think, 'even violence, suffering, war, and death, everything is constructed, fictionalised, constituted by and for the media apparatus. Nothing ever really happens. There is nothing but simulacrum and delusion.' While taking the deconstruction of artifactuality as far as possible, we must therefore do everything in our power to guard against this critical neoidealism and remember, not only that a consistent deconstruction is a thinking of singularity, and therefore of the event, of what it ultimately preserves of the irreducible, but also that 'information' is a contradictory and heterogeneous process. It can and must be transformed, it can and must serve, as it has often done, knowledge, truth, and the cause of democracy to come, and all the questions they necessarily entail.

Needless to say, Derrida's deconstruction of the 'event' of the September 11-'terrorist' attacks, carried out some 5 years after publishing these reflections on actuality and artifactuality (2002), is just such a 'thinking of singularity' which succeeds in demonstrating the – above all *political* – futility of 'enclosing' events such as these once and for all within the procrustean apparatus of mainstream media and hegemonic discourses (such as those of the Bush Administration) by insisting, 'uncritically', that they are 'constructed' in their entirety. As I have tried to show, Derrida's deconstruction unmasks these 'critical neoidealist' claims – regardless of the extent to which an 'event' like *September 11* has indeed, from one perspective, been 'constructed' in multiple ways by dominant discourses and iconic apparatuses (a fact acknowledged by him) as instances of 'passing the buck', refusing to accept political and philosophical responsibility for either the consequences or the unprogrammability of that which 'happens' or 'comes' unexpectedly, and which is, as such, irreducible to the encompassing productivity of technical and politico-discursive apparatuses. Only by relativizing the seductive claims of the petrifying Medusa-esque media-gaze, can the unprogrammability of history be acknowledged.

This is not to deny the crucial function, remarked on in the earlier discussion of Derrida's deconstruction of *9/11* as 'event', of the manner in which the ineluctable, repetitive and, moreover, cumulative weaving of the 'event' into a discursive fabric adds to, enhances and perhaps first constitutes it *as* 'event', making of it both more, *and* less than what it 'is'.

Paradoxically, *events* such as this one elicit conventional as well as creative elaborations precisely *because* their inassimilable singularity challenges the capacity of symbolic and iconic frameworks to accommodate them, generating, in the end, a reconfiguration of these contexts of comprehension. Even as humans elaborate on them, in the process enhancing them, 'making' them 'more' than what their initial 'impression' seems to suggest, they also, like the so-called sublime, escape our very best attempts to enmesh and domesticate them in our symbolic networks. In this respect philosophers' difficult task is to do justice to the many-sidedness of the phenomenon of the event – its political, social, cultural, epistemic and axiological implications – without shirking their duty to do so by executing some or other obfuscating reduction. In the process it is imperative to pay careful attention to what makes the specific historical moment unique, different from other, preceding (and perhaps successive) historical situations, as Derrida suggests (2002: 7) by referring to the 'new mediatic situation' which requires philosophers' as well as media professionals' careful consideration.

In fact, given the media-saturatedness of contemporary, postmodern society, philosophers should perhaps not only direct their philosophical-interpretive focus at the audiovisual images populating media-space, but actively promote the construction, generation or creation of *alternative* image-configurations. By 'alternative' I mean those images and image-sequences which would present the opportunity to viewers to distance themselves interpretively from the iconic constellation of dominant discourses and forces, specifically those representing global capitalism in its interwovenness with the 'homohegemonic' (Derrida 2002a) cultural, political and military powers – powers that are routinely, incessantly reinforced as the preferred nexus for identification on the part of media-viewers and listeners worldwide.[15] On this topic of creating the space for

15 See in this regard my article, 'Popular art, the image, the subject and subverting hegemony' (Olivier 2006), where I address at length the difficult question of the possibility of effective strategies for dislodging the stranglehold that images invested with capitalist value seem to have on the contemporary, 'globalized' world. In the course of the argument I engage with major thinkers and theorists, including Freud,

'alternative' cultural artefacts, such as films, and alternative film-traditions – which, to be sure, already exist, even if not enough viewers are attracted to them (yet?) – Derrida has the following to say (2002a: 54–55):

> If you want to fight the hegemony of the 'bad', 'Hollywood' production, you're not going to do it by closing the market, but by promoting, through education, discussion, culture, in France and elsewhere, occasions for preferring one kind of film over another and by promoting, at the same time, a production that escapes the bad, Hollywood industry, in France *and* in America. It's a struggle for which one can elaborate new discourses ... one can try to convince people, to ensure that the properly productive selectivity of those who were previously in the position of consumer-spectators can intervene in the market ... You've got to promote diversity of preference all over the world: preference for this film over another ... But if this struggle is not waged from the side of what are still called – provisionally – the 'buyers' or 'consumers', it is lost from the start.

Why is it necessary to emphasize the importance of iconicity, of images, here? What does it have to do with 'global terrorism', or with the question of how philosophers can and should respond to it and to related phenomena in the contemporary, twenty-first-century world? It is no exaggeration, I believe, to say 'Everything'. Earlier I referred to Derrida's argument, that the 'impression' of the 'event' of *9/11* was given form by a hegemonic system of interpretation, including language, communication, images and media (2003: 89). I believe that it has been shown persuasively by a variety of thinkers and theorists that media-images play a crucial role in patterns of identification on the part of viewers and audiences, and the ease with which people worldwide are subjectivized in terms of the interests and values of the intertwined, globally hegemonic economic and political systems, has a great deal to do with images offering sites of (never innocent) identification to viewers in and through mainstream media (see note 13 in this regard). It is to Derrida's credit that, unlike Habermas, he has given sustained attention to this problematic (which

---

Lacan, Deleuze and Guattari, Joan Copjec as well as Kaja Silverman, who have written compellingly on issues pertinent to this question, such as the provenance of the subject and the conditions of possibility of identification.

is closely connected to questions of power), as the present article shows. This strikes me as being quite ironic, given Habermas's reputation as the philosopher of 'communicative action' (see for example Brand 1990), and is comprehensible, I believe, in light of what I referred to earlier as his preoccupation with 'normative' critique – a strict focus on the normative foundations and counterfactual conditions for 'undistorted communication' would understandably distract one's attention away from the concrete, 'factical' historical circumstances (including contemporary patterns of identity-formation in relation to media-images invested with hegemonic interests) that comprise the foci of poststructuralists' analytical scrutiny. This is not to deny the conceptual-analytical usefulness of much of Habermas's work, for example his well-known distinction between 'strategic' and 'communicative action' (Brand 1990: 15–16) – a valuable tool in discourse-analysis for unmasking disingenuous attempts at wielding power, which masquerade as would-be acts of communication.

What light has the preceding discussion cast on the question regarding an appropriate philosophical response to 'global terrorism'? Performatively as well as constatively, both Derrida and Habermas are exemplary in demonstrating that there is such a thing as a distinctly *philosophical* response to this scourge of the present age, and, moreover, that it is a responsibility that philosophers cannot evade. Philosophers face the responsibility of elucidating the sometimes opaque, confusing or disconcerting occurrences of their time, without necessarily forgetting what links this era to (or distinguishes it from) former epochs. This responsibility entails, in the first place, the 'labour of reason' in the broadest sense; not merely Enlightenment reason, or analytical reason, or social-scientific, or hermeneutic-interpretive reason, but reason in the sense of philosophers availing themselves of every resource, capacity and nuance of human rationality to reach understanding of what is at hand – analysis, synthesis, various logics – from formal, informal and symbolic to quasi-transcendental; phenomenological or structural interpretation, discourse-analysis, psychoanalytic interpretation, performativity and more – not merely as an armchair activity, but with the social and political objective, to communicate such understanding to their fellow human beings in the hope of fostering insight into the conditions for peaceful co-existence as well as into the obstacles in the way of such a state of affairs.

Needless to say, as both of these thinkers indicate, this philosophical task entails everything from investigations into the historical preconditions of present problem-areas (such as Islamic 'fundamentalism') to the deconstruction of hegemonic cultural, political and military relations. It is especially important to note that, judging by their example – regardless of their differences in approach – no philosopher worthy of the name can be 'neutral' in the face of something as devastating to the thought of human solidarity as 'terrorism' in any guise (whether it is 'international', 'national', 'global' or 'state' terrorism, all of which descriptions require careful analysis). Philosophers should not (in fact, *cannot*, realistically) teach and practise their discipline with the objective of restricting it within the confines of academia, or indeed of the institutions of publishing. Although these are foremost as avenues for the dissemination of philosophical discourses within the ostensibly innocuous realm of intellectual debate, they are never limited in their effectivity to these domains, as every philosopher should know. All philosophical thinking faces the daunting responsibility of having to articulate its consequences and implications for social and political practice. As such, philosophy, in addition to being an intellectual or rational, linguistic activity or practice, is in principle also a social and political one, as both Derrida's and Habermas's contributions to the dialogue with Borradori on terrorism amply demonstrate. As for myself, I believe that Derrida succeeds even better than Habermas in this, simply because (as I hope to have demonstrated) his thinking moves on so many different levels compared to Habermas's. As such, it has the potential to awaken, not merely contemporary 'philosophers' from their dogmatic slumber, but ordinary citizens too, through the mediation of philosophers who are willing to practice their trade more widely – taking novel risks in the process, to be sure – for the sake of disabusing such citizens of the anaesthetizing prejudices inculcated in them by hegemonic powers through mainstream media.

It is time for the heirs of Socrates to follow the example of philosophers like Derrida and Habermas and confront the pressing philosophical problems raised by asymmetrical power relations in the contemporary world, and, importantly, to do so in those spaces which correspond, today, to ancient Athens's streets. These include e-mail and the internet, media such as television, radio and newspapers, universities' lecture halls, political meetings as well as any social, cultural or political spaces (such as arts festivals) that lend themselves to philosophical debates and reasoned calls to subvert hegemony and engage the (cultural, political, racial, gendered) *other* with a view to instantiating – or, at least, preparing the way for – democracy and justice which are, as Derrida says, always 'to come' (Borradori 2003: 168–172; Derrida in Caputo 1997: 16–19; 22–24). Philosophers must, lest they become even more socially and politically irrelevant than they already are, find inventive ways to become *activists* in a distinctively philosophical manner.

References

Borradori, G. 2003. 'Preface: Philosophy in a time of terror'. In: Borradori, G. (ed.). *Philosophy in a time of terror: Dialogues with Jürgen Habermas and Jacques Derrida*. Chicago: The University of Chicago Press, pp. ix–xiv.

Borradori, G. 2003a. 'Introduction: Terrorism and the legacy of the Enlightenment – Habermas and Derrida'. In: Borradori, G. (ed.), *Philosophy in a time of terror: Dialogues with Jürgen Habermas and Jacques Derrida*. Chicago: The University of Chicago Press, pp. 1–22.

Borradori, G. 2003b. 'Deconstructing terrorism: Derrida'. In: Borradori, G. (ed.), *Philosophy in a time of terror*. Chicago: The University of Chicago Press, pp. 137–172.

Borradori, G. 2003c. 'Reconstructing terrorism: Habermas'. In: Borradori, G. (Ed.) *Philosophy in a time of terror: Dialogues with Jürgen Habermas and Jacques Derrida*. Chicago: The University of Chicago Press, pp. 45–81.

Brand, A. 1990. *The force of reason. An introduction to Habermas' Theory of communicative action*. London: Allen & Unwin.

Baudrillard, J. 1996. 'The map precedes the territory'. In: Anderson, W.T. (ed.), *The Fontana postmodernism reader*. London: Fontana Press, pp. 75–77.

Caputo, J.D. (ed.). 1997. *Deconstruction in a nutshell. A conversation with Jacques Derrida*. New York: Fordham University Press.

Copjec, J. 2002. *Imagine there's no woman. Ethics and sublimation*. Cambridge, Mass.: The MIT Press.

Derrida, J. 2004. 'Terror, religion, and the new politics'. In: Kearney, R. *Debates in Continental Philosophy: Conversations with contemporary thinkers*. New York: Fordham University Press, pp. 3–14.

Derrida, J. 2003. 'Autoimmunity: Real and symbolic suicides – A dialogue with Jacques Derrida'. In: Borradori, G. (ed.), *Philosophy in a time of terror: Dialogues with Jürgen Habermas and Jacques Derrida*. Chicago: The University of Chicago Press, pp. 85–136.

Derrida, J. 2002. 'Artifactualities'. In: Derrida, J. & Stiegler, B., *Echographies of television. Filmed interviews*. Trans. Bajorek, J. Cambridge: Polity, pp. 3–27.

Derrida, J. 2002a. 'Artifactuality, homohegemony'. In: Derrida, J. & Stiegler, B., *Echographies of television. Filmed interviews*. Trans. Bajorek, J. Cambridge: Polity, pp. 41–55.

Derrida, J. 1994. *Specters of Marx. The state of the debt, the work of mourning, and the new international.* Trans. Kamuf, P. New York: Routledge.

Foucault, M. 1972. 'The discourse on language'. In: *The archaeology of knowledge & The discourse on language*. Trans. Smith, A.M.S. New York: Pantheon Books, pp. 215–237.

Habermas, J. 2003. 'Fundamentalism and terror: A dialogue with Jürgen Habermas'. In: Borradori, G. (ed.), *Philosophy in a time of terror: Dialogues with Jürgen Habermas and Jacques Derrida*. Chicago: The University of Chicago Press, pp. 25–43.

Habermas, J. 1987. *The philosophical discourse of modernity: Twelve lectures.* Trans. Lawrence, F. Cambridge, Polity Press.

Hardt, M. & Negri, A. 2001. *Empire*. Cambridge, Mass: Harvard University Press.

Hurst, A. 2004. 'Derrida's quasi-transcendental thinking'. *South African Journal of Philosophy* 23 (3), pp. 244–266.

Kovel, J. 2002. *The enemy of nature. The end of capitalism or the end of the world?* London & New York: Zed Books.

Norris, C. 1996. *Reclaiming truth: Contributions to a critique of cultural relativism*. Durham: Duke University Press.

Olivier, B. 2006. 'Popular art, the image, the subject and subverting hegemony'. *Communicatio (South African Journal for Communication Theory and Research)*, Vol. 32 (1), pp. 16–37.

Olivier, B. 2003. 'After the World Trade Center: Architecture at the crossroads'. *South African Journal of Art History 18*, pp. 94–103.

Olivier, B. 2003a. 'Discourse, agency and the question of evil'. *South African Journal of Philosophy*, Vol. 22 (4), pp. 329–348. Reprinted here, as Chapter 1 of this volume.

Olivier, B. 2002. '11 September 2001: A change in the status of the image'. *South African Journal of Art History* 17, December, pp. 140–143.

Olivier, B. 2002a. 'Time, technology, cinematic art and critique in *The Terminator* and *Terminator II – Judgement Day*: A philosophical interpretation'. In: *Projections: Philosophical themes on film*. Second, enlarged edition. Port Elizabeth: University of Port Elizabeth, pp. 95–110.

Olivier, B. 1998. 'Derrida: Philosophy or literature?' In: *Critique, architecture, culture, art*. Port Elizabeth: University of Port Elizabeth Publications, pp. 167–180.

Olivier, B. 1998a. 'The sublime, unpresentability and postmodern cultural complexity'. In: *Critique, architecture, culture, art*. Port Elizabeth: University of Port Elizabeth Publications, pp. 197–214.

Sorkin, M. & Zukin, S. (eds). 2002. *After the World Trade Center. Rethinking New York City*. New York: Routledge.

Steger, M.B. 2003. *Globalization: A very short introduction*. Oxford: Oxford University Press.

CHAPTER 6

Nature as 'abject', critical psychology, and 'revolt': The pertinence of Kristeva

> There looms, within abjection, one of those violent, dark revolts of being, directed against a threat that seems to emanate from an exorbitant outside or inside, ejected beyond the scope of the possible, the tolerable, the thinkable. It lies there, quite close, but it cannot be assimilated.
>
> — JULIA KRISTEVA

Julia Kristeva's thought is a rich repository of concepts with a powerful purchase on some of the most intractable problems faced by humans in the early twenty-first century. As a 'psychoanalytical philosopher' she brings together her extensive knowledge of the philosophical tradition and her psychoanalytical insights gained through a development of Freud's and Lacan's groundbreaking work on the formerly unacknowledged or hidden aspects of human subjectivity (McAfee 2004: 29–43). This means that, like these two thinkers, she rejects the misguided notion of the putatively autonomous, self-transparent 'liberal' subject, while simultaneously pursuing the project of coming to terms with the 'split' subject of psychoanalysis in all its complexities and ostensible contradictions.

Among the many fecund concepts that she has developed in the course of expanding and refining the Freudian and Lacanian intellectual legacy, those of 'abjection' and 'revolt' are particularly valuable, heuristically speaking, concerning a variety of societal problems generated in the course of the history of modernity. Here I would like to focus on one which affects all living beings on the planet, namely the relation between humanity and nature. As I have argued elsewhere,[1] there is increasing evidence that human society – particularly through the economic system known as capitalism – has reached a point in its history where it is exerting virtually unbearable pressure on natural ecosystems, with the result that natural degradation is abundantly and shockingly evident across the globe (as many writers, photographers and scientists have shown).[2] In light of this, any responsible human being who has taken note of the current state of affairs, cannot and should not avoid making use of every possible medium to create and expand an informed awareness of the situation, as well as a sense of urgency and the need to act, among as many people as possible. In my experience mere 'factual knowledge' is not sufficient to have the desired effect of galvanizing people into action – in the present 'information age' people with access to media (that is, the vast majority of people on the planet) are 'better informed' than in any previous era, but arguably just as apathetic as 'informed', judging by the deteriorating condition of natural resources.[3] Rather, therefore, by placing 'information' about the precarious state of the earth in the context of a philosophical-theoretical, but also, crucially, a critical-psychological interpretation, people are afforded the intellectual, psychological and ethical[4] means to

1 On a previous occasion I approached this question from the perspective of the effect of capitalism on natural (and social) ecosystems. See Olivier 2005.

2 See the special edition of *National Geographic* (2004; September), entitled: 'Global warning – Bulletins from a warmer world'. The various writers/photographers reporting on the current state of the globe adduce ample evidence that there is reason to be *very* concerned about global warming. They refer to, *inter alia*, the melting of ice in the polar regions and of Kilimanjaro's snows, as well as to the drastic effects that the increasingly warmer global climate is having on various species of animals.

3 No matter where one starts looking for evidence of such deterioration – in the vicinity where one lives, or in regions far from there – it is not difficult to find it. See, for example, Jackson, Baird & Els (2005), for a sustained scientific investigation of the (deleterious) effect of 'heavy metals' like zinc and lead on fresh-water organisms in the Zwartkops river (Eastern Cape, South Africa).

4 I am using 'ethical' here in a sense that is related to the word 'ethos', namely a 'sense of place', or of philosophical orientation in the world. It also bears the sense of something more 'fundamental' (but not *fixed*) than any specific, historically

appreciate what all this information means for them and for other creatures on the planet. Such critical awareness is decisive as far as individuals' actions are concerned – that is, whether such individuals, impervious to the psychological and ethical imperatives consequent upon newly awakened critical consciousness, will merely follow the contours of mainstream conventions (dictated largely by current capitalist economic practices), or instead evince the social-transformational marks of a kind of critical ecological practice (where 'ecological' bears on the interdependence of social and natural environments). Derek Hook (2004: 673), referring to several researchers' work, has highlighted the reinforcing function of institutional psychological practices as far as apartheid was concerned. Similarly, the institutional role of mainstream psychology, as an agent of the capitalist social *status quo*, could (and probably does) easily contribute to blindness on the part of patients or clients regarding the damaged condition of the natural environment, regardless of the potential impact of this (still deteriorating) environment on their own psychic health.

Hence, what I want to do here, is to activate the clarifying hermeneutical power of Kristeva's notions of the 'abject' and 'revolt' in relation to the humanity/nature relation, with a view to highlighting and emphasizing the conditionality of human actions and practices regarding the viability, integrity and 'sustainability'[5] of nature – and concomitantly, of society – as an encompassing ecosystem. Any critical psychology (or philosophy, for that matter) that does not approach the individual as an integral 'part' – that is, 'agent' – of an encompassing social and natural

---

actualised conventional system of morals. See in this regard Olivier 2005a, where this meaning of 'ethical' is elaborated in the context of Lacanian psychoanalysis.

5 I put 'sustainability' in scare quotes because it has attained buzzword-status today, with the result that its true meaning has become obscured behind the façade of political correctness. What I mean here is actually more a matter of 'self-sustainability', that is, the ability of nature as a whole (which arguably includes human beings) to maintain its (indispensable) resilience and self-reproducibility in the face of the tremendous pressure imposed on it by human development, through pollution or destruction of natural resources in various ways, including the global warming-effect of the emission of greenhouse gases into the atmosphere.

ecosystem, is ultimately powerless in its efforts of working towards a 'healthy' (or critically self-reflective) society.

It is probably superfluous to sketch in detail what is meant by the 'precarious' state of nature – it is safe to say that (as suggested above) the media have been, for a considerable time now, a constant source of information on the growing threat of global warming in various respects and contexts, for example concerning the unwillingness on the part of the United States (specifically the Bush administration) to sign the Kyoto Protocol regarding the control of greenhouse gas emissions which damage the ozone layer and thus contribute to global warming.[6] In other words, most people who are exposed to the media – and that would include most people in the 'developed' Northern hemisphere and a sizable number of people even in the 'developing' South – are likely to be aware, however dimly, of 'global warming' and the dire consequences that have predictively been linked with it, such as the desertification of many parts of the world, the possible melting of the icecaps and, in the event of this occurring, the probable flooding of the world's low-lying land-areas, not to mention the growing pace of the extinction of certain species of animals that have evolved under 'present' (or perhaps 'former') climatic conditions. All of this is related, as I have argued before (Olivier 2005), to a regrettable but unfortunately potentially decisive, destructive attitude towards nature on the part of humanity, one that can be summarized here by simply saying that, by and large, humanity has maintained an extremely negative, suspicious and repressive attitude towards the natural world – including the human body – for centuries, and practices such as so-called 'development', industrialization or 'modernization' (and today 'postmodernization') are the expression or embodiment of this destructive attitude towards the very natural realm that comprises the sphere of humanity's provenance as a distinctive species.

It is instructive in this regard to take note of the work of Berry (1996), who reminds one that religion is far from innocent as far as the destruction of nature is concerned. He shows that the historical break with an older,

6 See in this regard Sagan (1997: 71–138).

more nature-friendly tradition in Christianity (St Thomas, St Francis) occurred in the fourteenth century around the time of the Great Plague in Europe, when the world – and with it, nature – was experienced as evil, and escape from it through intense spirituality was advocated in various quarters. 'This deep aversion to the natural world', Berry remarks (1996: 3), 'has profoundly conditioned the entire western tradition ever since'. Needless to stress, this 'tradition' is not restricted to theology or philosophy, but includes western culture in its entirety.

For several centuries this 'aversion' (a word to note in the present context) to nature – which was admittedly challenged in some quarters, for example by the romantic movement of the nineteenth century – did not manifest itself on a large scale in the shape of visible, tangible damage to nature across the globe. To be sure, the effects of humanity's industrial-technological revolution already showed itself around the middle of the nineteenth century in densely populated urban areas like London, where the air as well as the water of the Thames was heavily polluted. But all of this has come to a head. In a powerfully argued text Joel Kovel (2002: 3–27) has assembled evidence that, in the last three decades of the twentieth century, the process that commenced centuries earlier has started yielding conspicuous symptoms of the earth straining under the immense pressure of humanity's inconsiderate industrial activities. It is impossible to list all of these manifestations of a veritable geo-physical and geo-biological pathology here. To mention but one far-reaching fact: the waters of the world's seas have warmed on average about 1.8 degrees Fahrenheit during the last century (arguably because of human industrial activity, resulting in 'global warming'), which has led to a major decrease in organic productivity, and probably to a change in thermo-weather patterns, to the death of a significant percentage of corals, and a decline of fish populations (further decimated by human overfishing), not to mention the contamination of coastal waters to such a degree that swimmers at popular beaches frequently fall ill from ingesting harmful bacteria and other contaminants (Kovel 2002: 17; see also the recent report on polluted water in Miami: Loney 2006). Having listed overwhelming evidence of this kind, Kovel observes (2002: 17): 'From these countless *environmental* events we derive a crisis of global *ecological* proportions'. Or, more elaborately (2002: 5):

> As the world, or to be more exact, the Western, industrial world, has leapt into a prosperity unimaginable to prior generations, it has prepared for itself a calamity far more unimaginable still. The present world system in effect has had three decades to limit its growth, and it has failed so abjectly that even the idea of limiting growth has been banished from official discourse. Further, it has been proved decisively that the internal logic of the present system translates 'growth' into increasing wealth for the few and increasing misery for the many. We must begin our inquiry, therefore, with the chilling fact that 'growth' so conceived means the destruction of the natural foundation of civilization.

The situation sketched above[7] can be approached very differently, however, from the perspective of the concepts of 'abjection' and 'revolt' as developed by Kristeva. The first of these concepts, 'abjection', may be grasped as something Kristeva hypothesized in the face of the inherited Lacanian conceptual apparatus being unsatisfactory – or perhaps leaving some gaps open – concerning the coming into being of the human subject. According to Lacan the infant subject is constituted developmentally via the structuring stages of the 'family complexes' or three 'imagoes', namely the 'maternal', the 'fraternal' and the 'paternal' imago, respectively, as well as the so-called 'mirror stage' (which gives the child access to the 'imaginary' register) and the child's entry into language or the 'symbolic order'. The 'maternal' imago functions, as the mirror image does at a later stage, to provide the infant with an exemplar of fullness and wholeness correlative to the child's own chronic deficiency. In fact, both of these, in particular the infant's mirror image, offer a locus of

7 What I have said briefly in the previous paragraphs has been thoroughly argued, with reference to a variety of corroborating sources – including the work of Carl Sagan and Joel Kovel – in the publication referred to earlier, with a view to uncovering the invidious role played by capitalism in the deteriorization of the natural world (Olivier 2005). Kovel (2002, especially pp. 3–5, 13–17), in particular, adduces what I believe to be incontrovertible evidence that humanity as a whole is facing an unprecedented crisis of colossal proportions, despite which most people across the globe are in a state of denial.

('real' and) imaginary identification, with the child misrecognizing the unitary image for itself. The 'fraternal' imago provides the structural means for the child to experience primordial rivalry and envy, something that also has its counterpart in the mirror image with which the child identifies and, simultaneously, 'competes' in so far as the image seems to possess everything the child feels it lacks: coordination, wholeness, unity, definition, and so on. Lacan's 'paternal imago' is (part of) his version of Freud's Oedipus complex – the child represses and sublimates its own sexuality in the face of the father's authority, on the unconscious and subversive understanding that the same paternal authority represents the paradigm of sexual maturity, *and* provides the opportunity for inventiveness on the developing child's part. The paternal imago is further inextricably linked to the child occupying his or her place in kinship and other social relations, with the concomitant implication that it is here, in terms of the structuring function of the paternal imago, that he or she acquires language. Without these quasi-structural stages, the subject would not be the human subject it is – and I call them 'quasi'-structural because, while every human being is historically (and universally) 'subject to' their functioning, it does not prevent him or her from being uniquely singular, in so far as the specific sense of self of every (so-called normal) human being is distinct from every other, not to mention what Lacan calls the subject's (unique) 'desire'.[8]

Why is Kristeva dissatisfied with these patently fecund theoretical elements of Lacan's conception of the subject? Because there are certain aspects of human experience that they do not account for. Lacan may have explained the genesis of the subject in affirmative terms (via identification with one's 'own' mirror image, for instance), but for Kristeva this is only one side of the coin, because it shows 'towards what' the subject develops. But what about that, which the subject wants to free her- or himself from? To account for this, she articulates the notion of the 'abject', which therefore compensates for what may be perceived as a gap in Lacan's theory of

8 Elsewhere I have elaborated on these and other facets of Lacan's poststructuralist, psychoanalytical theory of the subject. See Olivier 2004; 2005b and 2005c.

the subject. It theorizes the 'negative' or 'antecedent' side of the subject becoming a distinct and distinctive individual, someone with a sense of 'self'. The 'positive' side, or the 'towards what', is accounted for by the quasi-structuring function of the imagoes, the mirror stage and the entry into the symbolic,[9] discussed above, in so far as the subject is afforded a locus of and for 'identification' (precarious as that may be), but what about the 'from where'? How does the infant subject put the sphere of its (quasi-)genesis 'behind' it (although this 'behind' is never absolute)? Kristeva's notion of the 'abject' or 'abjection' as a process, addresses these questions, and also provides the means, I believe, to grasp the relation between humans and the natural world in the contemporary era.

It is well-known that Freud as well as Lacan noted the fact that the infant does not initially distinguish between itself and its immediate surroundings (McAfee 2004: 18–22) – which involves what Kristeva (1997: 35–37) calls the semiotic *chora* (that is, the generative quasi-spatial matrix) which, as a 'totality' comprising the infant's drives (as energy-impulses and their psychic correlates) is connected with the mother's body. While for Lacan, beyond the stage where the infant subject imbricates other objects and individuals, the imagoes and, concomitantly, the mirror stage inaugurate its distinctive, albeit potentially ever-revisable 'identity', Kristeva posits the process of 'abjection' to account for the infant's indispensable separation from its mother's body, or its distancing of itself from its parents' desire. 'Abjection' here means more or less the same as 'rejection', as a prerequisite for the infant subject's assumption of a position in the imaginary register via the mirror phase, and subsequently in the symbolic via language. The mother's body therefore functions paradigmatically as the prototypical 'abject', while reciprocally the infant may be termed 'abject' in relation to the mother (Kristeva 1997: 153–154). 'Abject' here implies a strong aversion to, a separation, distancing, or rejecting of something as 'other', a banishment of it to the periphery of consciousness in an attempt to keep it at arm's length, and, importantly, to attain a sense of self-with-

9 Later in this article I shall elaborate on what Kristeva calls 'the semiotic' as a necessary precursor to the 'symbolic' in the genesis of the human subject.

borders or boundaries. There are many instances of this. Apart from the mother or mother's body, Kristeva (1997: 230–232) refers to instances of food (for example the 'skin' on milk, which some people find nauseating) and to cadavers (corpses) to get her point across (Kristeva 1997: 231):

> The corpse (or cadaver: *cadere*, to fall), that which has irremediably come a cropper, is cesspool, and death; ... refuse and corpses *show me* what I permanently thrust aside in order to live ... If dung signifies the other side of the border, the place where I am not and which permits me to be, the corpse, the most sickening of wastes, is a border that has encroached upon everything.

'Abjection' as a process is therefore not synonymous with 'repression', which denotes relegating something experienced as traumatic to the unconscious; by contrast, what is abject is not wholly unconscious – it is always ambiguously situated in a quasi-conscious, quasi-unconscious limit-realm, from where it 'haunts' the subject as an other which nevertheless co-constitutes its sense of selfhood. Neither should the abject be conflated with 'object' – 'The abject has only one quality of the object', says Kristeva, '... that of being opposed to *I*'. She continues (1997: 230):

> If the object, however, through its opposition, settles me within the fragile texture of a desire for meaning, which, as a matter of fact, makes me ceaselessly and infinitely homologous to it, what is *abject*, on the contrary, the jettisoned object, is radically excluded and draws me toward the place where meaning collapses. A certain 'ego' that merged with its master, a superego, has flatly driven it away. It lies outside, beyond the set, and does not seem to agree to the latter's rules of the game. And yet, from its place of banishment, the abject does not cease challenging its master ... To each ego its object, to each superego its abject.

As the thinkers of the seventeenth century, who were obliged to account for the inauguration of modern science, demonstrated, subject and object are correlative: every subject implies an object and *vice versa*. As the child withdraws from the self-occluding embrace of the mother to win its 'independence' as individual subject, however, 'jettisoning' the mother's body as (retrospectively constituted) 'object', the latter is relegated to the (non-)status of the 'abject', from there 'metonymically' to spawn the endless series of 'abjects' that will threaten, nauseate, unsettle and menace the subject for the rest of its life.

It is my argument here that, reading Kristeva carefully within the present global context of the deterioration of natural ecosystems, it is almost irresistible to perceive in nature an instance (perhaps *the* instance) of the *abject* in relation to postmodern, technology-, media- and information-oriented subjects. And it is no accident that nature is traditionally depicted in feminine terms as 'Mother Nature' or the 'Great Mother' – in fact, for centuries before the advent of patriarchal religions, the earth was associated with a feminine deity or deities (Shlain 1998: 45–63). Perhaps, therefore, nature has in a certain sense instantiated the 'abject' in relation to the 'western' subject for some time, but if this is the case, I would argue that this has been reinforced in the process of nature being increasingly threatened by *homo technologicus*, especially in the course of the last 35 years since approximately 1970 (Kovel 2002: 3–5). This impression is reinforced by Kristeva's observation, that 'to each superego its abject', if one remembers that the normative or conventional dimension of society informs the function of the superego (broadly the axiological 'content' of conscience or the repository of societal authority – in patriarchal societies, paternal authority, secured by the transcendental signifier, the 'Name-of-the-Father'; see Olivier 2005a). In contemporary, globalized society technology arguably occupies a decisive position *vis-à-vis* authority (see Heidegger's critique of technology, below), hence the claim that its 'abject' counterpart is 'nature', cannot fail to be persuasive. And the more technophiliac society becomes (see Turkle 1997: 9, 18–19), the greater the aversion to nature.

There are various aspects to this aversion, of course. Consider the following excerpt from Hardt and Negri's *Empire* (2001: 135–136), where they discuss Céline's characterization of Africa as a place of ubiquitous disease:

> It is interesting in Céline's *Journey* that the disease of colonial territories is a sign not really of death, but of an overabundance of life ... The disease of the jungle is that life springs up everywhere, everything grows, without bounds. What a horror for a hygienist! The disease that the colony lets loose is the lack of boundaries on life, an unlimited contagion. If one looks back, Europe appears reassuringly sterile ...

> The horror released by European conquest and colonialism is a horror of unlimited contact, flow, and exchange – or really the horror of contagion, miscegenation, and unbounded life. Hygiene requires protective barriers.

The 'contagion' of jungled Africa encountered in the colonial imaginary and described here by Hardt and Negri is easily recognizable as a case of the 'abject' – that which Europe compulsively conquered and colonized in order to extract its variegated riches, but simultaneously kept at a distance as 'uncivilized', contagious and contaminating. It is therefore not surprising that Hardt and Negri (2001: 136) proceed to delineate the '*dark side of the consciousness of globalization*' similarly as '*the fear of contagion*', with the novel twist that this is a consequence of the fact that many erstwhile colonial boundaries (with the hygienic protection they afforded) have been destroyed, allowing 'multiple exchanges' and flows to occur – not merely economic exchanges, but also, significantly, of *the* 'global' (and globally feared) disease, namely AIDS. It is no accident, they point out (2001: 136), that AIDS-discourses remind one of colonialist ones, considering the frequency with which AIDS-proliferation is linked to lack of hygiene, promiscuity, and so on. But more importantly for my present purpose, Hardt and Negri's elaboration on the horrors of 'contagion', so conspicuously consonant with Kristeva's notion of the 'abject', establishes a connection with nature as 'abject' (manifested in the western aversion to the 'jungle', teeming with unrestrained life) which is crucial for my argument.

Perhaps a key concept for understanding the relation between the (especially, but not exclusively) 'western', or possibly 'global,' subject and nature as 'abject', is 'control'. Since its earliest beginnings, western science has been predicated on the possibility of controlling nature, as evinced in Descartes's seventeenth-century belief (1972: 119), that the wonderful new science (physics) would render humanity 'masters and possessors of nature'. Technology, initially the apprentice of science, was to carry out this task consequent upon science's reduction of nature to measurable, quantitative relations (Heidegger 1977: 118–123). Heidegger's (1977a) critique of technology has to be understood against this backdrop, and his characterization of the 'essence of technology' as 'enframing' (*Gestell*), according to the logic of which nature is 'set upon' or assaulted, reducing it to a 'standing reserve', can readily be interpreted in terms of Kristeva's notion of the 'abject'. For Heidegger (1977a: 4–5, 12–21, 27–29), technology cannot be seen merely as a 'tool' (a common misconception), but essentially as 'enframing' (or 'framework') which fundamentally directs the way in which people think and act in the present era, in the same manner that the middle ages were properly called 'theocentric' (that is, a time when questions and actions were decisively directed by the fundamental belief that God is the centre of all things). Yet, despite humanity's most strenuous attempts to subordinate nature to its technoscientific control – which has certainly met with 'success' in certain areas of experience such as the relatively effective combating of diseases like smallpox – it is arguably the case that, in many respects, natural phenomena such as hurricanes (think of the recent devastation caused by Hurricane Katrina in New Orleans; Desmond 2005: 491–492) and the appearance of new strains of viruses (the bird flu virus threatening the world at present, HIV, the Marburg, Hanta and Ebola viruses, the mutation of the malaria virus into resistant strains, and so on; Kovel 2002: 15–18) cast so-called human 'control' of nature in the light of a mere, paltry attempt, ultimately doomed to failure.

This obsession with control of nature is symptomatic, I would argue, of its status as 'abject', precisely, considering the fact that these perpetual efforts on the part of technophiliac humanity constitute nature as that which threatens the 'hygienic' space of measurement, calculation and 'control'. 'Nature' – that which threatens to engulf humanity, infect it, disrupt society's economic practices – like the cadaver, causes humans to 'fall'. People are horrified by its inaccessible, uncontrollable, amorphous, teeming proliferation of menacing 'things' – ranging from hurricanes, viruses, bacteria, insects, reptiles and sharks, to other predatory or 'lethal' embodiments of 'nature's intractable, intransigent and unmitigated hostility to human civilization. Everywhere (especially in media reports or movies about hurricanes, tsunamis or floods, as well as in films about killer sharks, spiders, and so on), it seems, the social imaginary confronts one with nature's ceaseless tendency to undermine coherent 'meaning', its refusal of the 'rules of the game' of civilization. Hence, people generally react to this image of nature (as the 'abject') in the form of 'abjection' – Hook (2004: 685) formulates this distinction well:

> ... whereas *abjection* is understood as a powerful, irrational and disturbing reaction, the *abject* is taken to be the source of such affects – that anomalous, uncontained and indefinable 'thing' which elicits fear, dread, anxiety ... the abject is above all that which threatens, that which constantly plagues and disturbs identity, system and structure.

One could object, of course, that there are many instances, at the level of the social imaginary, of nature in the guise of a benevolent, accommodating set of surroundings – think of images where rolling lawns, tranquil streams, trees and flowers frame two people embracing, for instance, as is the case on so many kitschy greeting cards. To be sure, but these representations of a 'natural' backdrop to human practices is one of nature tamed and domesticated, which is nature kept at bay, as it were. Needless to say, this contrasts starkly with that 'other' way of representing nature – one which has its representational roots in the romantic imagination of the late eighteenth and nineteenth centuries (Baumer 1977: 268–282) – as wild, untamed and inimical to human designs. It is the latter, I believe, which constitutes the 'abject', correlative to the technological drive to subjugate and control nature to an optimal degree. Besides, as Kristeva (quoted in Hook 2004: 687) reminds one: 'Abjection is coextensive with the social and symbolic order, on the individual as well as on the collective level ... abjection assumes specific shapes and different codings according to the various "symbolic systems"'. In other words, in a global culture which valorizes technology – a valuation iconically and symbolically projected ubiquitously in the contemporary media, and one that does not leave contemporary 'identities' untouched – what is felt to be a threat on the part of nature is bound to meet with abjection as '... a forceful physical, psychical and symbolic response, an expulsive response on all of these levels, a violent attempt at restitution of an apparent affront to wholeness be it of the body, of identity, or of socio-symbolic structure' (Hook 2004: 687).

In light of what has been adduced and argued concerning nature's current state of ruin or degradation, and its constitution in the social imaginary as (perhaps an exemplary instantiation of) 'the abject', the question arises as to a course of action: if one simply allows the status quo to prevail, the slide towards natural catastrophe will continue unabated; if one acts (with no guarantee of success), at least one could possibly bring about changed attitudes at individual and collective levels, possibly accompanied by interventionist action of a salutary kind (for instance actions aimed at limiting unrestrained economic growth, and preventing the construction of heavily polluting industries). This change of attitude, I want to argue further, could be promoted by critical psychological practices which take the relation between humanity and nature to be within its critical (theoretical and practical) scope. Importantly, however, it would require nothing less than what Kristeva calls 'revolt' or 'revolution', given the deeply entrenched, self-centred, conventional socio-economic practice of consumerism. To appreciate what is at stake, one has to take note of the rootedness of 'revolt' in the mode of signification dubbed the 'semiotic' by Kristeva.

The notion of the 'semiotic' serves a similar purpose as that of the 'abject' in Kristeva's work, namely, to 'fill in', as it were, a gap in Lacan's theory of the subject. Just as the 'abject' captures the negative side of the subject becoming an individual with a sense of 'identity', the semiotic captures the significance of all those signifying sounds, gestures and movements not easily accommodated by the symbolic. In her early work on poetic language (1984, especially 25–30), Kristeva already amplified the Lacanian theoretical arsenal by adding another signifying mode to Lacan's imaginary and symbolic, namely the 'semiotic', to account for certain kinds of signification not accommodated by Lacan's categories. Consider the following: the 'chain of signifiers', or language, which constitutes Lacan's symbolic realm, also has a conceptual side – the signifieds which are ineluctably 'attached' to signifiers. The concept of a tiger as a large, mammalian, carnivorous quadruped is inseparable from the written or spoken signifier 'tiger' (in any language); with the poststructuralist corollary, that the distinction 'signifier' and 'signified' is not as watertight as the structuralist Saussure believed: every signified is, again, a signifier. Given this conceptual aspect of language, Kristeva's notion of the 'semiotic' accommodates all those elements (McAfee 2004: 15–18) – sounds such as music, noise, audial rhythm, the timbre or sonic 'texture' of a voice; movement such as different kinds of dance and visual rhythm, and even tactile experiences such as smoothness, roughness, and so on – none of which have clear conceptual parameters, but which nevertheless clearly signify certain meanings, however vague, diffuse or intertwined these may be. Moreover, she links the 'semiotic' to Freud's theory of the drives and the so-called 'primary process' of the unconscious (Kristeva 1984: 25), in so far as the drives represent the social articulation of charges of energy (with their psychical correlates) on the infant subject's body, and therefore exhibit a 'structuring disposition' that, for Kristeva, 'points to' the semiotic as a 'distinctive' mode of signification.

The upshot of her innovative thought for the development of the infant subject is this: that, before entering the symbolic realm of (universalistic, conceptual) language, the child already participates in a signifying exchange with its mother (and other people) at the level of a variety of sounds, tactile sensations and movements (cooing, uttering what are initially merely repetitive sounds such as 'ma-ma' and 'da-da', singing of lullabies, smiling, stroking of hair, rocking the child to and fro, and so on). These experiences have 'semiotic' signification, and prepare the child for entry into the symbolic. Once such entry has occurred, however, the 'semiotic' continues to overlap and inform the 'symbolic' for the rest of the subject's life.[10] Importantly, given its rootedness in the energy of the drives (which exceed the symbolic), it therefore forms the basis of a subject's ability to challenge and transgress the established, conventional symbolic

10 It should be obvious why the distinction between the 'symbolic' and the 'semiotic' appears in a text titled *Revolution in poetic language* (1984) – poetry, or figural language generally, thrives on 'semiotic' signification as described by Kristeva. What would a poem such as Yeats's *The second coming*, or D.H. Lawrence's *Snake* be without the semiotic dimension of poetic language? The sensuous, 'semiotic' qualities of language in these, as well as other poems and novels (think of Ondaatje's exceptionally poetic novel, *The English patient*) are precisely what makes of them works of *literature*, as opposed to scientific or bureaucratic texts. It is striking that Kristeva establishes a connection, even in this early work, between a certain kind of signification (in literature) and 'political revolution' (1984: 17), thus paving the way for her later, related work on 'revolt'.

order in a 'revolutionary' manner, on a personal as well as a collective, political level (Kristeva 1984: 16–17). This is of particular relevance for the present theme, which presupposes this ability, on the part of individuals, to question conventional social practices and attitudes – specifically as far as the increasingly precarious state of nature is concerned – and if necessary, bring about a 'revolution' in thinking and acting. Small wonder that she thinks of humans as 'subjects in process' or 'on trial' (McAfee 2004: 29–30; the French word *procés* means 'process' as well as 'trial') – a static individual, with no evidence of challenging or overturning symbolic positions already attained in her or his life is as good as fossilized. At the same time it should be stressed that, in true poststructuralist fashion, she also denies the 'healthy' subject complete, unabated, 'semiotically' induced change – to be a 'self' at all, one requires a *relatively* stable iconic-symbolic 'identity', but also an indispensable, intermittently destabilizing semiotic 'subversion' of this 'identity' (McAfee 2004: 105–106), something (as will be argued) which is not without consequences for the broader social and political field of the subject's actions.

The concept of 'revolt' in Kristeva's (later) thinking is closely related to the revolutionary potential of the semiotic in her early work. She shows (2002: 100) that there is an etymological connection between 'revolt' and the Sanskrit root, meaning 'open, discover', as well as (2000: 1) the related Latin and Old French words for 'turn', 'return', 'vault' and 'roll'. 'I emphasize', she says about 'revolt' (2002: 85), 'its potential for making gaps, rupturing, renewing'. At the same time she argues passionately in favour of the *necessity* of revolt, appealing to the European 'tradition of revolt', without which culture would not have displayed great surges in innovative, rejuvenating activity, in this way suggesting a parallel between such 'cultural' revolt and the indispensable 'revolutions' in a 'healthy' individual's life (referred to earlier). One should not make the mistake of associating 'revolt' in this sense of creative transformation, born of a kind of 'permanent anxiety' (2002: 104), one-sidedly with *political* revolution in the usual sense, informed by the assumed meaning of historical 'revolutions', however. She hastens (2002: 102) to issue the cautionary reminder, that political revolutions like the French Revolution and the Russian Revolution had no sooner abolished old values in favour of new ones, than it forgot to *question* these new values, with the result that both degenerated into tyranny and dictatorship, in this way 'betraying revolt'. Revolt has to be a 'permanent' or recurrent feature of individual and social life (2002: 103), lest these similarly degenerate into the smug attitudes and 'standardized' practices born of a misguided assumption that 'the revolution' has happened once and for all. To prevent this from occurring – a danger prevalent in consumer society, with its misuse of the term 'revolution' to indicate what recommends the latest consumer product (2002: 104) – one has to remind oneself that there are also many paradigmatic cases of 'revolt' in the *salutary* sense in the history of western culture.

'Europeans are cultured', she claims (citing Descartes, Marx, Freud, Bauhaus, Stockhausen, Picasso and others; 2000: 6–7), 'in the sense that culture is their critical conscience ... The great moments of twentieth-century art and culture are moments of formal and metaphysical revolt'. Moreover, as psychoanalysis has taught us, nothing less than human fulfilment is at stake (2000: 7):

> Happiness exists only at the price of a revolt. None of us has pleasure without confronting an obstacle, prohibition, authority, or law that allows us to realize ourselves as autonomous and free ... on the social level, the normalizing order is far from perfect and fails to support the excluded: jobless youth, the poor in the projects, the homeless, the unemployed, and foreigners, among many others. When the excluded have no culture of revolt and must content themselves with ideologies, with shows and entertainments that far from satisfy the demand for pleasure, they become rioters.

The last sentence touches on something (already alluded to) that is extremely important for the present theme: the dominant culture, globally, is consumer culture, and it has proved to be unparalleled in the efficacy with which it anaesthetizes 'consumers' – the masses of spectators at soccer or rugby matches, millions of viewers in front of television screens, absorbed in the imaginary world of soapies – in this way effectively dulling the potential for revolt that still exists in the recesses of people's psyches.[11] From her allusion to 'ideologies ... shows and entertainments' in the above excerpt, it is clear that Kristeva is acutely aware of this, although she does not agree with those who mourn the psyche's *death*-by-media (2002: 82): 'The media doesn't kill the mind, as has been said, and we all like to have fun, but we also want to be able to say no'.

As Noëlle McAfee (2004: 107–108) indicates, Kristeva follows thinkers such as Guy Debord, author of *Society of the Spectacle* (and, one could argue, Heidegger in his seminal work, *The age of the world picture*; 1977), who argued that, in contemporary societies, 'life' is grasped as a series of 'spectacles' or shows (representations), which serve the dominant economic order (consumer capitalism) in so far as people's needs and 'desires' are manufactured for them by means of certain 'desirable' spectacles or representations. This occurs through all the major agencies of the dominant order, namely branding, advertising, 'information', 'entertainment' and propaganda (not necessarily of the overtly 'political' kind; capitalism is also an ideology, although it subtly hides this fact). McAfee (2004: 108) puts it succinctly: '... in the society of the spectacle, people are tools of the economy; their desires are not their own; desires are manufactured as surely as are the commodities meant to fulfil them'. Small wonder that, in *New maladies of the soul* (1995: 8–9), Kristeva (who is, apart from being a philosopher, also a practising psychoanalyst) elaborates on the 'loss of soul' on the part of contemporary (consumerist) people, who do not even know of this loss because they are 'swept away by insignificant and valueless objects ... [l]iving in a piecemeal and accelerated space and

11 See in this regard Olivier 1998, for an investigation (which confirms Kristeva's insights) into contemporary consumer culture's 'solutions' for problems foreseen by Freud regarding the 'discontent' on the part of humanity, caught between the need for pleasure or fulfilment, on the one hand, and the requirement of civilization, on the other, that these needs be repressed. As for what she says about people becoming 'rioters', instead of being still capable of satisfying or fulfilling 'revolt', perhaps contemporary society is witnessing a kind of turning point between mindless 'rioting' and regaining the capacity for 'revolt', judging by what Hardt and Negri (2005: 268–288) have argued about the contemporary symptoms of resistance, on the part of 'multitude', against the global forces of what they call 'Empire'. See in this regard also Olivier 2004a and 2007.

time' – clearly a reference to the manner in which capitalist consumerism speeds up everyday existence through the reduction of 'reality' to the perpetual, 'schizophrenic' present of endless, tantalizing money-invested images which pressure the consumer to 'Buy, Buy, Buy!!'.[12]

What is significant for the present argument, that critical psychology enlarge its 'critical and therapeutic scope' to include the largely forgotten, but indispensable relation between humans and nature,[13] is that, in the 'society of the spectacle' people are increasingly alienated from a fulfilling, meaningful psychic life. Moreover, without the re-inauguration or recollection of this relation with the natural world *as the domain of humanity's provenance, and its indispensable source of sustenance*, such a satisfying awareness of self within a potentially meaningful, encompassing natural environment is difficult, if not impossible, to achieve. The reasons for this have to do with the currently deteriorating condition of natural ecosystems – already referred to earlier, and a specific case of which will be discussed below – which does not and will not leave human societies unaffected. In fact, considering all the evidence of a deepening ecological crisis (see Kovel 2002: 3–27), which humanity ignores at its own peril, one is easily inclined to be pessimistic about the prospects of a cultural or social revolution or revolt which could possibly turn the process around. This is especially so if one remembers that the currently dominant political and economic system – state capitalism – which is demonstrably largely responsible for the ecological crisis (Kovel 2002: 28–86), is so powerful and entrenched that most people cannot even imagine an alternative. And yet, one should not despair about the ever-present possibility of such revolt (in Kristeva's sense as indicated earlier),

12 See in this regard Fredric Jameson's (1985) illuminating characterization of postmodern consumer society in terms of the spatiotemporal features of 'pastiche' and 'schizophrenia'.

13 I should point out that I am *not* under the misguided impression that 'nature' is ever accessible to humans in a direct, unmediated manner. It is always, *ineluctably*, a socially or culturally (or epistemically) mediated concept, as Kant, Nietzsche and many other subsequent thinkers have convincingly demonstrated (see Kovel 2002: 89).

evidenced in the following excerpt from Joel Kovel's relentless critique of capitalism as '*The enemy of nature*' (2002: 104):

> All of the powers of humanity, spiritual and practical, are available for addressing the social order and have the potential for transforming it, through a revolution if necessary. If nothing in nature stands still, how much more so is this the case for human beings and society! All things pass, and for us, the relevant question is whether the capitalist order will pass away before it causes humanity to pass away. But capital cannot pass away of itself; it has to be ushered out, through the transformation into an ecologically sane society.

The 'revolt' required is therefore in the first place a rediscovery and re-affirmation (in the *new* historical context of the twenty-first century) of the uncompromisable value of nature for humanity *as part and parcel of it* in an encompassing sense – one that goes *beyond* the relegation of nature to the realm of the 'abject'. This remark may strike one as incongruous, considering that 'nature' is always a social and linguistic 'construct' (Kovel 2002: 89), regardless of the intuitive awareness that 'nature' will continue existing beyond individual humans' limited lifespan. Perhaps the thought that humans can nevertheless *not* be separated from nature may seem less absurd to the millions of people who spend major parts of their lives in the virtual spaces of 'chatrooms' and Multi User Domains (enabled by the internet), if they took time to ponder the following insight concerning the question: 'What is life?', articulated by Kovel in exemplary manner (2002: 92–104):

> The boundary between the living and the non-living is not sharp, which is to be expected if life is a potential form of being hatched by nature. Nature is *formative*, that is, it has the dynamic potential to generate particular nodes of existence; and life represents a way-station of its formativeness (p. 92) ... Like all natural creatures, the human one has an imprint. The bat has sonar, the whale special capacities for diving (and its own kind of sonar), the bee its quantum dance, the venus flytrap its signature form of carnivorousness. Each creature in nature has its 'nature', its way of being, its point of insertion into the ecosystemic manifold, its peculiar mode of struggling. We regard 'human nature', or 'hummingbird nature', or 'bee nature', or 'maple tree nature' in this light – ... as the species-specific way of struggle in an ecosystemic world ... and also at a more concrete level, as the ensemble of powers, potentials and capacities that enable this way to be expressed ... To be is to struggle,

> and each point of difference in being is a different mode of struggling. In this way, living forms arise and take their place in ecosystemic manifolds, each, in their way, better, each *as* their way (p. 98).

Isn't this felicitous passage a veritable paean to the richness, variegatedness and difference, but simultaneously also the 'equal' intrinsic value of every living species, and every individual of every species – from bees, snails, snakes, tigers and antelope to dolphins, jellyfish and humans – in nature? To be able to see the interconnectedness of all the living creatures on this planet, as well as the inorganic substructure that comprises the basis for their emergence as organic beings since the simplest ones appeared about 3 billion years ago (Kovel 2002: 94), is a prerequisite for being receptive to the claim that nature is intrinsically valuable to all her creatures, including humans, and that this thought should form the inaugurating point for a 'revolt' against the relegation of nature to the realm of the 'abject'. With such a revolt, perhaps the transformation of the socio-economic system known as consumer capitalism may also begin, given its (well-documented) hostility to, and destructiveness towards, nature as well as human communities (Kovel 2002: 3–86; Steger 2003: 86–87; Olivier 2005).

But perhaps something more tangible should be adduced here. After all, what one *has* to remember, even if my attempt at highlighting the pertinence of Kristeva's psychoanalytical work for an urgently needed 'enlargement' of the scope of critical psychology (to include the relationship between humans and an encompassing 'nature') is affirmed, is the concrete, demonstrably precarious state of the natural world across the globe today. In this respect John Desmond's article on 'The dying Louisiana wetlands' (2005: 485–492) – and others like it – should function as a clarion call to action on the part of everyone who reads it. Desmond talks about these wetlands in reverential terms that some may regard as sentimentalist – talking about and even addressing them in the singular feminine pronoun ('she', 'her') – but anyone who is familiar with the age-old custom (mentioned earlier), rooted in mythology and ancient goddess-religions, of addressing the earth or *Gaia* as 'Mother',[14] would understand that this is one way of rekindling a much-needed respect and veneration for the earth as a living ecosystem, *of which the human species is an integral part*. I have used italics here to emphasize something that most people all over the world – but especially in developed countries – simply ignore, because taking note of it would entail a psychological reorientation which has serious consequences for their capitalist, technophiliac, wealth-oriented way of life, namely to abandon this way of life to some, if not a significant degree.

From Desmond's article it is clear that human interference, largely for economic gain, in the 'natural' processes which gave rise, over thousands of years, to the wetlands in question, is responsible for their current state of decline. This interference is multiple, and has consisted of the building of dams and levees in the Mississippi River to prevent flood damage to property (which, in turn, prevented life-promoting river-sediment from reaching the deltaic plain), the establishment of straight canals for the sake of mineral and oil exploration and extraction (with the result that there has been greater saltwater incursion into the marshes, compromising plant life, and accelerating subsidence), and human industry-induced global warming, with concomitant sea-level rise threatening the fragile – but life-giving – wetlands (Desmond 2005: 486–487). Ironically, the growing awareness of the wetlands' decline on the part of some people, has spurred them into preventative action, which is *again* predicated on the possibility of economic gain – the argument being that losing the wetlands would be economically disastrous (because of the increasing rise of the sea level; Desmond 2005: 487–488)! Desmond is adamant

14 See in this regard Leonard Shlain's remarkable book, *The alphabet versus the goddess* (1998: 45–63), for an extended discussion of the ancient veneration and worship of the earth as 'Mother' or of earth goddesses during a time when there was, by all accounts, a harmonious relationship between humans and nature – at least in the sense that, although humans depended, though hunting and gathering, on nature for their survival, they also venerated it precisely as indispensable source of life (albeit not without its own minatory aspect).

that this mainstream, economic approach to the wetlands – even if it may benefit the latter – is misguided (p. 488):

> This place takes special pleasure in revealing its soul to those who look and listen from a wider perspective which embraces a cultivation of humanity's restoration, not of the wilderness, but with the wilderness ... Eco-psychology is the search for and recognition of the world's soul. These wetlands, by and large, offer no hint of mankind. But through their slow death and retreat downward into the gulf they have awakened mankind, albeit through the pain of lost profits and foreboding expense.

I hope to have demonstrated, by drawing on various sources, that there is wide agreement about the deteriorating state of nature on planet earth, and that this is at least partly to be understood as manifestation of human abjection in the face of nature being experienced, by and large, as 'abject'. This state of affairs, moreover, calls for a 'revolt' or revolution – in the salutary sense that Kristeva has given to these notions – in human thinking and practice regarding 'standard' attitudes towards nature (as 'abject'). This is a much-needed revolt that critical psychology could hasten through its theory and practice by taking seriously the following remark by Joel Kovel (2002: 20), himself no stranger in psychoanalytical circles: 'Ecology takes on a human form, since humans are part of nature, and, like all other creatures, require a pattern of relationships to survive and flourish'. The relationships in question include, perhaps most fundamentally, the multifaceted one apparently ignored for so long at humans' own peril, namely that with humanity's natural environment. The well-being of the human subject is intimately tied up with the well-being of nature. If the latter suffers, so will humans – perhaps sooner than one thinks, judging by the impact of human activities on nature, and the reciprocal effects of the decline of ecosystems on humans' well-being, which have already become apparent.[15]

15 See Kovel (2002: 28–38), for an account of the Bhopal disaster of the mid-1980s, one of the most notorious instances in history of the impact of human industrial activity on nature and society – an event the after-effects of which, after more than 20 years, are *still* causing humans and the natural environment around Bhopal (in India) untold suffering.

References

Baumer, F. L. 1977. *Modern European thought. Continuity and change in ideas, 1600–1950*. New York: Macmillan.

Berry, T. 1996. 'The university: Its response to the ecological crisis'. Paper delivered before the Divinity School and the University Committee on Environment at Harvard University, April 11. http://ecoethics.net/ops/berrybio.htm.

Descartes, R. 1972. 'Discourse on method'. In: *The philosophical works of Descartes*, Vol. I. Trans. Haldane, E.S. & Ross, G.R.T. Cambridge: Cambridge University Press, pp. 79–130.

Desmond, J.M. 2005. 'The dying Louisiana wetlands'. *Janus Head* 8 (2), pp. 485–492.

Hardt, M. & Negri, A. 2001. *Empire*. Cambridge, Mass.: Harvard University Press.

Hardt, M., & Negri, A. 2005. *Multitude. War and democracy in the age of Empire*. New York: Penguin Books.

Heidegger, M. 1977. 'The age of the world picture'. In: *The question concerning technology and other essays*. Trans. Lovitt, W. New York: Harper Torchbooks, pp. 115–154.

Heidegger, M. 1977a. 'The question concerning technology'. In: *The question concerning technology and other essays*. Trans. Lovitt, W. New York: Harper Torchbooks, pp. 3–35.

Hook, D. 2004. 'Racism as abjection: A psychoanalytic conceptualisation for a post-apartheid South Africa'. *South African Journal of Psychology* 34 (4), pp. 672–703.

Jackson, R.N., Baird, D. & Els, S. 2005. 'The effect of the heavy metals lead (Pb2+) and zinc (Zn2+) on the brood and larval development of the burrowing crustacean *Callianassa kraussi*'. *Water SA* 31 (1), pp. 107–116.

Jameson, F. 1985. Postmodernism and consumer society. In: Foster, H. (ed.), *The anti-aesthetic. Essays on postmodern culture*. Port Townsend, Washington: Bay Press, pp. 111–125.

Kovel, J. 2002. *The enemy of nature. The end of capitalism or the end of the world?* London & New York: Zed Books.
Kristeva, J. 1984. *Revolution in poetic language.* Trans. Waller, M. New York: Columbia University Press.
Kristeva, J. 1995. *New maladies of the soul.* Trans. Guberman, R. New York: Columbia University Press.
Kristeva, J. 1997. *The portable Kristeva.* Ed. Oliver, K. New York: Columbia University Press.
Kristeva, J. 2000. *The sense and non-sense of revolt: The powers and limits of psychoanalysis, Vol. I.* Trans. Herman, J. New York: Columbia University Press.
Kristeva, J. 2002. *Revolt, she said. An interview by Philippe Petit.* Trans. O'Keeffe, B. Los Angeles: Semiotext(e).
Loney, J. 2006. 'Beachgoers at risk from polluted water'. *Yahoo!* NEWS. http://news.yahoo.com/s/nm/20060524/hl_nm/environment_beaches_dc (accessed May 25, 2006).
McAfee, N. 2004. *Julia Kristeva.* New York: Routledge.
National Geographic, 2004 (September): 'Global warning – Bulletins from a warmer world'.
Olivier, B. 1998. 'Freud and Lyotard on Civilization'. *South African Journal of Philosophy* 17 (2), pp. 126–141.
Olivier, B. 2004. 'Lacan's subject: the imaginary, language, the real and philosophy'. *South African Journal of Philosophy*, Vol. 23 (1), pp. 1–19.
Olivier, B. 2004a. 'The (im-)possibility of communication'. *Communicare*, Journal for Communication Sciences in Southern Africa, Vol. 23, (1), pp. 79–91.
Olivier, B. 2005. 'Nature, capitalism, and the future of humankind'. *South African Journal of Philosophy* 24 (2), pp. 121–135.
Olivier, B. 2005a. 'Lacan and the question of the psychotherapist's ethical orientation'. *SA Journal of Psychology* 35 (4), pp. 657–683. Reprinted here, as Chapter 3 of this volume.
Olivier, B. 2005b. 'Lacan and narrative identity: *The Piano Teacher*'. In: *Word, (wo)man, world: Essays on literature. Festschrift* for Ina Gräbe. Oliphant, A.W. & Roos, H. (eds). Pretoria: UNISA Press, pp. 94–112. Reprinted here, as Chapter 2 of this volume.

Olivier, B. 2005c. Philosophy and the pursuit of one's desire: Mathilde's project. *Janus Head*, Volume 8.2, Winter 2005/6, pp. 473–483. Also published online at http://www.janushead.org (http://www.janushead.org/8-2/Olivier.pdf).

Olivier, B. 2007. 'Communication' in the era of 'Empire' and 'multitude'. *Communicatio* (South African Journal for Communication Theory and Research), Vol. 33 (1), pp. 42–61.

Sagan, C. 1997. *Billions and billions. Thoughts on life and death at the brink of the millennium*. London: Headline.

Shlain. L. 1998. *The alphabet versus the goddess. The conflict between word and image*. New York: Penguin Arkana.

Steger, M.B. 2003. *Globalization. A very short introduction*. Oxford: Oxford University Press.

Turkle, S. 1997. *Life on the screen: Identity in the age of the internet*. London: Phoenix.

CHAPTER 7

Negotiating the 'paranoiac structure' of human knowledge: Fowles's *The magus* and Lacan

The desire for knowledge bears no relationship to knowledge.

— JACQUES LACAN: *The other side of psychoanalysis* (2007: 23)

The basic principle of life is hazard ... If one goes deep enough in atomic physics one ends with a situation of pure chance. Of course we all share the illusion that this can't be so.

— LILY DE SEITAS in John Fowles's *The magus* (1983: 627–628)

Apparently humanity has a deep-seated fear of being deceived – how else can one explain Descartes's (1972: 144–157) strenuous attempt to exorcise the *malin genie*, born of a powerful 'will to truth' or 'will to knowledge', that exerts certain 'constraints' on other types of discourse – as Foucault (1972: 219) thinks of it – or the ostensible smug satisfaction, if not joy, with which humanity regards its 'edifices of knowledge': the sciences, technological achievements, the so-called 'knowledge society'? But, considering the arguments as well as the evidence adduced by thinkers such as Schopenhauer (see for example 1969: 103–104) and Lacan, humans seem, simultaneously, to desire being deceived, to want to cling to illusions. This smugness or joy regarding the vaunted achievements of human civilization would be short-lived, in other words, if the human race should take seriously Jacques Lacan's (1977: 17; 1977a: 3) claim, that the structure of human knowledge is 'paranoiac', that is, that human knowledge is built on illusion. What does Lacan mean by this? And, if one could come to a cogent understanding of his claim, how should one account for it? In terms of the 'will to truth'? Whatever answers are available to these questions from thinkers such as Foucault and Lacan, I believe that John Fowles's novel, *The magus*, puts one in a position to appreciate the extent to which human beings are driven by an irresistible 'will (or desire) to know' – one that does not cease functioning even when indications are that one is constantly being deluded by what ostensibly amounts to evidence supporting certain interpretations and conclusions. Moreover, Fowles's novel also seems to point in the direction of an alternative to the blind adherence to epistemic mirages, an alternative predicated on a more modest claim, compatible with the paradoxical Socratic dictum, 'I know that I do not know'.

If one considers that the notion of *Bildung* or self-cultivation (self-formation) originated in medieval mysticism, became important for eighteenth-century thought, and fundamentally informs the thought of Hegel in the nineteenth century (Gadamer 1982: 10–18) – as the 'series' of forms assumed by consciousness on the developmental path from self-alienation to self-knowledge (Hegel 1966: 136) – it is not difficult to grasp it as underpinning the development of the narrative in *The magus*, albeit not straightforwardly, as in a conventional *Bildungsroman*. The narrative concerns what one might call the counter-*Bildung* – the simultaneous *Bildung* and its own subversion, in contrast with the *Bildung* of the protagonist, Pip, in Dickens's *Great expectations* (1993) – of the narrator and protagonist (perhaps anti-hero), Nicholas Urfe. The latter is a young, simultaneously (over-)confident and unsure Oxford graduate in literature, who fancies himself a 'discoverer' or 'adventurer' of sorts, not least when it comes to women. The following excerpt captures his character well (Fowles 1983: 21):

> I suppose I'd had, by the standards of that pre-permissive time, a good deal of sex for my age. Girls, or a certain kind of girl, liked me; I had a car – not so common among undergraduates in those days – and I had some money. I wasn't ugly; and even more important, I had my loneliness, which, as every cad knows, is a deadly weapon with women. My 'technique' was to make a show of unpredictability, cynicism, and indifference. Then, like a conjuror with his white rabbit, I produced the solitary heart.

> I didn't collect conquests, but by the time I left Oxford I was a dozen girls away from virginity. I found my sexual success and the apparently ephemeral nature of love equally pleasing. It was like being good at golf, but despising the game. One was covered all round, both when one played and when one didn't. I contrived most of my affaires in the vacations, away from Oxford, since the new term meant that I could conveniently leave the scene of the crime ... I became almost as neat at ending liaisons as at starting them.
>
> This sounds, and was, calculating, but it was caused less by a true coldness than by my narcissistic belief in the importance of lifestyle. I mistook the feeling of relief that dropping a girl always brought for a love of freedom. Perhaps the one thing in my favour was that I lied very little; I was always careful to make sure that the current victim knew, before she took her clothes off, the difference between coupling and marrying.

It is impossible to do justice to the long and complex narrative; here only the briefest of summaries can be provided, in addition to which relevant information will be provided as the need arises in the course of the theoretical discussion. Nicholas meets an Australian girl, Alison Kelly, with whom he falls in love without really acknowledging it to himself, given his 'self-absorption' (Fowles 1983: 35). She starts working as an air hostess; he goes off to teach English at a boys' school on a Greek island in the Aegean – Phraxos – in search of a 'new mystery' (1983: 19), with a certain ambivalence regarding his feelings for Alison, but with a tentative agreement between them to meet when she is in Athens. At the school on Phraxos he learns about a mysterious man called Conchis, who lives at an estate called Bourani on the other side of the island, where some of his predecessors at the school, according to their communication with Nicholas, had puzzling experiences. To cut a long story short, Nicholas's curiosity impels him to make contact with Conchis, and as their acquaintance grows – in the course of weekend visits to Bourani – he becomes deeply aware of the intellectual and psychic power of the older man, who shares with Nicholas his personal experiences as a soldier in World War I, as well as in his role of medical doctor and psychiatrist. In the course of these visits, which increasingly exercise a veritable mesmerizing effect on him – despite his belief that he is able to maintain a certain sceptical distance from Conchis – Nicholas is introduced to a beautiful young woman, Lily, who seems to be play-acting the role of Conchis's (deceased) beloved from his youth, and with whom he (Nicholas) becomes infatuated. Parallel to these developments, he experiences what he describes as 'mysteries' (incomprehensible experiences of visions as well as several of an auditory and olfactory nature, which seem to be connected with Conchis's narration of salient episodes from his life) – a description that, needless to point out, powerfully resonates with the spirit of the bygone realm of ancient Greek mystery religion and tragedy, in the context of an atmospheric landscape which still inescapably evokes that ancient world. These 'mysteries' initially seem inexplicable, but gradually Nicholas comes to believe that they are staged for his benefit – his edification – by Conchis, with the help of a number of elusive 'actors' who perform their roles (of ancient Greek deities, among other personages) with chilling conviction.

Nicholas manages to befriend 'Lily', and attempts to uncover the purpose behind Conchis's increasingly elaborate 'masque'. He also discovers that she has a twin sister, June, that her 'real' name is Julie Holmes, and that they were initially hired in England by the wealthy Conchis as actresses to star in a film he was to produce, only to find themselves enmeshed in the elaborate scheme aimed at simultaneously deceiving and enlightening Nicholas – hence my initial characterization of *The magus* as a kind of counter-*Bildung* novel. Conchis, having become aware of the contact between Nicholas and Lily/Julie, advises Nicholas to act with the utmost care regarding her well-being, as she is a patient of his who is suffering from schizophrenia, and can therefore not be relied upon as a rational interlocutor. Needless to stress, in the face of conflicting messages from various individuals, together with the sometimes disturbing experiences to which he is privy, as well as his irresistible attraction to Julie, Nicholas finds himself vacillating between what he believes to be insight into the 'truth' about Conchis's intentions, on the one hand, and utter confusion, accompanied by anger in the face of apparent deceit, on the other. In fact, at one point he acknowledges to himself that (Fowles 1983: 294): 'Every truth in his world was a sort of lie; and every lie a sort of truth'.

By now it should be apparent that the theme – announced at the outset of this paper – of the 'will to truth', or in Lacanian terms, the 'will to illusion', is powerfully deployed in the narrative. With consummate, tantalizing mastery, step by step, Conchis lures Nicholas further along the way to what seems to be the promise of an eventual revelation of the truth about him, about Bourani, about Lily/Julie, Rose/June, about the elaborate masque ostensibly staged for his (Nicholas's) benefit, and – perhaps most important – about Nicholas himself in the guise of some profound variety of self-knowledge. One might say that the narrative is driven by the Socratic injunction, to 'know thyself', except that the object of this quest appears to be elusive, and – as the narrative progresses – its presupposition, that there is some 'self-knowledge' worthy of the name, to be discovered, illusory. This narratively structured insight as embodied in Fowles's novel, I want to argue here, is consonant with Lacan's claim – to be unpacked shortly – that the structure of human knowledge is 'paranoiac' (that is, illusory or even delusional).

The narrative culminates in a series of events so startling that it sometimes catches the reader unawares – who, for reasons of ineluctable identification with the first-person narrator of the story (see in this regard Olivier 2005a & 2006), sometimes vicariously registers the shocks and surprises on the part of the protagonist with remarkable intensity. Every time that Nicholas is convinced, apparently with good reason, that he has finally discovered what the true state of affairs is, this 'ground' is knocked from under his feet, and he is, once again, propelled onto a roller-coaster of events that point to yet another possibility, rendering his previous belief that he has discovered the true state of affairs, null and void. The remarkable thing is, however – and this is the point that is germane to the theme of this paper – that he never seems to give up the belief that there is some final, conclusive opportunity waiting for him, some ultimate discovery of the 'truth', no matter how many masquerades he has to brave in the interim. In this respect, I believe, the character of Nicholas represents the human condition. Along the way, it should be mentioned, Nicholas meets Alison in Athens, from where they embark on a simultaneously wonderful and (for their relationship) disastrous journey to Mount Parnassus, at the end of which Nicholas breaks ties off with her. As a sequel, he later receives the devastating news (resulting in some serious soul-searching on his part) from a friend that Alison has committed suicide – only to learn, much later in the narrative, that she is alive and complicit in the *masque* to which he has been subjected.

The crucial event in the novel, as far as Nicholas's counter-*Bildung* is concerned – a kind of simultaneously climactic and anti-climactic *dénouement* – is, to my mind, the 'trial' to which Nicholas is subjected by a group of people who claim to be human scientists: psychologists, psychiatrists and psychoanalysts, including 'Dr' Conchis and Lily/Julie, who also turns out, supposedly, to be a psychologist (named Dr Vanessa Maxwell) – and one who does not hesitate to engage in participative research in the guise of her relationship with Nicholas, which 'ended', just before the 'trial', in a passionate sexual encounter between them. All of his experiences relating to Conchis, Lily/Julie, Rose/June, the elaborate *masque*, and even to Alison, are made the subject of the trial – where Nicholas is bound like some sacrificial animal, but at the conclusion of which, subsequent to the scientists' judgment of him, he is invited to deliver his own judgement of them in turn. Things do not end here either – before being released, he is subjected to a gruelling series of 'de-briefing' encounters, in the position of involuntary spectator, with the enactment of various 'primitively Dionysian' sexual encounters between Lily/Julie and her lover, a black American psychologist previously known to Nicholas as 'Joe', one of the 'actors' in Conchis's *masque* or symbolic enactment of events for Nicholas's benefit. It is significant that, in the end, Nicholas discovers that even Alison's 'death' was part of the *masque*, and the novel ends with a puzzling, ambivalent encounter and eventual parting between them, with the apparent (uncomfortable) realization, on his part, that he has lost something very valuable through his inability to embrace her love for him – and perhaps also his (unacknowledged) love for her – instead of which he has persisted in chasing an elusive and illusory goal dangled like a carrot before his nose by Conchis, the Magus of the narrative.

The final question that confronts the reader of this – to my mind profound – novel, is: has Nicholas learned anything worthwhile through his trials and tribulations? Has there been *Bildung* comparable to Pip's in Dickens's *Great expectations*, or only a breaking-down (an un-*Bildung* or de-cultivation) of his ability to trust his faculties? And if the latter, or perhaps a paradoxical combination of the two, what could one learn from it? The role of Conchis in this regard appears to be that of an epistemic catalyst (perhaps even that of a psychoanalyst) who assists Nicholas in 'assuming his desire', in the process disabusing him of his epistemic illusions and misguided beliefs. It seems to me, therefore, as if Fowles's novel is consonant with certain aspects of Jacques Lacan's psychoanalytic theory of the human subject.

In 'The mirror stage' (1977a: 3) – where Lacan shows how the primitive ego develops through a dialectic of *méconnaissance* ('misrecognition'), on the part of the infant, of its mirror image as 'itself' (see Olivier 2004) – he talks of '... the social dialectic that structures human knowledge as paranoiac'. In 'Aggressivity in psychoanalysis' (1977: 17), referring to a 'stagnation' of one of the stages of organization of the ego and of objects (which are experienced as 'events in a perspective of mirages'), he elaborates as follows:

> ... this formal stagnation is akin to the most general structure of human knowledge: that which constitutes the ego and its objects with attributes of permanence, identity, and substantiality, in short, with entities or 'things' that are very different from the *Gestalten* that experience enables us to isolate in the shifting field, stretched in accordance with the lines of animal desire ...
>
> What I have called paranoiac knowledge is shown, therefore, to correspond in its more or less archaic forms to certain critical moments that mark the history of man's mental genesis, each representing a stage in objectifying identification.

One has to be very clear on what Lacan is claiming here. He is in fact extrapolating (Lacan 1977: 20) what he has shown regarding the genesis of the subject's sense of self as 'ego' in the imaginary register – that it emerges from a kind of alienating projection of vaunted 'permanence' into a mirror image which is then mistakenly taken as being the subject 'itself', despite really being a fictional construct distinct from the 'I'-position from which one speaks (Lacan 1977a: 1–7) – to the world of objects which, in the 'shifting field' of quotidian experience, lacks the ostensible 'permanence' or substantiality attributed to it through this gesture of 'stagnation'. In brief: the dynamic field of experience is constituted by humans as if it consists of relatively unchanging objects identical to themselves.

If this seems startling to some, one might remind oneself that Kant (1964: 1–24; 90–94) already, in the eighteenth century, argued that human reality is constituted as 'manifold of experience' by way of the synthetically structuring, *a priori*, transcendental functioning of forms of intuition (space and time) in combination with the categories of the understanding (such as causality and substance). What Kant argued as transcendental thinker, sets the scene for Lacan's argument – without the synthetic role of the cognitive faculties of reason, there is no coherent 'reality'; outside of the constitutive functioning of the faculties of reason, there is only the 'I know not what' of what Kant called the *Ding an sich* (thing in itself) – the unknowable or noumenal 'ground' of the phenomenal world. As psychoanalytical theorist, and in contrast with Kant, Lacan places the genesis of human (phenomenal) reality in a developmental schema, and – like Kant before him – intimates that 'reality', or the world of egos and objects, is a function of human cognitive exigencies: reality is constituted as an amalgam of the imaginary and symbolic registers ('entered' by the subject at successive stages in its life), and is breached from within by the 'real' in so far as it resists being assimilated into human reality (see Olivier 2004; 2005). To be sure, by attaching the epithet 'paranoiac' to knowledge of such a world, Lacan does seem to put a different complexion on things compared to Kant (who believed that 'objective' knowledge of phenomenal reality is possible precisely because human subjectivity is the condition for objectivity) – after all, 'paranoia' is a delusional psychosis (Lacan 1997: 3–4), and even if one assumes him to be using it as a metaphor where he describes human knowledge as 'paranoiac', it still seems to imply that there is something about it which makes it illusory. Why such an apparent overstating of the case? It is instructive in this regard to turn to Lacan's theory of the 'four discourses'.

For this theory to make sense, it bears repeating that the world – or human reality, as intimated above – is structured (quasi-)transcendentally (that is, conditioned regarding its possibility as well as its 'impossibility' or 'impurity') through perception and language, or (what amounts to the same thing) iconically, at the level of the imaginary register, and linguistically, at the level of the symbolic register. The fact that one always, ineluctably, comes up against the limits of the imaginary (imagination) and the symbolic (language) when they falter in the face of an unassimilable, traumatic experience, or of an inexplicable scientific discovery (or anomaly) of some kind, announces the elusive operation of Lacan's third register, the so-called 'real'. Nevertheless, it is through language (and, as will become apparent, discourse) as well as iconicity that the organization of experience into quasi-stable entities occurs – those entities which supposedly comprise the correlates of human knowledge in the encompassing field known as (social and natural) 'reality'.

Lacan refers to the 'production of the four discourses' – those of the master, the university, the hysteric and the analyst. Think of these as four different kinds of operation of language, each of which constitutes and structures both the subject and social reality differently in cratological terms – that is, structurally as far as identity and interpersonal or social power relations are concerned. In his Seminar 17 – *The other side of psychoanalysis; 1969–1970* (Lacan 2007: 13) – he intimates that he thinks of discourse as something by means of which several 'stable relations' are established, and within which 'conduct' or 'acts' can be 'inscribed' as within a kind of 'framework' of 'primordial statements'. As an instance of validation regarding these claims concerning the character of discourse, he alludes to psychoanalytic experience, where one encounters, for example, such 'stable relations' in the form of the superego. It is not difficult to grasp this – the superego, in so far as it is recognizable as a psychic structure of authority and subjugation by which the subject's actions are constrained – as an exemplary instantiation of the operation of discourse.

How do the four discourses differ (see Fink 1997: 129–136; Bracher 1994: 115–126)? Lacan gives phylogenetic and ontogenetic priority to the *discourse of the master* – the subject is first constituted by its (nonsensical) subjection to language or the master signifier, which alienates it irreversibly from the real by introducing a split into it, in this way rendering the lacking subject, forever divided between consciousness and unconsciousness. However, the master's discourse systematically hides or represses the unconscious 'knowledge' of its incompleteness – it shows no interest in knowledge as such; as long as things 'work'. The discourse of the master is the discourse of power (today, that of liberal democratic capitalism), which, unlike the discourse of the university, is not concerned with knowledge, but simply with whether the system of dominant power relations works.

The *university discourse* is in the position of the slave (whose knowledge serves the master), and is predicated on the attainment of knowledge, but knowledge putatively of a specific kind, namely systematic, factual or encyclopaedic knowledge regarded as being, in principle, 'completeable'. As such, it functions to support the discourse of the master in so far as the latter claims unquestionable power – one finds here an acknowledgement, on Lacan's part, that the university as an institution more often than not serves the dominant powers of the age.

The *discourse of the hysteric* comprises that epistemic position from which the master's discourse (and by implication that of the university) is relentlessly questioned concerning the justifiability of its claims. Interestingly, Lacan associates this – the hysteric's discourse, and not, as one may expect, that of the university – with authentic science, because the questioning or problematization of the master's discourse by the hysteric's exemplifies the structural 'uncertainty' or indeterminacy at the heart of science. Needless to say, this insight dispels the illusory claims and aspirations of the master's as well as the university's discourse, by uncovering a logic which limits, and therefore subverts all claims to the justifiability of unconditional power, and to presumed wholeness of 'knowledge' from within, as in the case of Heisenberg's 'uncertainty (indeterminacy) principle' (Fink 1997: 133–134). This explains why Lacan increasingly identified the discourse of the hysteric and the discourse of science (Fink 1997: 133).

In its turn, the *discourse of the analyst* marks that discursive position from which the subject's certainties (its master signifiers) are symptomatically decoded as being indicative of its desire – in other words, the analyst's discourse, representing the real (the impact of which requires the reconfiguration of one's symbolic horizon), mediates between the subject's explicit claims (whether these belong to the university's discourse or to the hysteric's) and its repressed or hidden desire, in the process uncovering the master signifiers driving the subject, and submitting them to a relativizing dialectic by implying that the subject is never 'master' of her or his discourse. Nevertheless, as Bracher (1994: 123–124) reminds one, for Lacan the analyst's discourse does not enable one to break with the master's discourse once and for all; the crucial difference here is that, instead of being subordinated to master signifiers imposed from the outside, the subject learns to 'produce' them her- or himself. The analyst's discourse therefore functions paradoxically to disabuse the subject of the implicit claims to authoritativeness and completeness of the discourses of the master and the university, while acknowledging the ineluctable need, on the subject's part, to be temporarily empowered in order to act. The analyst's discourse therefore enables the subject to resist the illusion of conclusive empowerment by master signifiers and final enlightenment by their servant, the university discourse, in the place of which he or she is encouraged to settle for knowledge that is open-ended and revisable.

Although it is not the main focus of this article, it should be noted that Lacan formalizes the relation of the four discourses (Fink 1997: 130–136) to one another by assigning a symbol-schema to each, and placing these, in turn, in the positions, respectively, of 'agent' over 'truth', on the left side, and 'other' over 'product/loss' on the right side, with an arrow (→), representing the function of 'addressing', pointing from the left side position of the 'agent' to the right side position of the 'other'. Every time the formal schema of these four symbols is rotated in a counter-clockwise direction, it changes the power relations fundamentally, with the result that each turn gives rise to the representation of (the emergence of) a different discourse. For example, the master's discourse is represented with the symbol (S1) of the master in the position of 'agent', over the 'truth' (the split subject, \$), addressing (→) the 'other' (S2; knowledge), over 'product/loss' (a, or object a, representing, in a capitalist system, surplus enjoyment, for example). In the university's discourse, the symbol for knowledge (S2) occupies the position of 'agent', while in the hysteric's discourse the split subject \$ (that is, the subject divided between conscious and unconscious, which the master cannot afford to recognize) occupies that position, and in the analyst's discourse the agent-position is occupied by the symbol (a) for the cause of desire. The upshot of this, as Fink (1997: 132) notes, is to suggest a kind of 'historical movement from the master's discourse to the university discourse' as its 'legitimation'. The hysteric's discourse, in turn, which represents a challenging of prevailing systems of knowledge in the university discourse (and indirectly that of the master, served by the university), as well as that of the analyst, which represents the repressed desire of the subject, may plausibly be seen as having emerged historically after those of the master (grasped as such by Hegel) and of the university (or Hegel's 'slave'), namely in the late nineteenth century. The power of this theory derives from the fact that, as represented by the different permutations of the symbols representing the four discourses, it may be used as analytical or 'hermeneutic' schema to make sense of a wide variety of discursive power relations as well as the conditions under which they may be challenged or changed.

The first of these four kinds of discourse – the master's discourse – operates through master signifiers that create the illusion on the part of its speakers that they are, in fact 'whole, undivided, self-identical' (Bracher 1994: 121) – a clear indication that this corresponds with the putative paranoiac structure of human knowledge, although the university's discourse in its epistemically supportive function should be added here, given its founding principle of systematic knowledge as 'the ultimate authority', where 'everything has its reason' (Fink 1997: 132). Philosophy, in its traditional guise of rational discipline *par excellence*, instantiates the discourse of the university in its role of 'rationalizing and propping up the master's discourse' (Fink 1997: 132; Lacan 2007: 20–22). Instances of the master's discourse are afforded by all ideological and religious systems, which comprise closed 'paranoiac' or 'delusional' totalities, where meaning subsists in an undiluted plenum. By contrast, the discourse of the hysteric, in so far as it questions the discourse of the master, registers the refusal, on the body, to submit to such master signifiers (Bracher 1994: 122), and the delusional claims of both the master's discourse and its servant discourse, that of the university, are symptomatically apparent precisely there where symptoms such as nervous tics or stammering become manifest in subject's actions. Lest the impression be created that it is only in pathological hysterical behaviour that the illusory claims to wholeness on the part of the discourses of the master and of the university become visible, consider Mark Bracher's illuminating extension of the hysteric's discourse in the following (1994: 122):

> The hysterical structure of discourse also characterizes other instances of resistance, protest, and complaint – from the plaintive anthems of slaves to the yearning lyrics of lovesick poets to the iconoclastic rhetoric of revolutionaries. The hysterical structure is in force whenever a discourse is dominated by the speaker's symptom – that is, his or her unique mode of experiencing *jouissance*, a uniqueness that is manifested (in experiences such as shame, meaninglessness, anxiety, and desire) as a failure of the subject, *$*, to coincide with or be satisfied by the master signifiers offered by society and embraced as the subject's ideals.

In what, precisely, can one detect the paranoiac structure of human knowledge, then, where the four discourses are concerned? The master's discourse functions unreflectively through the exercise of power, and the discourse of the university proceeds on the assumption that knowledge in the guise of scientific disciplines in principle comprises a plenum, and that only considerations of an empirical nature stand in the way of erecting the final storeys of its edifice. In brief: these discourses are committed to the illusion (if not delusion) that knowledge comprises a systematic whole. The fact that Lacan associates the hysteric's questioning, challenging discourse with science – something that would strike most people as counter-intuitive – is a stark reminder of the distance that separates mainstream opinion from this insight. After all, as Fink (1997: 138) remarks, standard conceptions of science (especially in America) entail the naïve belief that the conclusions of 'hard science' are agreed-upon in scientific circles, and are virtually unassailable, in contrast with the true state of affairs, that there is wide disagreement among scientists at any given time concerning the question, what makes science into science.

While the characterization of human knowledge as 'paranoiac' is evidently metaphorical on Lacan's part, it is instructive to consider his commentary on paranoia in a pathological sense, because it enables one to flesh out the analogy with knowledge. In *The psychoses* (*The seminar of Jacques Lacan, Book III*; 1997: 85), commenting on Freud's case of the delusional Judge Schreber, Lacan makes the following observation:

> What is the psychotic phenomenon? It is the emergence in reality of an enormous meaning that has the appearance of being nothing at all – in so far as it cannot be tied to anything, since it has never entered into the system of symbolization – but under certain conditions it can threaten the entire edifice.

Clearly, human knowledge as 'paranoiac' cannot be identified with psychosis or paranoia in this strict sense – for one thing, the 'meaning' of knowledge is always made manifest in the symbolic system, unlike the 'enormous', un-symbolizable delusional 'meaning' on the part of the psychotic subject. Its delusional, psychotic status is shown by the fact that, despite its enormity, it appears to be 'nothing at all' – that is, it does not connect with the normal, pragmatic state of affairs, which is regulated by linguistic exchange. In contrast to this, knowledge – for instance the 'rational' disciplines taught at universities – apparently does 'connect' with pragmatic life through symbolic exchanges. (Psychological theories on personality types offer psychologists pragmatic guidelines for working with clients, for example.) So where is the analogy? It lies precisely in the description: 'an enormous meaning that has the appearance of being nothing at all'. In the case of the paranoid person, this is a delusion which manifests itself 'in the real' (Lacan 1997: 86–88), that is, as a bodily symptom of sorts (a hallucination, for example), which resists linguistic articulation. In the case of systems of knowledge, it lies in the enormity of the system, which – as systematic totality – appears to be 'nothing at all', that is, metaphorically speaking 'delusional' in the sense of not taking account of all those anomalies which are the 'real' driving force of true science. Speaking of the university's discourse in Lacan's thought, Bruce Fink (1997: 132–133) says:

> ... the kind of knowledge involved in the university discourse amounts to mere rationalization ... We can imagine it, not as the kind of thought that tries to come to grips with the real, to maintain the difficulties posed by apparent logical and/or physical contradictions, but rather as a kind of encyclopedic endeavor to exhaust a field (consider ... Auguste Comte's goal of a total sociology).

Lacan's discussion of psychosis offers another basis for an analogy with 'paranoiac' human knowledge. The psychotic subject, he points out (Lacan 1997: 87), 'substitutes for symbolic mediation a profusion, an imaginary proliferation'. With this in mind, it appears to be no accident that 'paranoiac knowledge' is mentioned in Lacan's 'The mirror stage' (1977a: 3), where he outlines the subject's entry into the imaginary register via its identification with its own mirror image – which it mistakenly regards as being 'itself'. This 'misrecognition', according to Lacan, comprises the ambiguous ground for the subject's sense of identity as well as its alienation from itself: it functions 'orthopaedically' (Lacan 1977a: 4) in so far as the infant subject lacks and desires the ostensible wholeness and unity of the mirror image, and it operates in a rigidly restrictive fashion, like an armour of sorts, as far as other possibilities on the part of the subject are concerned. The upshot of this is that the subject's 'identity' as 'ego' (*moi*) is of a fictional nature, and must be fundamentally distinguished from its position as 'I' (*je*) in the symbolic register, which is located where it exceeds the domain of conscious deliberation and control, that is, at the level of the unconscious (Lee 1990: 40–41). In fact, Lacan counsels that, for the subject to participate in the narrative of its own story (in dialogue with the analyst and in relation to the role of the unconscious via *parapraxes*, like slips of the tongue), the 'empty speech' of its alienating ego- or *moi*-position in the imaginary register should be uncovered for what it is, namely an illusory construct (Lacan 1977b: 41–50). Because the imaginary 'proliferation' which characterizes it is not susceptible to symbolic articulation, psychosis, strictly speaking, therefore differs from imaginary identification on the part of 'normal' subjects, which always overlaps the functioning of the subject in language. But one cannot ignore the fact that the imaginary component of the subject's complex structure – ironically, that which is usually regarded as marking its 'true' identity, namely its 'ego' – introduces a fictional or illusory dimension into it, albeit tempered by its imbrication with the other registers of the subject's articulation, namely the symbolic and the real (see in this regard Olivier 2004, 2005 & 2005a). It is here where the pertinence of Lacan's metaphorical description of human knowledge as 'paranoiac' is apparent: the role of the imaginary as common element in psychosis (minus symbolization) as well as in the (illusory) identities of 'normal' individuals explains what may to some seem to be an unjustified epithet for one of humanity's most prized achievements, namely systems of 'knowledge'.

There is another source in Lacan's work that casts light on the puzzling comparison of human knowledge with paranoia, namely what he described, in his early work, as one of the 'imagoes' – the *maternal*, *fraternal* and *paternal* (Lee 1990: 14–15) – which fulfils a psychically structuring function in the life of the infant, namely the 'maternal imago'. These three structuring complexes correspond with the registers of the real, the imaginary and the symbolic, respectively (see Olivier 2005a for an elaboration on this in relation to the question of narrative identity). While the fraternal imago – born of envy, rivalry and identification with siblings – anticipates the quasi-transcendental imaginary function of the 'mirror stage', and the paternal imago the societal or Oedipal (superego-) subjectivization accompanying the child's entry into the symbolic sphere, it is especially the maternal imago which strikes one as being pertinent to the illusions that accompany human cognitive aspirations, despite being located at the level of the real. This becomes more apparent when one learns that the maternal imago is correlative to the infant's 'congenital deficiency', signalled by its dependence on the mother's breast as source of fulfilment of its bodily needs (Lee 1990: 14). It is but a small step from here to conceiving of the structuring function of this 'maternal' imago as paving the way for all (fundamentally discursive) quests for a totality of some kind, whether political, religious or 'philosophical' (that is, metaphysical), in so far as these register the interminable lack on the part of the subject in the face of whatever *plenum* it desires (behind which the experience of the maternal breast lurks; Lee 1990: 14). Lacan's own formulation is telling as far as the connection between the maternal imago and the illusory character of human knowledge is concerned (quoted in Lee 1990: 14):

> If it were necessary to define the most abstract form where it is refound, we might characterize it thus: a perfect assimilation of the totality of being. Under this formulation with a slightly philosophical aspect, we can recognize these nostalgias of humanity: the metaphysical mirage of universal harmony, the mystical abyss of affective fusion, the social utopia of a totalitarian guardianship, and every outburst of the obsession with a paradise lost before birth or of the most obscure aspiration toward death.

In *The ethics of psychoanalysis* Lacan offers an additional insight into the grounds for the human drive towards (illusory) knowledge. In a discussion of Aristotle's ideas on the problem of human intemperance, in the face of accompanying 'knowledge' (that is, despite 'knowing better') – or on a 'syllogism of the desirable' – he says (1997: 29–30):

> Beside the major premise – one must always taste what is sweet – there is a particular, minor premise, i.e., this is sweet. And the principle of wrong action is to be found in the error of a particular judgment relative to the minor premise. Where is the error found? Precisely in the circumstance that the desire which is subjacent to the major premise causes the wrong judgment to be made concerning the reality of the supposed sweetness toward which the action is directed.

The major premise is abstract, conceptual, while the minor premise depends upon something intuitive and particular – perception – where desire leads judgment astray. In other words, the error of the minor premise – which is no doubt followed by the inference: 'Taste this' – results from ascribing pleasure anticipatorily to something particular *because* it is desired. One witnesses here the ingenious twist given by psychoanalysis (in Freud, who is discussed in the same section as Aristotle, referred to above, and developed by Lacan) to the transcendental tradition going back to Kant. According to Kant, it will be remembered, the rational faculties of intuition (space and time) and the concepts or categories of the understanding are the conditions of the possibility of there being a (human) reality or world. These faculties fulfil an indispensable constitutive or structuring role regarding what is 'given' to perception from the side of the un-objectifiable noumenon. It was Freud, however, who added something which made Kant's 'rational faculties' look anaemic and sterile in retrospect, infusing the constitution of 'reality' with that unmistakeable human element, namely *desire* – or what Freud referred to as the singular *Wunsch* peculiar to every human being universally (Lacan 1997: 24; see also in this regard Hurst 2006: Chapter 2, especially pp. 35–37). In brief: knowledge of 'reality' is not merely a synthetic function of perceptually 'given' content and rational forms; it is ineluctably affected or distorted by desire. This is consonant with what Lacan terms the 'paranoiac structure of human knowledge': desire affects judgment, it may even cause wrong judgment or illusion; because one desires a certain kind of knowledge, especially in particular or specific situations (as Lacan argues in the passage cited above) – for example coherent, systematic, clear and distinct conceptual knowledge – the inclination asserts itself to construct such 'knowledge' on the basis of specific, desire-induced perceptions, that is, perceptions that are guided by the desire for an encompassing, complete, ultimately closed system. Even in the philosophy of science the phenomenon of 'theory-laden perception' is well-known (Hurst 2004: 20–23; Chalmers 1982: 25–38) – the way in which theory is said to precede observation in the sense that observation is guided by theoretical or hypothetical expectations. This would be related to what Lacan is arguing here, although – given the status of desire as unconscious – the two things are arguably not synonymous.

I mentioned at the outset in this article that Fowles's *The magus* (1983) constitutes a kind of counter-*Bildung* novel, which eschews the narrative effect of the protagonist growing wise through painful experiences, embodying a process of incremental disillusionment instead. (At an advanced stage in the narrative Nicholas considers all the instances where, what was presented to him by, or through the mediation of Conchis, and correspondingly, what he initially regarded as 'true' – that is, as 'knowledge' which had been imparted to him – turned out to be false or fictitious in varying degrees at a later stage; see Fowles 1983: 576–583) One witnesses a tantalizing epistemic relation between Conchis and Nicholas – at one point the latter actually tells Conchis that he is sometimes 'very tantalizing' (1983: 109) – so much so that its unfolding could be read as a model for the paranoiac structure of knowledge, on the one hand, and a way of negotiating its pitfalls in a paradoxical manner, on the other: Nicholas constantly desiring to know (of Conchis, of Bourani, the secluded estate on Phraxos where Conchis lives, of the reasons for Conchis's interest in him, of the mysterious experiences that he is privy to at Bourani, of Lily's true identity, then of Julie's, and so on), and Conchis constantly luring him further; Nicholas ostensibly satisfied, at least intermittently, then disappointed by the unmasking of his presumed knowledge as illusory, only to be lured further on the supposition that he has discovered the 'true state of affairs', then to be disillusioned again, and so on and on.

The dynamic is therefore one of presumed knowledge followed by ostensible discovery, calling for revision of an initial supposition; revision of an earlier position, followed by further discoveries calling for further revisions if not reversals, culminating in several 'showdowns', first, between Nicholas and Conchis, later between him and Lily de Seitas (the twins' mother, whom he tracks down in England), and finally between Nicholas and Alison. While one gets the impression, especially from his final meeting with Lily de Seitas (Fowles 1983: 622–631), that the rigorous, if alternatingly exciting and infuriating ordeal that Conchis has imposed on Nicholas has not been without some salutary effects concerning the young man's conspicuously enriched and comparatively increased, nuanced understanding of himself, of others, and more broadly of life, the same cannot be said of his final meeting with Alison (Fowles 1983: 647–656), which he craves unbearably before it finally happens. This encounter is highly ambiguous, in so far as they do not seem to be able to get through to each other. It seems to suggest that Nicholas has not really learned anything about the importance of smiling in the face of one's ineluctable mortality, of all loss, and of the indispensable place of love in human life. I would suggest that this has to do with what I shall discuss below, namely human fallibility and finitude – especially Nicholas's in this encounter – and the ineluctable responsibility that one's decisions and choices impose on one. But before one gets to this point in the narrative, there are many lessons to be learned.

In passing, I should note that the novel ends on an exemplary, self-reflective literary-theoretical note, which bears on the difference between literature as art, on the one hand – where the actions in fictional space occupy a kind of 'eternity' in the sense that they will stay the same, frozen, for all time – and social reality, on the other – where things change irreversibly. Unless this is kept in mind, readers would find the last paragraph endlessly puzzling. On this note, a perceptive critic has suggested footnoting the literary-theoretical aspect of this article by referring to the work of literary theorists Robert Con Davis and Isaiah Smithson, which would certainly be illuminating. As a counter-suggestion I believe that what Deleuze and Guattari write in their volume, *What is philosophy?* (1994), where they discuss the differences between art (including literature), philosophy and science, captures exactly what I argue here as far as literature is concerned (1994: 163):

> The young man will smile on the canvas for as long as the canvas lasts. Blood throbs under the skin of this woman's face, the wind shakes a branch, a group of men prepare *[sic]* to leave. In a novel or a film, the young man will stop smiling, but he will start to smile again when we turn to this page or that moment. Art preserves, and it is the only thing in the world that is preserved. It preserves and is preserved in itself (*quid juris?*), although actually it lasts no longer than its support and materials – stone, canvas, chemical color, and so on (*quid facti?*).

As they proceed to argue further in this chapter (Chapter 7), art differs from philosophy in so far as it creates 'percepts' and 'affects', embodied in the characters, shapes, movements, and so on, which are preserved in art and, in turn, preserve it. Philosophy (and one may include the theorizing in which I am engaged here), by contrast, creates (novel) 'concepts' through which the world is reconfigured. One of the exemplary ways for a theorist to proceed is to bring the percepts and affects embodied in a narrative such as *The Magus* into a productive heuristic constellation with illuminating concepts such as those drawn here from (mainly) Lacan's work. In this way literature, philosophy and psychoanalytic theory may enter into a fruitful collaborative relationship.

Returning to the narrative in question, during one of his first visits to Bourani Nicholas already feels constrained to change his mind about Conchis, whom he initially regarded as being merely an eccentric old man (Fowles 1983: 102):

> I was increasingly baffled by Conchis. At times he was so dogmatic that I wanted to laugh, to behave in the traditionally xenophobic, continentals-despising way of my race; at times, rather against my will, he impressed me – not only as a rich man with some enviable works of art in his house. And now he frightened me. It was the kind of illogical fear of the supernatural that in others made me sneer; but all along I had felt that I was invited not out of hospitality, but for some other reason. He wanted to use me in some way.

Later during the same visit, in the face of what he calls Nicholas's 'pessimism' (which seems more like nihilism or cynicism to me), Conchis proposes to show the young man 'the innermost secret of life' (Fowles 1983: 146). Because this scene contains something that is crucial for assessing the epistemological and axiological position of *The magus*, I shall quote it almost in full (Fowles 1983: 146–147):

> It was a stone head, whether of a man or a woman it was difficult to say. The nose had been broken short. The hair was done in a fillet, with two sidepieces. But the power of the fragment was in the face. It was set in a triumphant smile, a smile that would have been smug if it had not been so full of the purest metaphysical good humour. The eyes were faintly oriental, long, and as I saw, for Conchis put a hand over the mouth, also smiling. The mouth was beautifully modelled, timelessly intelligent and timelessly amused.
>
> 'That is the truth. Not the hammer and sickle. Not the stars and stripes. Not the cross. Not the sun. Not gold. Not *yin* and *yang*. But the smile.' ...
>
> He was right. The little sunlit thing had some numen; or not so much a divinity, as a having known divinity, in it; of being ultimately certain. ...
>
> 'Tell me where it came from.'
>
> 'From Didyma in Asia Minor.'
>
> 'How old is it?'
>
> 'The sixth or seventh century before Christ'. ...
>
> The little head watched our watching; bland, certain, and almost maliciously inscrutable. It flashed on me that it was also the smile that Conchis sometimes wore; as if he sat before the head and practised it. At the same time I realized exactly what I disliked about it. It was above all the smile of dramatic irony, of those who have privileged information. I looked back up at Conchis's face; and I knew I was right.

This scene (and the important place of the smile in it) connects with several other scenes in the narrative, such as the one (Fowles 1983: 531), where Nicholas has just been coerced into witnessing a scene of passionate lovemaking between Lily/Julie/Dr Maxwell and her black lover, Joe, apparently in the roles of Desdemona and Othello. Conchis approaches him and informs him that he is 'now elect', and when Nicholas, who is gagged, shakes his head violently, indicating his rejection and contempt for the process that he has been subjected to, Conchis insists that he has 'no choice', and urges Nicholas: 'Learn to smile, Nicholas, learn to smile.' The significance of this for the overall theme of the novel should not be underestimated. That is, it should be seen in relation to the theme of 'hazard', suggested to Nicholas several times by Conchis (see, for example, Fowles 1983: 87, 88) but probably the most eloquent formulation of which is given by Lily de Seitas, mother of Lily and Rose (or Julie and June), when Nicholas meets her after his return to London from Greece, desperately trying to make sense of his ordeal in retrospect. She tells him (Fowles 1983: 627–628; see also p. 294 regarding the 'equivalence' of truth and lie in Conchis's world):

> 'Nicholas, if one is trying to reproduce, however partially, something of the mysterious purposes that govern existence, then one also has to go beyond some of the conventions man has invented to keep those purposes at bay. That doesn't mean that in our ordinary lives we think such conventions should be swept away. Far from it. They are necessary fictions. But ... we start from the premise that in reality all is fiction, yet no single fiction is necessary.' ...
>
> 'The basic principle of life is hazard. Maurice [Conchis] tells me that this is no longer even a matter of debate. If one goes deep enough in atomic physics one ends with a situation of pure chance. Of course we all share the illusion that this can't be so.'

The first thing that strikes one about this is its resonance with Lacan's (2007: 23, 33–34) contention, that knowledge or science corresponds to the discourse of the hysteric, which proceeds by relentless questioning, and not – as one might expect – with that of the university (underpinned by a commitment to 'complete', systematic knowledge of what is). The upshot of this is that the discourse of the hysteric is predicated on the structural impossibility of a 'complete' system of knowledge, no matter what the discipline. Interestingly, Foucault (1972: 222–224), too, argues that disciplines are characterized by a paradoxical tension between their vaunted open-endedness (in the sense that something novel or fresh can always be added to them, adding to their growth), on the one hand, and the fact that at any given stage in their development, only a limited number of statements or hypotheses can be accommodated by them – as his example of the work of Mendel, which could not be accommodated in biology when it first appeared, demonstrates: Mendel was not (yet) 'within the true'. This is not where the correspondence between Lacan, Fowles and Foucault on this question ends, either. What Foucault says in *The discourse on language* (1972: 216) on the function of discourse in society is uncannily close to Lily de Seitas's words, quoted above, on conventions being 'necessary fictions' that 'keep those [existence-governing] purposes at bay'. Foucault intimates that the function of the principles governing the generation of discourse – and I believe this statement is consonant with Lacan's theory of the four discourses – is primarily to provide a medium for 'controlling' it, lest society fall apart:

> I am supposing that in every society the production of discourse is at once controlled, selected, organised and redistributed according to a certain number of procedures, whose role is to avert its powers and its dangers, to cope with chance events, to evade its ponderous, awesome materiality.

In other words, for Foucault as for Lacan (and one could add the names of other poststructuralist thinkers such as Derrida, Kristeva and Deleuze), the ideal of an encompassing, all-inclusive, *coherent* system of knowledge, is an illusion – or, in other words, it is paranoiac.

Derrida's (1978: 285) deconstructive reading of Lévi-Strauss's distinction between the *bricoleur* (tinkerer) and the engineer is a particularly striking example of this, while simultaneously exemplifying the paradoxical or aporetic logic of poststructuralist thinking. On the one hand, he points out, the concept of the *bricoleur* signifies someone who always uses 'the means at hand' (no matter how adequate or inadequate it may be) to construct what is needed, while, on the other, the 'engineer' represents the person who constructs 'the totality of his language' – a formulation that strikingly reminds one of what Lacan calls the 'paranoiac structure' of human knowledge, that is, an epistemic totality or all-inclusive system. Derrida hastens to point out, however, that this conception of someone who is the origin of his or her own discourse is a myth (and probably one produced by the *bricoleur*). Most importantly, however, he insists that humans cannot stop believing in such an 'engineer', because as soon as they do, the very distinction between the *bricoleur* – who always, inevitably, has to avail him- or herself of the available historical discourse(s) – and its opposite, the engineer – who stands for a discourse which starts afresh, with precise, clear rules and instruments of exactitude – breaks down, and the meanings of the two opposing concepts collapse. In other words, for Derrida as for Lacan, we cannot ever choose definitively between the paradigm of 'absolute', certain knowledge (the engineer, the discourse of the university) and the epistemic paradigm of always already 'ruined' or 'uncertain' knowledge (the *bricoleur*, the discourse of the hysteric). We have to learn to negotiate the difficult terrain constituted by their difference. Clearly, Fowles's position in *The magus* is consonant with this one.

What about the smile? The smile functions as the image of a kind of paradoxical Socratic *docta ignorantia* (as metaphor of what has been argued above): an 'I know that I do not know', captured in Lily de Seitas's remark (quoted above), that, although it is beyond debate that life is governed by the principle of hazard (chance, risk, danger, uncertainty), 'we all share the illusion that this can't be so'. That is as much as reiterating Lacan's claim concerning the paranoiac structure of human knowledge: regardless of its semblance of systematicity (Derrida's 'engineer') and the repeated attempts to ground such knowledge 'empirically', human systems of knowledge are vitiated by their mostly unacknowledged subjection to the principle of hazard or chance (Lacan's discourse of the hysteric; Derrida's '*bricoleur*'). And yet, we cannot do without this illusion – like Nicholas in the novel, every human being has to act on the basis of presumed knowledge, and further, in the course of our quest for knowledge, as if every discovery of the illusory nature of an explanation or account of knowledge points forward to a better, alternative explanation. In this way human beings move the epistemic, cognitive goalposts every time, in the ineluctable (but illusory) belief that, sooner or later, we shall discover the 'true state of affairs'. Hence, the smile signifies, metaphorically, the knowledge and acceptance of hazard as the inescapable law of life, accompanied by the reflective knowledge of this knowledge – hence Nicholas's feeling that the smile signifies 'privileged information' (Fowles 1983: 147).

My argument here is that, in the light of what has been shown, Fowles's *The magus* may be understood as offering the reader a sustained narrative account, consonant with that of Lacan, of the paranoiac or illusory structure of human knowledge (with Nicholas in the role of the exemplary human subject), on the one hand, but also, on the other, a way of negotiating this ostensibly hopeless state of affairs in such a manner that it would induce a paradoxical smile of 'informed ignorance'. This smile, I would further contend, is a metaphor for the manner in which

Lacan's discourse of the hysteric and that of the analyst function together with the other two discourses, those of the master and the university (just as Derrida's paradigmatic figures of the *bricoleur* and the engineer cannot function on their own). To be sure, from one situation to the next, Fowles emphasizes different aspects of the smile. When Conchis shows Nicholas the ancient, sculpted head with its enigmatic smile, it will be remembered, its embodiment of good humour is highlighted; by contrast, where Conchis tells Nicholas that he should 'learn to smile' (referred to earlier), it is noteworthy that something different from good humour is foregrounded (Fowles 1983: 531):

> It came to me that he meant something different by 'smile' than I did; that the irony, the humourlessness, the ruthlessness I had always noticed in his smiling was a quality he deliberately inserted; that for him the smile was something essentially cruel, because freedom is cruel, because the freedom that makes us at least partly responsible for what we are is cruel. So that the smile was not so much an *attitude* to be taken to life as the *nature* of the cruelty of life, a cruelty we cannot even choose to avoid, since it is human existence.

What at first sight may seem like a blatant contradiction in the text, starts making sense when it is kept in mind, firstly, that all signifiers – including iconic ones such as a smile on a person's face – are ineluctably multivocal. We cannot get away from the fact that what may appear to be 'one and the same' signifier generates a different meaning in a new context – in accordance with the one movement of what Derrida (1982: 7–9; see also Olivier 2005b) calls *différance*, namely *spacing* or the endless, 'aneconomic' deferral of meaning (as opposed to its counter-movement, namely *temporization*, or the 'economic', temporary stabilization of meaning) – and it is understandable that the two different contexts involved here would generate very different meanings of 'the smile'. In the first, relatively early in the narrative, Nicholas was Conchis's guest, and was being regaled and impressed by every new piece of information about the older man's world that Conchis could conjure up; hence the predominant impression of good humour projected by the smile on the sculpted face. By the time Conchis accosts the shackled Nicholas, he has been through an ordeal he could not imagine before; hence the impression of cruelty.

What exactly does Fowles mean by 'cruelty'? By equating it with 'human existence' here he gives one an important clue, which resonates with the interpretation that has been given of Lacan's puzzling claim concerning the 'paranoiac structure of human knowledge', specifically that human aspirations to 'timeless' systems of knowledge betray a desire for the kind of knowledge that would overcome, once and for all, the inescapable imprint of time on human knowledge, as conveyed in the relentless questioning of the master's and the university's discourses by that of the hysteric. Such questioning signifies human finitude (including suffering) and fallibility, and it seems clear that this is what the 'cruelty' detected by Nicholas in Conchis's smile intimates as well: the unmitigated contingency of human existence is characterized by the impossibility to avoid suffering of some kind, even if it is true that it usually affords the individual his or her share of joy and pleasure as well.

A brief Nietzschean digression – which would simultaneously demonstrate the compatibility between Nietzsche, Lacan and Fowles – would clarify what is at stake here. Just how close the latter two thinkers are to the German, is evident from Nietzsche's elaboration, in *Beyond good and evil* (1966: 35), on the 'will to knowledge' as being underpinned by a more profound 'will to ignorance' – a phrase that resonates with Lacan's notion of the 'paranoiac' structure of human knowledge, and with Fowles's contention, in *The magus*, that 'in reality all is fiction' (even if humans cannot do without such fictions, whether in the shape of conventional beliefs or scientific theories). But secondly, regarding the interpretation of the 'cruelty' signified by Conchis's smile (suggested above), namely, that it signifies the utter finitude and contingency of human life, which one has to learn to accept, it is instructive to note that Nietzsche establishes what is arguably an ethical connection (see Olivier 2007 for an elaboration on this question) between the so-called 'eternal recurrence' and human finitude by way of what he calls the 'spirit of revenge'.

One could say that, for Nietzsche, by affirming the contingent or chance events which inevitably occur in one's life, one simultaneously affirms or activates the 'eternal recurrence', in so far as *chance* events are, in this way, tied into the circle of *necessity*, of the 'eternal recurrence'. Ethically, the latter doctrine implies the exhortation to do the 'impossible', namely to affirm one's life as something that one 'wills' to recur 'eternally', regardless of the amount of joy or suffering experienced by the person in question. And those rare individuals who are capable of such unconditional acceptance of their *finitude* (their inability to reverse what has happened once), and therefore of their *mortality*, in this way succeed in overcoming what Nietzsche, in the persona of Zarathustra (1984: 252) calls the 'spirit of revenge': '... the will's ill will against time and its "it was"'. Such individuals would also attain 'singularity' in so far as acceptance of the finitude or (in Fowles's idiom) 'cruelty' of human life is linked with the affirmation of the unique, albeit contingent actions performed by an individual, in this way imparting a certain 'necessity' to them (see Olivier 2007 for a thoroughgoing examination of this problematic in Nietzsche's work). It is precisely such an affirmation of the 'cruelty' of life – signified by the ability to smile – that Conchis asks Nicholas to perform in *The magus*. The ability to smile would signify one's affirmation that 'freedom is cruel', and the fact that Fowles links this to one's responsibility (in the above excerpt), confirms the correspondence between Fowles's and Nietzsche's (and Lacan's) positions regarding human finitude: freedom is 'cruel' because, tied as it is to contingent situations in which one has to make decisions in the absence of anything or anyone else who could take responsibility for our decisions, each human being bears the *terrible* burden of responsibility for the consequences of her or his choices and decisions. This is why Sartre (1956: 567) says: '... I am condemned to be free'.

To conclude, it seems to me that Fowles provides a degree of corroboration of the interpretation put forward here, which aligns his position in *The magus* with Lacan's notion, that human knowledge exhibits a paranoiac, or illusory (if not delusional) structure, but one that may nevertheless be negotiated in a paradoxical fashion. This entails 'unlearning' one's perhaps naïve attachment to conventional beliefs (instances of the master's discourse), as well as overcoming a superior attitude, born of a degree of 'higher learning', like Nicholas's at Oxford (the university's discourse), in the place of which one learns to 'smile' in the face of one's fallibility and the concomitant realization that one has to negotiate, or alternate between relentless questioning of conventional morality (the hysteric's discourse) and revisable beliefs in the necessity of (questionable) convention, without which no one could live (as shown by the analyst's discourse, represented by Conchis and Lily de Seitas). In the Foreword to the revised edition of *The magus* (1983: 10) Fowles remarks apropos of the novel:

> If there was some central scheme beneath the (more Irish than Greek) stew of intuitions about the nature of human existence – and of fiction – it lies perhaps in the alternative title, whose rejection I still sometimes regret: *The Godgame*. I did intend Conchis to exhibit a series of masks representing human notions of God, from the supernatural to the jargon-ridden scientific; that is, a series of human illusions about something that does not exist in fact, absolute knowledge and absolute power. The destruction of such illusions seems to me still an eminently humanist aim; and I wish there were some super-Conchis who could put the Arabs and the Israelis ... through the same heuristic mill as Nicholas.

Compare this excerpt from Fowles's reflection on *The magus* with Lacan's observation, in *The other side of psychoanalysis* (2007: 23), that '... the desire to know is not what leads to knowledge. What leads to knowledge is ... the hysteric's discourse'. From what was said earlier about the hysteric's discourse it should be apparent that it represents those discursive practices which are structurally characterized by relentless questioning, from within, of the (illusory) claims and aspirations regarding the systematic completeness, or encompassing, of the realm of the knowable on the part of the master's as well as the university's discourse. It is not difficult to discern here, too, a 'destruction of ... illusions' comparable to those thematized by Fowles in *The magus*. And, in my judgment, to disabuse human beings of their illusions, in the place of which a practice of coping with the difficulty and complexity of life is encouraged, can in the final analysis only be a way of promoting psychic health.

Needless to stress, the upshot of this article is the insight that both Fowles and Lacan are ambivalently located in the Enlightenment tradition of largely rationalist-scientific western thought – neither is prepared to throw the baby of knowledge out with the bathwater of rationalist illusions; hence their respective complexifications or problematizations of knowledge, or more broadly, of human existence. The radicality of this mode of thinking should not be overlooked, in the erroneous belief that radicality requires resolute 'opposition' to conventional ways of thinking – in this case, sticking to one's charge (derived from Lacan), that human knowledge is 'paranoiac' in structure. This would simply be to collapse into the paralysis of binary thinking once again, instead of which Lacan and Fowles (together with other poststructuralist thinkers like Derrida, Lyotard, Foucault and Kristeva) introduce a truly revolutionary way of thinking opposites together in an aporetic manner, which preserves the irreducibility of each member of the opposition, in this way acknowledging the inescapable complexity of life. In the face of Hegel's optimistic belief in the possibility of conclusive, consummate *Bildung*, Lyotard (1992: 1, 8–16) counters with the 'experimental' (*not* pessimistic) spirit of the *avant-garde*.

In retrospect, therefore, the structure of knowledge *in a complexified sense* turns out to be not quite paranoiac – as the conceit on the part of the university's discourse would suggest, taken by itself – but instead paradoxical or aporetic: we know *and* we don't know; that which provides (illusions of certain) knowledge fulfils an epistemic function for a limited time, until the hysteric's persistent interrogations point in the direction of possible revisions, open-endedness and alternative understanding or explanations. To learn this, constitutes a kind of counter-*Bildung* on the part of the person fortunate enough to be disabused of the illusions keeping the vast majority of people captive, one that inculcates a radical humility in the face of inescapable epistemic finitude and the 'cruelty' of existence – a humility accompanied by the smile of 'learned ignorance'.

References

Bracher, M. 1994. 'On the psychological and social functions of language: Lacan's theory of the four discourses'. In: Bracher, M., Alcorn Jr, M.W., *et al. Lacanian theory of discourse. Subject, structure and society*. New York: New York University Press, pp. 107–128.

Chalmers, A.F. 1982. *What is this thing called science? An assessment of the nature and status of science and its methods*. 2nd edn. Milton Keynes: The Open University Press.

Deleuze, G., & Guattari, F. 1994. *What is philosophy*? Trans. Burchell, G. & Tomlinson, H. London: Verso.

Descartes, R. 1972. 'Meditations on first philosophy'. In: *The philosophical works of Descartes*, Vol. I, pp. 144–199. Trans. Haldane, E.S. & Ross, G.R.T. Cambridge: Cambridge University Press.

Derrida, J. 1978. 'Structure, sign, and play in the discourse of the human sciences'. In: *Writing and difference*. Trans. Bass, A. Chicago: The University of Chicago Press, pp. 278–293.

Derrida, J. 1982. '*Différance*'. In: *Margins of philosophy*. Trans. Bass, A. Chicago, University of Chicago Press, pp. 1–27.

Dickens, C. 1993. *Great expectations*. Ed. Cardwell, M. Oxford: Clarendon Press.

Fink, B. 1997. *The Lacanian subject. Between language and* jouissance. Princeton: Princeton University Press.

Foucault, M. 1972. The discourse on language. In: *The archaeology of knowledge*. Trans. Smith, A.M.S. New York: Pantheon Books, pp. 215–237.

Fowles, J. 1983. *The magus. A revised version*. London: Triad/Panther Books.

Gadamer, H.-G. 1982. *Truth and method*. Trans. and ed. Barden, G. & Cumming, J. New York: Crossroad.

Hegel, G.W.F. 1966. *The phenomenology of mind*. 2nd edn. Trans. Baillie, J.B. New York: Humanities Press Inc.

Hurst, A. 2004. *The sciences, the humanities, research and hermeneutics*. Port Elizabeth: PE Technikon.

Hurst, A. 2006. *Derrida or Lacan: The revolutionary's choice. On the 'plural logic of the* aporia*' in deconstruction and Lacanian psychoanalysis.* PhD dissertation, Villanova University, Pennsylvania, USA. Published by ProQuest. This has since been republished, in enlarged form, as Hurst, A. 2008. *Derrida* vis-á-vis *Lacan. Interweaving deconstruction and psychoanalysis.* New York: Fordham University Press.
Kant, I. 1964. *Critique of pure reason.* Trans. Meiklejohn, J.M.D. New York: Dutton.
Lacan, J. 1977. 'Aggressivity in psychoanalysis'. In: *Écrits: A selection.* Trans. Sheridan, A. New York: W.W. Norton & Co., pp. 8–29.
Lacan, J. 1977a. 'The mirror stage as formative of the function of the I as revealed in psychoanalytic experience'. In: *Écrits: A selection.* Trans. Sheridan, A. New York: W.W. Norton & Co., pp. 1–7.
Lacan, J. 1977b. 'The function and field of speech and language in psychoanalysis'. In: *Écrits: A selection.* Trans. Sheridan, A. New York: W.W. Norton & Co., pp. 30–113.
Lacan, J. 1997. *The ethics of psychoanalysis; 1959–1960. The seminar of Jacques Lacan, Book VII.* Trans. Porter, D. New York: W.W. Norton & Co.
Lacan, J. 2007. *The other side of psychoanalysis; 1969–1970. The seminar of Jacques Lacan, Book 17.* Trans. Grigg, R. New York: W.W. Norton & Co.
Lee, J.S. 1990. *Jacques Lacan.* Amherst: The University of Massachusetts Press.
Lyotard, J.-F. 1992. 'An answer to the question, what is the postmodern?' In: *The postmodern explained.* Trans. and ed. Pefanis, J. & Thomas, M. Minneapolis: University of Minnesota Press, pp. 1–16.
Nietzsche, F. 1966. *Beyond good and evil. Prelude to a philosophy of the future.* Trans. Kaufmann, W. New York: Vintage Books.
Nietzsche, F. 1984. *Thus spoke Zarathustra.* In: *The portable Nietzsche.* Trans. & ed. Kaufmann, W. New York: Penguin Books, pp. 103–439.
Olivier, B. 2004. 'Lacan's subject: the imaginary, language, the real and philosophy'. *South African Journal of Philosophy*, 23 (1), pp. 1–19.

Olivier, B. 2005. 'Lacan and the question of the psychotherapist's ethical orientation'. *SA Journal of Psychology* 35 (4), pp. 657–683. Reprinted here, as Chapter 3 of this volume.

Olivier, B. 2005a. 'Lacan and narrative identity: *The Piano Teacher*'. In: *Word, (wo)man, world: Essays on literature. Festschrift* for Ina Gräbe. Oliphant, A.W. & Roos, H. (eds). Pretoria: UNISA Press, pp. 94–112. Reprinted here, as Chapter 2 of this volume.

Olivier, B. 2005b. 'The contemporary context of relativity and relativism'. *Acta Academica Supplementum*, (2) (Special edition on *Relativity and relativism*), pp. 73–104. Reprinted here, as Chapter 4 of this volume.

Olivier, B. 2006. 'Popular art, the image, the subject and subverting hegemony'. *Communicatio (South African Journal for Communication Theory and Research)*, Vol. 32 (1), pp. 16–37.

Olivier, B. 2007. 'Nietzsche, immortality, singularity and eternal recurrence'. *South African Journal of Philosophy*, 26 (1) (Special edition on Nietzsche.), pp. 70–84.

Sartre, J.-P. 1956. *Being and nothingness. A phenomenological essay on ontology*. Trans. Barnes, H.E. New York: Pocket Books.

Schopenhauer, A. 1969. *The world as will and representation*, Vol. I. Trans. Payne, E.F.J. New York: Dover Publications.

CHAPTER 8

Trauma and literature: Derrida, *9/11* and Hart's *The reconstructionist*

Jack Harrington, a psychiatrist, has an uncommonly beautiful, but evidently unhappy, sister, Kate. From time to time she requires of him to help her, lest she 'sink', or 'fall'. Sometimes this assistance assumes the form of a ritual, initially resisted by him when she sets it in motion, where they dance together in a quasi-formal manner, naked, with their clothes neatly folded on a chair, to music that only they can hear. And always, always, Jack has to be alert to the minutest signal that Kate is about to disintegrate. As the story unfurls its various layers, one realizes that, lurking somewhere in their shared memories, but with more lethal gravity for her than for him, there is some unspeakable thing, some trauma, which has ruptured the psychic canopy of their lives, for her perhaps in an irreparable way. Nevertheless, when the need arises, he 'repairs', or 'reconstructs', it as best he can with the means at his disposal, which are, largely, linguistic – Freud's 'talking cure' – in conjunction with other symbolic, signifying acts.

Jack is divorced, as is Kate, but marriage has been proposed to her by a very wealthy member of the London upper class and a civilized, intelligent and understanding man into the bargain, someone who just might be able, at last, to give her the symbolic protection she so desperately needs, and that Jack has always provided in her life. But then he is compelled to return to the family house (aptly named *Malamore*) in Ireland where he and Kate grew up together, and in retrospect the terrible circumstances of the traumatic event that interrupted their childhood re-emerge piece by piece. The question then obtrudes itself irresistibly, namely, what should be done about the house to ensure Kate's psychic survival. When the reader of the tale that I have briefly reconstructed here, finally discovers (near the end of the narrative) what this 'event' was, it is fully evident, for the first time, *why* Jack is, or has had to be, the eponymous 'reconstructionist' of the narrative. It also drives home to the reader that the narrative of Josephine Hart's novel, *The reconstructionist* (2002), crucially revolves around, or turns on, a specific trauma. To put it differently, 'trauma' turns out to be the central literary, intra-textual, narratological category in terms of which the narrative thread spins itself out in this novel. However, I suspect that *The reconstructionist* is but one of many literary works where 'trauma' occupies such a central place as an intra-textual generative principle regarding the dynamics of the narrative. This 'suspicion' is what I want to focus on here: if it can be shown that it occupies an indispensable structural and hermeneutic position in *The reconstructionist*, is it the case that 'trauma' is an important, even constitutive, category for understanding the unfolding of at least some important literary (and cinematic) narratives – and not merely contingently, but structurally, given the very nature of trauma? What is this 'nature', and why are such narratives important for literary and psychoanalytic theory?

To most English-speaking people the word 'trauma' is no stranger, especially if one happens to live in a country riddled with random, unpredictable instances of violent criminal activity.[1] It is probably safe to say that in common parlance the term is associated with something which disrupts one's life so severely that it is difficult, if not impossible, to 'pull oneself together' any time soon after the traumatic, traumatizing event (or 'come to terms with it'), such as a car hijacking, a robbery or mugging, an assault, a rape, and so on. It is not only violent crime that inflicts trauma, however – a car accident or a mountain-climbing mishap that ends in severe injury or death, and even the life-disrupting insolvency of a family, may be equally 'traumatic', and it takes time for individuals concerned to recover from its devastating effects. But beyond the everyday understanding of 'trauma' there is a more 'technical' theoretical concep-

1 See in this regard Olivier 2007a and 2007b, for a psychoanalytical interpretation of the excessively brutal violence in South Africa, partly in terms of trauma.

tion of it, encountered in psychology and psychoanalysis, among other disciplines. If I am right in surmising that what I have described above as a common understanding of such disastrous occurrences is more or less correct, it seems to me that it might be compatible with the more conceptually refined understanding of it, even if one could not directly infer, from the everyday conception, what the theoretically sophisticated version of 'trauma' entails. In other words, from the perspective of the theoretically refined account of 'trauma', the commonsensical notion seems intuitively right, but the inverse is not the case; from the perspective of the latter, the complexities uncovered by the former would not be immediately, or necessarily, apparent.

I make this distinction because of the assault, of late, on all kinds of theory by the representatives of so-called 'post-theory' – a current, everyday knowledge-oriented version of what was earlier referred to as 'positivism' (broadly, the belief that the true objects of knowledge are 'facts', without considering that a 'fact' may be described as 'an agreed-upon interpretation'). Against this I want to argue that 'theory' in all its variants is indispensable if one desires to come to an understanding of phenomena that not only surpasses the relative vagueness and multivocality of vernacular appropriations, but succeeds in articulating the distinctiveness of such phenomena within the conceptual context of specific disciplines – something that imparts to it a systematic coherence and a phenomenal clarity and distinctiveness it would otherwise lack, and in so doing allows it to function in a heuristic and hermeneutically fruitful and generative manner. A theory is like a metaphoric lens through which something becomes apparent that would otherwise have remained 'invisible'. To be sure, it is not difficult to agree with Žižek (2001: 4–5) that post-theory serves the valuable function of pulling theorists up short, as it were, in the face of the temptation to surrender to the ostensibly useful but ultimately obfuscating role of jargon (theory's 'jargonistic imitation'), reminding them that theory has to illuminate, or flesh out, for example, the character of literature, or of communication, in the process engaging with certain social or cultural phenomena, practices or artifacts. Far from having outlived its usefulness and epistemic value, therefore, as 'post-theory' would have us believe through its rather comical reduction of theoretical work to no more than a caricature (Žižek 2001: 4), 'theory' is still as indispensable as ever. Žižek (2001: 9) articulates this by means of the distinction between talking *about* something and actually *doing* it:

> ... in philosophy, it is one thing to talk about, to report on, say, the history of the notion of the subject (accompanied by all the proper bibliographical footnotes), even to supplement it with comparative critical remarks; it is quite another thing to work in theory, to elaborate the notion of 'subject' itself.

With this in mind, what I want to do here is to 'elaborate' or 'work' in the domain of the theory of literature, and – to borrow yet another expression from Žižek *a propos* of the cinematic art of Kieslowski (2001: 9) – I would like to 'refer to' Hart's novel, *The reconstructionist* (2002), 'in order to accomplish the work of theory' as far as the concept of 'trauma' is concerned, specifically in an intra-textual (and possibly inter-textual) narratological, but in the main not in an extra-textual sense.[2] (I use 'textual' in the narrower meaning of the word here, rather than the encompassing sense that would make of the whole of social life, as well as of nature, the 'text' of the world, according to which every interpretable constellation of signifiers, from the ecology of a tidal pool to an esoteric religious book, would comprise a fragment of the 'textual' totality). Whenever one embarks on such a theoretical enterprise, which is, like a journey by ship, fraught with risk, Gadamer's (1982: 111) account of the etymology of the word, which derives from the ancient Greek *theoros*, meaning a spectator at the performance of a drama (a comedy or a tragedy), is a

2 Regarding the matter of trauma as an intra- and possibly inter-textual category, what I intend doing here is not the same as what was done in Miki Flockemann's essay (2004) on the question of what happens when 'traumatic experiences' are 'translated' into a cultural form such as literature. Her work in this article focuses on questions surrounding the 'fictionalisation' of 'actual' (or 'historical') traumatic experiences (which belong in the category of what I refer to, above, as the 'extra-textual'), such as those instances of violence to which people were frequently subjected during the apartheid era. My own project, by contrast, is an exploration, chiefly, of the intra-textual narrative function of trauma – something that may well prove to have intertextual and extra-textual implications (although this is not my main concern at present).

salutary reminder that theory has never been (or rather, should never be) a frivolous undertaking. The *theoros* who attended the performance of a comedy or tragedy was indeed an onlooker – to this extent the word 'theory' accurately captures the 'distance' between the spectator and the events which unfold on the stage. But 'distance' here does not mean an unbridgeable chasm. On the contrary: by beholding the dramatic action on the stage, the *theoros* participated or shared in the action which, by implication, represented a cosmic order of which he or she formed a part. The 'distance' was therefore a prerequisite for understanding one's own relation to fundamental cosmic, sometimes putatively divine, laws. Hence, 'theory', which sometimes may seem abstruse and distant from the density of the quotidian – so distant that 'post-theorists' reject its legitimate epistemic and ontological function – requires precisely such distance to be able to cast phenomena, experiences, events or artifacts in a new and revealing light. In this respect 'theories' are like extended metaphors, or 'transfer points', where the familiarity of everyday experience is suspended by way of a de-familiarizing peeling away that brings different textures and colours to the surface. These remarks about theory are by no means irrelevant, given the present theme; they go to the heart of the kind of theoretical work I engage on here. With this in mind, I turn to Derrida and Lacan's philosophical-theoretical understanding of 'trauma'.

Jacques Derrida's (2003) perceptive deconstructive interpretation of the 'event' of *September 11* renders, among other things,[3] a theoretical account of the phenomenon of 'trauma', as I shall attempt to show.

3 Among the other things that Derrida does here, is his persuasive demonstration that he is no mere, solipsistic 'textualist' who lacks the theoretical means to escape from the carceral confines of language or the text – something that some scholars still do not seem to understand (see Butler 2002: 16–21; Terblanche 2004), despite many available arguments to the contrary, from Derrida himself as well as from others (see Caputo 1997; Hurst 2004; 2006). Instead he shows that he is able, no less than Lacan, to account for the pivotal function of what passes by the name of the 'real' in Lacan's theory of the subject – that which cannot be assimilated into language or the symbolic register, or which, according to Copjec's (2002: 95–96) formulation, constitutes the 'internal limit' of language itself, the fact that language can only, endlessly, refer to itself, even or especially when 'something' unforeseen or

Purist psychoanalytical scholars may disagree, but any open-minded theorist would discern the correspondence between Derrida's conception of trauma and Lacan's, both discussed below. (I should stress that I focus here on specific elaborations of the concept of trauma in these thinkers' work; I do not claim to give an exhaustive overview of differently nuanced accounts in their or any other psychoanalytical theorist's work.) Moreover, if anyone would object that *9/11* does not qualify as an event that could be considered from the perspective of trauma, because psychoanalysis is concerned solely with 'psychic' trauma (that is, in terms of repressed materials at the level of the unconscious, which manifest themselves symptomatically), the obvious response is that *9/11* may be regarded as precisely representing psychic trauma at an individual as well as collective level – this is borne out by Derrida's analysis, reconstructed below.

The quasi-transcendental logic[4] of Derrida's thinking is immediately apparent in his analysis of the 'event' of *9/11* at various levels, not least of which is that of the very notion of it being a 'major event'.[5] Furthermore, Derrida (2003: 86–94) does not hesitate to problematize this notion mercilessly. He concedes that it is 'at least *felt*', with ostensible immediacy, to be an event of an 'unprecedented' kind, but questions the authenticity of such a feeling of immediacy, pointing out that (2003: 86):

---

apparently incomprehensible – such as *9/11* – which does not readily find a place in extant language, has happened.

4 On this, see Andrea Hurst's (2004) exemplary exposition, including a discussion of a number of telling instantiations – such as the gift and justice – of this quasi-transcendental pattern of Derrida's thinking.

5 The concept of the 'event' signals one of the Heideggerian roots of deconstruction, as Derrida acknowledges in the Borradori interview. As he points out (2003: 90), Heidegger's notion of *Ereignis* ('event'), which bears on the '… *appropriation* of the proper (*eigen*)', is inseparable from the countervailing movement of '… a certain *expropriation* that Heidegger himself names (*Enteignis*)'. He elaborates (2003: 90): 'The undergoing of the event, that which in the undergoing or in the ordeal *at once opens itself up to and resists experience*, is, it seems to me, a certain *unappropriability* of what comes or happens'. This is essential for Derrida's understanding of the 'event', as will become clearer in what follows here. See in this regard also Olivier 2007.

> ... this 'feeling' is actually less spontaneous than it appears: it is to a large extent conditioned, constituted, if not actually constructed, circulated at any rate through the media by means of a prodigious techno-socio-political machine.

The fact that one does not 'yet really know how to identify' this event would perhaps explain why the 'minimal deictic' of the date is resorted to as a way of naming this ineffaceable, (but also ineffable – 'like an intuition without concept') 'thing' that has occurred (2003: 86). Besides, describing it as an act of 'international terrorism' is hardly what one might call a 'rigorous concept' that would capture the utter 'singularity' of what has happened. The powerlessness of language to assign this event a horizon of signification, Derrida insists (2003: 86), shows itself in the 'mechanical repetition' of the date – an observation which marks his canny interpretive use of psychoanalytic theory. The conspicuous similarity of Derrida's remark (concerning the 'impotence' of language when faced with the singularity of *September 11*) to Jacques Lacan's claim, that the register of the so-called 'real' announces itself precisely there, where language comes up 'against its own limits', can hardly be ignored.[6] He emphasizes the pertinence of this psychoanalytical insight when he elaborates on the necessity of repeating the date like a mantra (Derrida 2003: 87):

> ... on the one hand, to conjure away, as if by magic, the 'thing' itself, the fear or the terror it inspires (for repetition always protects by neutralizing, deadening, distancing a traumatism, and this is true for the repetition of the televised images we will speak of later), and, on the other hand, to deny, as close as possible to this act of language and this enunciation, our powerlessness to name in an appropriate

6 Joan Copjec explains Lacan's notion of the 'real' as follows – effectively precluding the temptation to equate it with the Kantian *Ding-an-sich* (2002: 95–96):

> Lacan's definition of the real is precisely this: that which, in language or the symbolic, negates the possibility of any metadimension, any metalanguage. It is this undislodgeable negation, this rigid kernel in the heart of the symbolic, that forces the signifier to split off from and turn around on itself. For, in the absence of any metalanguage, the signifier can only signify by referring to another signifier ... Far from positing the existence of an elsewhere, the real as internal limit of the symbolic – that is, the very impotence of the signifier – is the obstacle that scotches the possibility of rising out of or above the symbolic.

> fashion, to characterize, to think the thing in question, to get beyond the mere deictic of the date: something terrible took place on September 11, and in the end we don't know what.

What Derrida here refers to as a 'traumatism' is central to the thesis I want to put forward here concerning Hart's *The reconstructionist*, and other narratives like it. In the face of all the conspicuous repetitions of the 'event' responsible for the trauma or 'traumatism', in various guises – as image-sequences on television, in the form of discussions and analyses in the media, in academic articles and books – one has no option but to admit that the degree to which what he calls the 'thing' that has happened, eludes one's grasp, is proportional to the amount of linguistic, communicational and informational attention paid to it. After all, one should not delude oneself that reason in the guise of clear, distinct conceptual language is adequate to grasp what happened that day. In effect, Derrida is reminding latter-day rationalists like Habermas[7] that, what is known in psychoanalysis as the 'repetition compulsion' (which he explicitly names later in the interview), has precisely the function to make the unbearable bearable, *but* at the cost of falsifying the 'thing' that has inflicted the trauma, which one tries repeatedly to pin down, to nail, in language and image-replay. For no matter how apparently efficaciously one succeeds in inscribing it in the symbolic fabric or dominant discourses of the time – and even if one articulates it in terms of esoteric ones – or how familiar the sequence of images depicting the mesmerizing implosion of the twin towers, one after the other, may have become, the 'event itself' will always prove to be elusive. The function of the repetition is precisely to weave a web of iconic and symbolic familiarity around the 'event' constituting the trauma, within which it will be (and has to a large extent already been) archived 'historically' (where one should remember that there is not only one account of historical events). But in so far as it has the status of the 'real' of psychoanalysis, it escapes one the moment you think you have managed to 'name' or capture it. It is important to note, however, that

7 Habermas (2003) also features (via an interview) in the book where Derrida's piece on *9/11* appears in the form of an interview with Giovanna Borradori.

this does not mean one should avoid articulating it in language as best one can – on the contrary, as Derrida emphasizes (2003: 87–88):

> I believe always in the necessity of being attentive first of all to this phenomenon of language, naming, and dating, to this repetition compulsion (at once rhetorical, magical, and poetic). To what this compulsion signifies, translates, or betrays. Not in order to isolate ourselves in language, as people in too much of a rush would like us to believe, but on the contrary, in order to try to understand what is going on precisely *beyond* language and what is pushing us to repeat endlessly and without knowing what we are talking about, precisely there where language and the concept come up against their limits: 'September 11, September 11, *le 11 septembre, 9/11*'.[8]

8 Here, again, it is clear that Derrida's remark is perfectly consonant with Lacan's articulation of the register of 'the impossible real'. Moreover, for those scholars referred to earlier (in note 3), who still labour under the misapprehension that Derrida does not acknowledge anything '*beyond*' language – no matter how difficult it may be to invoke, suggest, hint at or allude to it – his analysis of *9/11* should remove all doubt that he does in fact affirm such a dimension. Andrea Hurst (2006, especially chapters 2 and 6) has argued persuasively that Derrida's notion of *différance* is here the equivalent of Lacan's notion of the 'real'. One should perhaps recognize how easy it is to fall into the trap of erroneously attributing to Derrida the status of a neo-idealist in 'textual' terms, or to give the impression that one does this, through hasty or non-nuanced formulations – I recall a time when I gave an interlocutor, friend and fellow-scholar, Marius Scholtz (who argued strenuously, and accurately, in favour of the position that Derrida's work testifies to a recognition of something 'beyond' the text), the unfortunate impression that I was making exactly that mistake through careless formulation on my part. A major reason why so many people still overlook the implications of Derrida's complex interweaving of traditional binary motifs into an aporetic logic that surpasses it, is the fact that many scholars do not read Derrida's own texts thoroughly and patiently, easily opting for one of the abundant, but mostly misleading commentaries on his work. Even Richard Rorty, who welcomes the 'playful' side of Derrida while lamenting the supposedly persistent 'metaphysical' side to his work, gets it wrong, precisely because he reduces the French thinker's work to a binarism (see in this regard Hurst 2004 for a thorough debunking of Rorty's well-meaning, but misguided appropriation of Derrida). It is by no means easy to say exactly *how* Derrida gets beyond binary thinking, however. In addition to Hurst's texts mentioned above, one of the works

As I shall attempt to show in the case of Hart's *The reconstructionist*, the inescapable need to inscribe a traumatic event in language (no matter how inadequately or provisionally), to 'reconstruct' it time and time again, repeatedly, is at the heart of coming to terms with it – not to *reduce* it to language and iconicity, believing in the end that is all there is to it, but precisely because something that resists the symbolic weave of language, that cannot be assimilated to it, nevertheless has effects in language, and on the bodies of living human beings. Articulating it in as many symbolic frameworks and contexts as possible, elaborating on it in the precise sense of 'working on and through' it, ravelling and unravelling it, is all one *has* to try and understand, and perhaps, eventually, come to terms with it. After all, as Gadamer says (1982: 432): 'Being that can be understood is language'. This leaves open the question of that which surpasses language, and what its relation to language, intelligibility and reason is. As mentioned earlier, for Lacan this register that cannot be assimilated to language or iconicity is that of the 'real' (in contrast to the registers of the imaginary and of the symbolic; see Olivier 2004 for an elaboration on these). The following formulation by Lacan, with which Derrida's remark on 'traumatism', above, resonates, indicates the connection between trauma and the 'real' (Lacan 1981: 55):

> The function of the *tuché*, of the real as encounter – the encounter in so far as it may be missed, in so far as it is essentially the missed encounter – first presented itself in the history of psycho-analysis in a form that was in itself already enough to arouse our attention, that of trauma.
>
> Is it not remarkable that, at the origin of the analytic experience, the real should have presented itself in the form of that which is *unassimilable* to it – in the form of the trauma, determining all that follows, and imposing on it an apparently accidental origin?

This elaboration on the 'real' in relation to trauma occurs in the context of Lacan's distinction (1981: 52–64) between two types of causality, borrowed from Aristotle, namely *tuché* and *automaton*, where the former

---

that most successfully shows the complexity of his truly *poststructuralist* thinking, is John Caputo's delightfully written *Deconstruction in a nutshell* (1997).

(which Lacan describes as 'the encounter with the real') denotes that which always escapes us, but with which we will nevertheless inescapably have a meeting of sorts (the 'missed encounter' of the above quotation). As Lacan puts it (1981: 53): 'For what we have in the discovery of psychoanalysis is an encounter, an essential encounter – an appointment to which we are always called with a real that eludes us'. In other words, one faces a causality here: something is set in motion by something else, which remains hidden, but nevertheless asserts its force powerfully, *in absentia*, by means of certain lingering traces of sorts. In contrast, the *automaton* refers to the type of causality that operates in the realm of the symbolic (language) and the imaginary or iconic, within the 'network of signifiers' (Lacan 1981: 52), in other words, the sphere of 'reality' (as opposed to the 'real'), where the pleasure principle holds sway, where causal links between antecedents and consequents may be readily discerned, for example: water boils when heated. Not so with the *tuche*. Lacan invokes it in connection with repetition which, he points out (1981: 54) '… is always veiled in analysis'. Moreover (p. 54): 'What is repeated … is always something that occurs … *as if by chance*'.

The echoes, here, with Derrida's analysis of *9/11*, above, should be clearly audible. *September 11* belongs to the causal realm of the *tuché*, of the traumatic missed encounter with the 'real', that which happens 'as if by chance', as opposed to the domain of the *automaton*, that is, of language, visibility, predictability and anticipatability – the domain of the empirical and social sciences in the broadly positivist sense of 'science', where so-called 'facts' are located or understood within the framework of testable hypotheses and explanatory theories. If it is objected that *9/11* could have been anticipated (and, as Derrida reminds one, an attack of that nature was indeed foreseen as early as in 1994 by certain architects; see Derrida 2003: 186–187; note 6), it should be pointed out that this is not what is at stake. For a 'terrorist attack' to be 'predictable', is one thing; for an 'event' like *9/11* to be anticipatable in so far as it is 'more' than just a terrorist attack, and belongs properly to the order of the 'missed encounter', is another. It is therefore necessary to pursue Derrida's analysis a little further to be able to understand the event and advent of a trauma, to the point where he problematizes the very question, whether *September 11* 'really' constitutes an 'event' in this sense of something, some traumatic 'thing', which tantalizes our resourcefulness in naming, in inventing conceptually appropriate appellations to inscribe it, finally, in the archive of a putatively shared social and political history. Accordingly, he proceeds to unravel the paradoxical logic of 'eventspeak', agreeing (2003: 88) with Borradori, that one could speak of the 'impression' of a '*major event*' here, reminding her, however, that the 'menacing injunction' to repeat the name, *September 11*, issues from a constellation of dominant powers, themselves dominated in turn by 'the Anglo-American idiom', from which this impression cannot be separated in its rhetorical, interpretive, globalized guise. However, one should distinguish rigorously between the 'impression' as a supposedly 'brute fact', and the interpretation pertaining to it. 'We could say', he observes (2003: 89):

> ... that the impression is 'informed', in both senses of the word: a predominant system gave it form, and this form then gets run through an organized information machine (language, communication, rhetoric, image, media, and so on). This informational apparatus is from the very outset political, technical, economic.

In the case of *9/11* there is therefore a 'resemblance' between the 'impression' as a global effect and the 'thing' that produced it by means of a web of mutually reinforcing agencies (the media, technoscience, as well as military, economic and diplomatic institutions), although neither the 'thing' nor the event is *reducible* to this impression (Derrida 2003: 88–89).

This becomes more comprehensible when he explains (2003: 89), that the '*event*' comprises the '*thing*' itself as that which 'happens' ('event' is also 'advent' or 'arrival'), together with the '*impression*' (simultaneously 'spontaneous' and 'controlled') created by it. From this it seems that one is not permitted to say that the ineffable 'thing' *is* in any meaningful sense separable from the agencies which produce the 'impression', but one might say it is 'refracted' through these agencies as through a prism, so that it first becomes 'visible' as event in its constituent 'colours' when it has 'passed through' the prism of language, dominant discourses, images, media and communication channels. Here one is confronted by the limits of language – an unmistakable sign that one has encountered the Lacanian 'real' – for the prism-metaphor only partly captures the relation between the 'thing' and the 'impression'. It is important to note, however, that whatever it is that becomes 'visible' (and therefore intelligible) must unavoidably do so in terms of the spectrum of humanly visible 'colours', which here represents language and iconicity in their most encompassing sense. This is significant for comprehending the indispensable function of the 'reconstructive' language, especially on the part of Jack, in the narrative of *The reconstructionist*, because one learns from the above that language and iconic representation function ambivalently, paradoxically even, in the face of a traumatically experienced event – it knits an intelligible, protective fabric around one even as it alienates one from the 'thing' which wields inscrutable power over one's life; obscurely, as if from a distance.

Nowhere does this become clearer than where Derrida's deconstructive thinking delineates the 'other side' of the 'constructedness' of the 'event' of *9/11*. Every successive linguistic or iconic appropriation of the 'event' evinces the functioning of a cumulative process: with each appropriation (iteration, description, discussion, analysis, framing) something is added to it, complexifying it, enhancing it, constituting it *as* 'event'. But concomitantly it increasingly assumes the character of something 'sublime' in the aesthetic sense of being, strictly speaking, 'unpresentable'.[9] In this way it highlights the paradox, that the more the event is 'put in perspective' by what is said or written about it, the more it recedes from humans' attempts to incarcerate it, as it were, in the 'prison-house' of language in the widest sense, and the more it asserts its irreducibility. At the same time as the symbolic network progressively appears to assimilate or appropriate the event (*Ereignis*), therefore, the countervailing process of 'expropriation' (*Enteignis*) or withdrawal occurs in a corresponding manner, intimating that 'something' escapes it. And it is this traumatically experienced 'something' – the 'thing' that inflicted the traumatic event of *9/11*, and similarly that unspeakable event which traumatized Kate in *The reconstructionist* – which continually, *repeatedly*, returns, challeng-

9 For an extended discussion of the sometimes countervailing aspects of the sublime as 'unpresentable', specifically in the context of postmodern culture, see Olivier 1998.

ing and exhorting one to appropriate it interpretively in an attempt to exorcise its effects. This is why (Derrida 2003: 90–91):

> … there is no event worthy of its name except insofar as this appropriation *falters* at some border or frontier. A frontier, however, with neither front nor confrontation, one that incomprehension does not run into head on since it does not take the form of a solid front: it escapes, remains evasive, open, undecided, indeterminable. Whence the unappropriability, the unforeseeability, absolute surprise, incomprehension, the risk of misunderstanding, unanticipatable novelty, pure singularity, the absence of horizon.

Even the most therapeutically efficacious linguistic exchange or communication, enacted between people to ward off the debilitating *Nachträglichkeit* (its enigmatic 'causal' working long after the occurrence) of a trauma, seldom, if ever, succeeds in exorcising it exhaustively. The compulsion to repeat – manifestation of what Freud (1968: esp. 38, 47 & 53) named the 'death drive' (initially translated as 'death instinct') – calls for repeated, 'interminable' reconstructive interventions, because they tend to 'falter' to a greater or lesser extent before the elusive (non-) frontier of the thing that conceals itself even as its impact exacts its price.

In *The reconstructionist* Kate Harrington's brother, Jack, is the one who bears the responsibility for these therapeutic interventions, made more significant than is usually the case by the fact that they are siblings – unusually close siblings; a fact not lost on some of their acquaintances (Hart 2002: 94). As intimated earlier, unless he stays on the alert for these occasions, she might disintegrate. From the outset, Hart judiciously imparts just enough information to the reader to create a varying and expanding, as well as deepening sense of anticipation, blended with dread. The narrative opens with a section cleverly titled 'Afterwards' – a reference to the aftermath of the traumatic event, which simultaneously signals that the entire, subsequently unravelling narrative thread will be enigmatically determined by what happened there – which depicts Jack and Kate, as children, sitting opposite each other in the hallway of their childhood home, tellingly named (as the reader gradually realizes in the course of the unfolding narrative) *Malamore*.[10] Here already, in the opening sentence, Hart (2002: 1) introduces the psychoanalytic theme of verbal 'reconstruction' which is inescapable in the aftermath of a traumatic event: '... We were asked to reconstruct the event'. One gathers that their father had instructed them to sit there, waiting for people who would inevitably arrive. Significantly, the narrator, Jack, describes the instant when these people broke the window and entered the house, in retrospect as '... the first moment of dispossession' – a description the symbolic implications of which could not be lost on anyone familiar with psychoanalytic theory either. This marks the retrospective activation of the trauma, as it were, something that explains why even the best efforts on the part of those into whose custody their father entrusted Kate and Jack could not entirely wipe out the memory of the event which, decades later, still exercises its grave spell on them, but more gravely on Kate.

After 'Afterwards', the narrative abruptly switches, like a cinematic flashforward, to the narrative present, where Jack is a practising psychiatrist, and the troubled Kate is worrying about the advisability of marrying for a second time. Again, inserted smoothly into the sequence of narrated occurrences, there is (like on so many occasions throughout the novel) a 'symptomatically' pertinent moment when Kate's erstwhile mother-in-law says to Jack (Hart 2002: 48): 'Giving birth is nothing. What is required of parents is dedication to the art of helping their children save their own lives.' And a few paragraphs further, resonating with what one already knows about the siblings' past, including their father's role in entrusting them to the care of a family member in the wake of the 'event', apparently 'abandoning' them forever, Kate confides in Jack (p. 49): 'You see, Jack, I feel that he [Harold, the man who has proposed marriage to her] could build a wall around me and that I could hide behind it'. When Jack does not reply, she says softly (p. 49): 'I'm sinking again. I'm sinking. Please Jack. Please'. And, knowing when it is inescapably his duty to rescue her, here through the still mysterious enactment of a strange, almost – but

10 '*Malamore*' may be divided into 'mal' and 'amore', which would mean something like 'evil' (or 'bad') 'love'.

not quite – incestuous ritual, the dance (macabre, the reader realizes in due course), Jack concedes. Having folded their clothes neatly and placed them on facing chairs, they dance, at shoulder's length, in the nude, to silent music. As the story progresses (or perhaps 'retrogresses'), one discovers that this is an imitation, or re-enactment, of a ritual enacted by their parents, and secretly observed by the children on more than one occasion, including immediately prior to the shattering event. Moreover, the ritualistic re-enactment of the dance by Jack and Kate whenever the (repressed) memory of the traumatic event threatens to overpower Kate in the shape of some obscurely anticipated lapse, is itself metonymically interwoven with the function of the 'talking cure' mediated by the therapist-reconstructionist (here, Jack).

The fact that Jack is burdened with the responsibility to keep Kate from falling apart by 'reconstructing' her – their – past when called upon to do so, is framed by narrative information concerning Jack's regular patients, his psychiatric-therapeutic practice and his relationship with various other people, in conversation with whom he reveals valuable glimpses into the past that he shares with his sister, Kate. It is clear from his relationship with each one of them that he has an uncommon gift – the capacity to listen, discern and observe even the minutest clue (verbal and physical) on their part, which would signal something significant, negative or positive, to him. As the narrative peels away each layer that still separates the reader from the pathology-inaugurating, traumatic event, one gains a better understanding, not only of Kate's repetition compulsion, but also of the provenance of Jack's uncanny ability to home in on any important sign or symptom on the part of either his patients or his damaged sister. It is as if the catastrophe of their youth predisposed him to being a psychiatrist, given the fact that he was entrusted by his father with the responsibility of 'looking after' Kate subsequent to the catastrophic event in question. But more than this, and hand in hand with it, all the stages of the narrative are connected to, and impelled by, this event which, in its turn, is inextricably intertwined with the passionate love relationship between Jack and Kate's parents, Michael and Catherine Trainor, the frequent dramatic-erotic expression of which the children sometimes witnessed. In fact, this awareness on the part of brother and sister, of the passionate nature of their parents' relationship – determined, on the one hand, by their mother's almost desperate adoration of her husband, and on the other hand by his strength, wisdom and ability to 'handle' his wife's excruciatingly fiery desire for him (up to a point) – is crucial to, and conditions the impact of what eventually happens.

Hart even provides, interwoven with the narrative, a hermeneutic key to the theoretical understanding of trauma – one which is conceptually compatible with that derived from Derrida and Lacan for the purposes of the present analysis (not surprisingly, given Hart's explicit attribution of familiarity with Lacan's work to Jack; see Hart 2002: 50). Not only does she explicitly connect 'trauma counselling' to Jack (2002: 56), but also provides, in the guise of a speech written by him, reflections on the limitations of such counselling. Significantly, in his intended speech Jack situates himself in the contemporary field of psychoanalytic theory (Hart 2002: 57):

> MY POST-FREUDIAN QUESTIONS THEREFORE ARE, HOW DEEP SHOULD WE GO IN EXAMINATION OF OUR SELVES AND OUR PAST? DO WE UNDERSTAND ITS DANGERS? ... INDEED THAT IT IS POSSIBLE TO FALL AND VANISH INTO ONE'S PAST? ... ARE WE SPENDING LARGE SWATHES OF TIME BANGING ON THE DOOR OF TIME PAST, WHICH IN TRUTH IS ALWAYS LOCKED AGAINST US?

Isn't this statement a clear indication of the novelist's appropriation of what Lacan calls the 'missed encounter' (with the 'real') in the traumatic event? That it is in principle impossible to confront the 'thing' (as Derrida describes it) head-on, face to face, because it remains faceless? This impression is reinforced when Jack's written text continues, referring to the speech of the patient (Hart 2002: 59–60):

> ... THE LANGUAGE WE CHOOSE AND THE VOCAL EMPHASIS WE GIVE TO OUR CHOICE ILLUMINATE NOT WHAT HAPPENED, BUT OUR OWN COMPLEX REACTION TO THE MEMORY OF THAT EVENT. A MEMORY WHICH OVER THE YEARS IS REINTERPRETED IN THE LIGHT OF NEW EVENTS. AUTHENTICITY IS THEREFORE MOST OFTEN A CHIMERA.

Here, again, one witnesses a confirmation of the Lacanian/Derridean version (discussed above) of the quasi-efficacy of therapy: what matters, is not whether the traumatic event has been captured, '*wie es gewesen ist*', but the quasi-efficacy of the subsequent interpretations and re-interpretations – the question, to what extent the event has been bearably inscribed in experience through language or discourse (Lacan 1977: 48; Derrida 2003: 87–88). In his speech Jack acknowledges his awareness of these inadequacies, but simultaneously commits himself to the 'endeavour' of limited, but indispensable efficacy (Hart 2002: 60–61), one which no doubt also bears on his reconstructive interventions regarding his sister:

> THAT OF AIDING THE PATIENTS WHO COME TO ME – WHEN THE VERSION OF REALITY THAT WORKED PREVIOUSLY FOR THEM IS BREAKING DOWN – TO BE 'EQUAL TO CIRCUMSTANCE' ...
>
> WHAT IS NEEDED, OVER TIME, IS A METHOD OF DISTANCING THEMSELVES SO THAT SOME FORM OF PERSPECTIVE MAY BE ACHIEVED. ONE WHICH WILL AT LEAST ALLOW LIFE IN A REASONABLE FORM TO CONTINUE.

Within the unfolding story, these self-reflective words on Jack's part explain his own therapeutic work regarding his patients' perceived needs, but crucially also his sister's. Structurally, Hart's narrative (which has to be adequately, albeit succinctly reconstructed here for my interpretation to be intelligible) resembles the temporality peculiar to psychoanalysis: just as the therapist systematically works back (see Freud 1957), through different stages of the analysand's history or personal anamnesis towards the final knot to be 'disentangled' – if this can conceivably be done at all – or, alternatively, reconstructively reinscribed in a safety zone persuasively experienced as such by the analysand, so, too, the narrative inexorably works through present and a series of receding, past layers, until one finally comes 'face to (veiled) face' (recall the earlier discussion of Lacan on trauma as the 'missed encounter') with what might have been inferred or guessed correctly by then. Even so, the horror of it is almost as unbearable, when the reader re-lives it ('impossibly') in her or his imagination, as it conceivably was for Kate (and to a lesser extent, Jack) at the time. By the time one gets here, one knows that Jack believes Kate's prospective husband (number two), Harold, to be, in all probability, a good prospect as far as Kate's well-being goes. Not only is he a wealthy member of London's upper classes, but for various reasons he sees Kate as his last opportunity to 'make good' in marriage, and welcomes it when Jack intimates that he would have to 'take responsibility' for Kate (as 'reconstructionist' in Jack's place) once they are married.

One has also been told that Kate and Jack's father, Michael Trainor, has spent time in prison after being convicted of 'manslaughter', and that he has moved to America, where Jack is able to contact him, on strict instructions, *only* in the event of emergencies. The incongruity of different surnames has been explained, too – after the watershed event they were entrusted to the enduring care of an English uncle, Edmund, whose surname, Harrington, they eventually assumed. In fact, Jack's house, which is home as well as clinical premises to him, in Harley Street, London, used to be Uncle Edmund's home. And although Jack has therapeutically protected Kate by repeatedly spinning and re-spinning a protective web around her, painstakingly, ritualistically reconstructing her life whenever cracks appeared in the edifice – usually signalled by her saying something like, 'Please Jack', or 'I'm falling again', or simply 'What happened?' – it is when he discovers that Harold Abst intends buying *Malamore* as a well-intended wedding gift for Kate when it is put on the market, that Jack has to intervene. He decides to purchase their childhood home himself, first, to have it demolished, lest Kate be propelled headlong into disaster by unwittingly revisiting the scene of primordial disaster. This act holds the promise of an eventual liberation of sorts for both of them (Hart 2002: 194):

> Soon the Malamore of my childhood, the internal landscape of the house, will be destroyed and with it the catalyst to devastating memory. A memory which could pull down around me the construction within which Kate has for so long been protected.

In the process of returning to the estate in Ireland, Jack himself enters, at last, upon a re-living, a personal working-through, of the fateful happenings of their youth at *Malamore*. This is where the psychoanalytic structure of the narrative is most conspicuous – once in the house, crucial, mind-shaping episodes from his and Kate's youth are resurrected in Jack's memory (Hart 2002: 143–177; 212–216): memories of witnessing, from a hiding place, some of the passionate (and often puzzling) encounters between their parents, as well as angry confrontations between their father and their grandfather concerning Catherine, his daughter and their mother – furious exchanges not fully comprehensible to a child because they involved accusations of infidelity, references to passion and to erotic devotion. There are memories, too, of Michael Trainor bearing the brunt of a vicious dog's attack to protect Kate and Jack, and pacifying their mother when she berates Kate for provoking the attack. Throughout these memories a red thread runs, as it were: Jack and Kate's incomprehension and bewilderment in the face of the strange, ambiguous passion that binds Michael and Catherine together – sometimes ecstatic, sometimes ostensibly painful (judging by the erotic sounds their unwittingly observed parents make, and the expressions on their faces), but always palpably fraught with the possibility of imminent disaster. For example, they witness their mother banging her fists against their father's chest, making dire threats against a woman who works as a nurse for Michael's mother. This anamnesic journey on Jack's part culminates, here, in a lengthy recall of the sequence of events that converges with, and expands on, the 'afterwards'-scene with which the narrative opens – Jack and Kate sitting opposite each other, waiting, on their father's instructions, for the people who would, and do, inevitably come to *Malamore*; a sequence of bewildering happenings, including being questioned by the police, that leads, finally, to their Uncle Edmund coming to their grandfather's house and taking them back to London with him the next morning.

What is achieved through the narrative reconstruction of these events is not merely imparting to the reader crucial information on the context which frames the traumatic event in Kate and Jack's lives, but simultaneously a performance of 'working through', on Jack's part, of these events. As he acknowledges near the end of the tale (p. 216) concerning his own part in rescuing Kate via 'the talking cure' and its ancillaries (apart from his father's decisive part): 'And my reward? I helped. He knew that would save me too. I had a job to do and, honestly, fourteen is not all that young to start'. This negotiation of that treacherous terrain in memory is what 'finally' delivers Jack, too, from its clutches.

The reader has to wait almost until the end of the narrative to arrive at the remembered, and simultaneously covered up, traumatic moment from which Jack has been protecting Kate all along. Before this is narrated, Jack returns to London from Ireland, and has to face the important, indispensable task of passing the baton, as it were, to Harold Abst by providing him with an acceptable 'version' of that 'something' which has cast a shadow over his future bride's life (surmised by Harold to have occurred, of course, given his knowledge of Kate's personality by this time). This account of events (Hart 2002: 196–197) casts their father, Michael, in the role of one who accidentally committed manslaughter by wounding their mother, Catherine, fatally with a gun when Jack was fourteen and Kate eight and a half. Jack knows that, armed with this account of events, Harold would be in a position to catch Kate if she should ever fall again. It requires a fine calculation on Jack's part – how much to tell Harold, how to let him feel that he is assuming responsibility, without allowing him too much, lest he should feel justified to improvise his own recipe for 'handling traumatic history' (Hart 2002: 197). Jack also allows Harold the satisfaction of a partial truth, when the latter surmises that the 'secret' Jack has shared with him has been 'the bond' between brother and sister ((Hart 2002: 200).

Having returned from his meeting with Harold, Jack receives a phone call from Kate, who has sensed that she may have reached a point where she will be relatively free from the persistent, insistent echo of the past, sheltered by the embrace of the man she is about to marry (Hart 2002: 202):

> 'Why do I feel it's all ending?'
>
> I know what she's talking about. I sense in her voice that she is now caught in the loop of hope, which is as contagious as despair. I, too, have taken a careful bet on the future. Fundamental to which was the historical perspective I had, this evening, painted for Harold. The story, which will guide him to certain strengths from his own repertoire, which will make him more beloved by her.

Harold, in other words, has become Kate's 'reconstructionist' in Jack's place, with the responsibility of shielding her from the long-term effects of trauma. Hart's keen insight into the exigencies of psychotherapy – that it is the degree to which the patient believes an account of the pathologizing events to be true that matters, and not the question whether it corresponds to 'what actually happened' – is striking here (see Lacan 1977: 47–48).

This is where the culminating sequence of events – which brings the originary traumatic moment (inaccessible as it is in its pure 'originality'), and the 'end' of the narrative, together – starts unfolding. Jack knows that a certain rite of passage faces him too: a newspaper article and photograph of his father, referring to the day the latter was released from prison, trigger a series of reminiscences on his part – how he met his father at the station, the older man's reluctance to see and talk to him (believing, as he did, that the best thing for his children was minimal or no contact with him, in order to bury the past under a blanket of silence), his father's stated intention to go to America, with a woman lawyer whom he had met in prison (a sure sign that Michael Trainor's enigmatic charm still worked), and the abrupt way he ended the conversation and left. Too agitated by the memory of that day of parting to settle down, Jack rings his father's 'emergency number' in America for what he believes will be the last conversation between them. He needs to share with the older man the belief that Kate may henceforth be 'safe', that the re-enactment of his own intermittent, ritualistic, dance macabre with his sister has been obviated at last. In a very significant passage (with tragic echoes of Shakespeare's *Hamlet*), Michael Trainor provides insight into the grounds of the passion that constituted a kind of *hamartia* on Catherine's part, and conditioned their tempestuous relationship, so incomprehensible to their children at the time (Hart 2002: 210):

> 'She lived high up on some other plain, in a kind of passionate dream of me. The smallest thing threatened the giddy high-wire act of Catherine and Michael. She wanted it seamless. As though we'd been knitted into one another.[11] Even a single

11 Catherine's passion, on this account, corresponds largely with Aristophanes's version, in Plato's *Symposium*, of love (or, more appropriately, the sexual drive for union with the other) – unlike Socrates's own version of love, which stresses 'lack' on the part of the lover (implying that one never 'really' reaches the object of one's love,

loose thread was a prophecy of unravelment to her. I let her fall. I wasn't careful enough. The rest is a technicality. It's a heavy burden, a woman's adoration. Anyway, it's to be feared. With good cause, in my case. You've carried this a long time, Jack. I'm grateful. Well ... goodbye now'.

This is not yet the culminating moment of returning to the scene of the 'crime' as it were. Being a psychiatrist – and a Lacanian one, as Hart (2002: 50) intimates – Jack knows that, having taken care, as best he could, of Kate's future well-being, he has to shuffle off his own burden of suffering, in the rich sense of passion, too. After all, for someone as sensitive, and as much of an observer, as himself, his decades-long vigilance has not been neutral, innocuous. In true Lacanian fashion (see Lacan 1977: 40–49), he knows that he has to introduce a new, changed perspective into the narration of his own story. Hence (Hart 2002: 211–212):

It's time, as my father said, to finish it.

I will now lose Kate. I must now lose her. I must let her go – which is just another way of saying it. She is the love of my life. She is my great love affair. Though not in the sense the words usually mean ...

The great thing is over.

Kate and I will no longer dance. She will not ask me. She too has sensed her own survival. How strange that I never felt a single spark of desire for her, not even when we danced naked together.

No, that was a communion. A ritual to celebrate the moving tableau that was our last vision of them, our utterly beautiful parents, naked, dancing, not in their bedroom but in the attic where new guns, and old treasures, were carefully locked away. The forbidden place, to which we had followed them, ambivalently, excitedly, secretly. Looking for the answer to the mystery of parental love. A fatal quest, as I learned young and relearn weekly in my consulting rooms. Not all of us are lost parents but most of us are, at some time, lost children.

---

which is actually aimed at the cultivation of an outonomous self; see Plato 1965: 82–83; 92–94). There is evidently also a measure of desire, the passion accompanied by the dread of human groundlessness, on Catherine's part, though. In his Seminar XX (1999), Lacan elaborates on the differences among these 'passions'. I am indebted to Andrea Hurst for my very provisional understanding of this very difficult aspect of Lacan's work.

This is not the place to elaborate on Hart's wisdom, commensurate with Lacan's (and across the millennia, with Plato's), that – contrary to what most people naively believe, there is not only one kind or form of love, or passion. Clearly, Jack's 'love' for Kate, his sister, has not been of the erotic, sexual kind, but it has been a kind of passion nevertheless – perhaps most accurately described as *the desire to free her* from the cold clutches of the past, of that thing which perpetually threatened to pull her down. In short, she has been his *desire* in psychoanalytic terms (explained below). His means to protect her has been, of course, the version of events that he has had to 'reconstruct' as the need arose – that version according to which her father was convicted of manslaughter for the death of her mother, but which she intermittently doubted. Is there another version? Here the reader, finally, has to look the terrible, traumatic 'truth' in the eye, when Jack recalls, near the end of the narrative – which here comes full circle – that day, long ago, when he and Kate hid behind a chest of drawers in the attic and watched, mesmerized, as their parents danced, naked, ecstatically, until Catherine suddenly stopped and started beating her husband on his chest with her fists, threatening (Hart 2002: 213):

> 'Oh, Michael, I will kill you, I will truly kill you if you ever, ever, touch …'
>
> And then, our world exploded and burned out. What is noted in the moment of conflagration remains indelible. Though not everything is noted. A sensation of emotional vertigo does not allow for precision as layers of presumed reality collapse, the way trembling buildings do in an earthquake. But of this I'm certain. Her face as she fell dead to the floor, did not look frightened.

The anamnesic narrative retrogression having worked through layer after layer metonymically bearing, but also covering over, the unsayable traumatic kernel, has finally stripped away the 'last' one, revealing – what? Something tangible, or an abyss? A traceable implosion of horizons of meaning? These are difficult questions to answer, but Hart's is as accurate an evocation of the anatomy of trauma as any, if one compares it to Derrida's and Lacan's characterizations, outlined earlier. What she describes is the counterpart of the 'event' or of the 'thing' that happens, like a bolt from the blue, the 'real' rupturing the canopy of 'reality' fatally.

But how did Catherine die? Who shot her? That it should have been Michael, her husband and lover who, seconds before, had been dancing the dance of Eros with her, is surely incongruous. Hart gently peels away this last layer of memory covering up the elusive moment of traumatic impact: (2002: 214–215):

> There is not a day I do not hope that in her last seconds she saw it all and sensed how sublime he would be. Yes, that's the word. He was sublime. In a split second he lifted from Kate the burden of her guilt, a primitive guilt which is, and always has been, unendurable.[12] He wrenched it from her and carried it away. It requires supernatural strength ...
>
> ... He did not cry out as his wife slipped from his arms but as though a primitive impulsion drove him, turned and threw himself headlong across Kate, who stood there, paralysed. He took the gun, seeming to wipe it from her hand, as though it were a stain.[13] Then, as his huge body blocked Kate's vision, with studied precision he fired over the body of his dead wife.
>
> In that strange state, which follows trauma and which destroys or suspends human responsiveness, we remained silent and becalmed ... And as though in a dream I listened to him as he whispered to her over and over that poor Daddy had done a terrible thing, that there had been the most dreadful accident and that maybe Daddy would have to go away ...
>
> Afterwards, he sat us opposite each other in the stone hallway and rehearsed us in the reconstruction of the event.

12 What Hart is invoking here is the well-known feminine counterpart of the Oedipus complex, namely the so-called Electra complex, according to which the daughter loves the father to the extent that she would, like the eponymous Electra in ancient Greek drama, murder the mother in his defence, or to avenge him.

13 'Stain' is another telling word that connects the narrative to Lacanian theory here. Metaphorically speaking, the 'stain' marks what Lacan calls the *objet petit a* (or *object a*, 'little other object'). Very succinctly stated, it represents the 'stain', fragment or 'knot' that 'frames' one's desire, or from the perspective of which one's desire may be deciphered. In this case, it is ambiguous – it could either denote Kate's desire for her father's endless affection, or Michael's desire for Catherine, in which case it would mark his sense of guilt about not anticipating the possibility of the catastrophe. See in this regard Žižek 1993: 206–207.

The last sentence in the above passage connects the narrative, near the end of its unravelment (appropriately, in psychoanalytic terms), with the word that commences, instigates the narrative: 'Afterwards'. Not only does Hart demonstrate, in these lines, her keen grasp of the conditions of possibility (and of comprehensibility) of trauma and its consequences, as well as of its possibly effectual treatment (Michael initiates the work of 'reconstruction' of Kate's world, something that Jack afterwards has to take over from him), but she simultaneously shows her insight into something, going back to the ethics of Immanuel Kant, and strikingly thematized in the work of Jacques Lacan, namely, what it means to act ethically.[14] This is properly framed in the language of *desire* – a truly ethical act does not necessarily coincide with what conventional morality dictates; on the contrary, it is, more often than not, transgressive in respect of convention, because it presupposes that the acting person has 'taken up' his or her desire (which is, paradoxically, what is unique or singular about the person, but also a differentiating characteristic that she or he has in common with all other people). However, the further test of whether someone who has assumed his or her desire is capable of acting ethically, consists in his or her ability to sacrifice this very irreducible desire. And this is what Michael does, fully accepting the consequences of giving up his desire – living, in a fundamental sense, to fulfil the reciprocal desire of Catherine – when, faced with the dreadful fact of Catherine's demise at the hands of his daughter, who heard in her mother's threat the possibility of losing her beloved father, he immediately stepped into the breach and assumed culpability in Kate's place. In sacrificing his desire like this, creating for his daughter at least a *chance* to live a 'normal' life one day, he paradoxically confirms it, for he simultaneously honours what would arguably – as Hart intimates through Jack's thoughts – have been Catherine's own wish, too. He takes the rap. And this is what makes him, as Jack tells the reader, sublime; which means 'unrepresentable' in

14 See in this regard Olivier 2005, for an investigation into the question of the ethical (in relation to various agents and contexts) in Lacan's work. For further elaboration, see also Lacan 1997: 243–287; Zupancic 2000; and Žižek 2000.

philosophical terms – that is, his is an act that cannot be articulated in ordinary, conventional terms.

The narrative ends where the virtuoso 'reconstructionist', Jack, having just listened to a message from Cora – who has him 'in her sights' – decides that he has reached a point where he can allow himself the luxury of being 'willing'. He, too, has in a sense been saved (Hart 2002: 218):

> But tonight, before I sleep, I'll play that reel of memory just one more time before I finally erase it. Just once more ...
>
> Then I'm swimming to the surface and this time I'm going to stay there.

One cannot overestimate the importance of Hart's insight into the nature of psychotherapeutic work in the shape of 'reconstruction' – it should be emphasized that, in effect, this amounts to the reconstruction, *time and time again*, of what Lacan understands as the *symbolic* sphere of a person's life (as distinguished from the *imaginary* and the 'real' registers of human existence). This has already been discussed in the theoretical section, above, but what has not been adequately emphasized (although it is implicit in what was said earlier), is the inescapable need for *repeated* (primarily linguistic) 'reconstruction' of the symbolic fabric of a person's life – in the first place, of a person like Kate, who has experienced an unbearably traumatic thing; so much so that it had to be repressed out of sight, but the intermittent symptomatic manifestation of which continually impinges upon her disruptively, necessitating the reconstructive interventions on Jack's part. But there is a second psychoanalytic lesson here from Hart, detectable in her treatment of some of her minor characters – including Harold Abst, Rose (Jack's erstwhile mother in law) and Cora (Jack's current girlfriend) in the novel: a 'healthy' person, no less than a 'damaged' one, requires intermittent 'reconstructions' of her or his personal symbolic horizon (either by the person her- or himself, or with the help of a friend or a therapist), lest one become victim to the (usually ideological) illusion that there is some permanent, time-resistant conceptual framework that remains intact throughout the vicissitudes of life and history. The need for *reconstruction* is interminable, and implicitly requires as its counterpart, one might say, interminable '*deconstruction*' of one's own life (either by oneself, or by someone else) in the Derridean sense of uncovering the groundlessness of a belief in inviolable wholeness, atemporal hierarchies, foundations and origins – in ordinary language, broadly, a resolute acceptance of one's own finitude, mortality and fallibility. This is something which is probably undertaken *explicitly* by very few people, although the regular or intermittent linguistic appropriation of one's own life in conversations with friends and family members presupposes the potential of such a questioning (even if it is not acknowledged), as shown in Rose's conversation with Jack in the novel.[15]

Here a Derridean and a Lacanian approach are in agreement, their terminological differences notwithstanding: one cannot do without the relative, albeit 'mobile', stability of something like language, while simultaneously learning to live with the 'certainty' that such 'stability' is itself subject to *uncertainty*. After all, what Derrida (in Caputo 1997: 23) calls the 'messianic' structure of experience – the fact that, strictly speaking, the future is not predictable in its temporal and historical specificity, that something could (and does) arrive or happen unexpectedly, that one should always 'expect the unexpected' – is consonant with Lacan's 'real' as that which cannot be symbolized, which constitutes the internal limit of language against which our very best efforts, literary as well as scientific, to name the 'cause' of events, shatter, thus evoking the ineffable. The religious and ideological dream of a final, conclusive, totalising, overarching framework, metanarrative or metalanguage has been debunked, incontrovertibly, as an illusion by poststructuralist thinkers such as Lacan, Derrida, Foucault, Lyotard, Kristeva and Deleuze. The alternative is not acceptance of an anything-goes relativism in epistemological and ethical terms (see Olivier 2005), but a willingness to live with, and learn

15 In a conversation with Jack, early in the narrative, for example (Hart 2002: 31), Rose (Jack's former mother-in-law) uses the opportunity of having a conversation with Jack to do some minor 'reconstruction' of her own life – from offering gratuitous judgements of Jack's home decorations (a way of re-affirming Jack's knowledge of her personality), through speculating about the reason why Ellie (Jack's former wife) left him, to informing him about her own past life, which she regards as 'a minor masterpiece' (p. 34).

to negotiate the difficult, complex structures and textures of existence, which means negotiating the tensional relations among the imaginary, the symbolic and the 'real'. To this end, poststructuralist thinkers such as Derrida and Lacan, and novelists like Josephine Hart, have contributed indispensable insights.

What this investigation has brought to light, it seems to me, is that 'trauma' is a crucial motif in the narrative of Hart's *The reconstructionist*. It is not difficult to think of other literary works where this is the case – Toni Morrison's *Beloved* and *Love* spring to mind, as do Golding's *Lord of the flies*, Richard Adams's *The girl in a swing*, Fowles's *The magus* and Rushdie's *Fury*. Cinema, too, yields promising candidates – thinking of films from Nicolas Roeg's oeuvre alone, for example: *Bad timing*, *Don't look now* and *Track 29* are all susceptible to a reading in terms of a narrative dynamic impelled by a trauma of sorts. Interestingly, in *Bad timing* it seems at first glance to work in a retrospective manner, where the narrative events culminate in a trauma which, when retrospectively reconstructed, is perceived as being virtually ineluctable. In all of these narratives there is some traumatic 'thing' that impels the narrative unfolding of events, some knot that the symbolic weave circles around even when it seems to be moving forward, and which, ultimately, does not really allow 'closure' – even when the narrative 'ends' – but rather a temporary suspension of the process of symbolic ravelling. Moreover, and perhaps most significantly, such novels and films enact, metonymically, the inescapable human symbolic activity predicated on the primordial trauma of being born, namely, to spin a web of words, a 'talking cure' of sorts, repairing or restoring it over and over – because webs get torn, ruptured, and blown to pieces – in an effort to catch some bits of sense, of meaning, in its threads. As the creative symbolic activity *par excellence*, literature may be understood, like Penelope's ravelling and unravelling in the face of Odysseus' 'traumatic' absence, as that which continually stitches up the intermittently (or perhaps perpetually) torn fabric of human existence. And sometimes – as in the case of Hart's *The reconstructionist* – the symbolic stitching is done so as to mark, even accentuate, the tear in life's cloth, but with such mastery that its textile beauty is enhanced, not spoilt.

References

Adams, R. 1980. *The girl in a swing*. London: Allen Lane.
Butler, C. 2002. *Postmodernism: A very short introduction*. Oxford: Oxford University Press.
Caputo, J.D. (ed.). 1997. *Deconstruction in a nutshell. A conversation with Jacques Derrida*. New York: Fordham University Press.
Coetzee, J.M. 2000. *Disgrace*. London: Vintage.
Copjec, J. 2002. *Imagine there's no woman. Ethics and sublimation*. Cambridge, Mass.: The MIT Press.
Derrida, J. 2003. 'Autoimmunity: Real and symbolic suicides – A dialogue with Jacques Derrida'. In: Borradori, G. (ed.), *Philosophy in a time of terror*. Chicago: The University of Chicago Press, pp. 85–136.
Derrida, J. 2004. 'Terror, religion, and the new politics'. In: Kearney, R., *Debates in Continental Philosophy: Conversations with contemporary thinkers*. New York: Fordham University Press, pp. 3–14.
Flockemann, M. 2004. 'Traumas and transformations: Fictions which play with what "they say", by Zakes Mda and Lindsey Collen'. *Journal of Literary Studies* 20 (3/4), pp. 248–264.
Fowles, J. 1983. *The magus. A revised version*. London: Triad Panther.
Freud, S. 1957. 'The origin and development of psychoanalysis'. Trans. Chase, H.W. In *A general selection from the works of Sigmund Freud*. Rickman, J. (ed.). New York: Doubleday Anchor, pp. 3–36.
Freud, S. 1968. 'Beyond the pleasure principle'. In: Strachey, J. (ed. and trans.), *The standard edition of the complete psychological works of Sigmund Freud*, Vol. XVIII. London: The Hogarth Press, pp. 7–64.
Gadamer, H.-G. 1982. *Truth and method*. Trans. and ed. Barden, G. & Cumming, J. New York: Crossroad.
Golding, W. 1970. *Lord of the flies*. London: Faber and Faber.
Habermas, J. 2003. 'Fundamentalism and terror: A dialogue with Jürgen Habermas'. In: Borradori, G. (ed.), *Philosophy in a time of terror*. Chicago: The University of Chicago Press, pp. 25–43.
Hart, J. 2002. *The reconstructionist*. London: Vintage.

Hurst, A. 2004. 'Derrida's quasi-transcendental thinking'. *South African Journal of Philosophy* 23 (3), pp. 244–266.

Hurst, A. 2006. *Derrida or Lacan: The revolutionary's choice. On the 'plural logic of the aporia' in deconstruction and Lacanian psychoanalysis*. PhD dissertation, Villanova University. Published by ProQuest. This has since been republished, in enlarged form, as Hurst, A. 2008. *Derrida* vis-á-vis *Lacan. Interweaving deconstruction and psychoanalysis*. New York: Fordham University Press.

Lacan, J. 1977. 'The function and field of speech and language in psychoanalysis.' In: *Écrits: A selection.* Trans. Sheridan, A. New York: W.W. Norton, pp. 30–113.

Lacan, J. 1981. *The four fundamental concepts of psycho-analysis*. (Seminar XI). Trans. Sheridan, A. New York: W.W. Norton & Co.

Lacan, J. 1997. *The ethics of psychoanalysis. 1959–1960. The seminar of Jacques Lacan* – Book VII. Trans. Porter, D. New York: W.W. Norton.

Lacan, J. 1999. *On feminine sexuality. The limits of love and knowledge. The seminar of Jacques Lacan* – Book XX. Encore 1972–1973. Trans. Fink, B. New York: W.W. Norton.

Morrison, T. 1987. *Beloved*. New York: Alfred A. Knopf.

Morrison, T. 2004. *Love*. London: Vintage.

Olivier, B. 1998. 'The sublime, unpresentability and postmodern cultural complexity'. In: *Critique, architecture, culture, art*. Port Elizabeth: University of Port Elizabeth, pp. 197–214.

Olivier, B. 2002. '11 September 2001: A change in the status of the image'. *South African Journal of Art History 17*, pp. 140–143.

Olivier, B. 2004. 'Lacan's subject: the imaginary, language, the real and philosophy'. *South African Journal of Philosophy*, Vol. 23 (1), pp. 1–19.

Olivier, B. 2005. 'Lacan and the question of the psychotherapist's ethical orientation'. *SA Journal of Psychology* 35 (4), pp. 657–683. Reprinted here, as Chapter 3 of this volume.

Olivier B. 2007. 'The question of an appropriate philosophical response to "global" terrorism: Derrida and Habermas'. *Freiburger Zeitschrift für Philosophie und Theologie* 54 (1/2), pp. 146–167. Reprinted here, as Chapter 5 of this volume.

Olivier, B. 2007a. 'Geweld: Waarom ons vir mekaar 'n "ding" word'. (Violence: Why we become a 'thing' for the other.) *Die Vrye Afrikaan*, Jaargang 4, Nr. 1 (Vol. 4, No. 1), 16 February, p. 16.
Olivier, B. 2007b. 'Why SA violence turns horrific and brutal'. In: *Mail & Guardian Online*, at http://www.mg.co.za/articlePage.aspx?articleid=303071&area=/insight/insight_comment_and_analysis/, March 27.
Plato. 1965. *The symposium*. Trans. Hamilton, W. Harmondsworth: Penguin Books.
Rushdie, S. 2001. *Fury*. London: Jonathan Cape.
Terblanche, E. 2004. 'That "incredible unanimal/mankind": Jacques Derrida, E.E. Cummings and a grasshopper'. *Journal of Literary Studies* 20 (3/4), pp. 218–247.
Žižek, S. 1993. '"The thing that thinks": The Kantian background of the *noir* subject'. In: *Shades of* Noir – *A reader*. Copjec, J. (ed.). London & New York: Verso, pp. 199–226.
Žižek, S. 2000. 'Foreword: Why is Kant worth fighting for?' In: Zupancic, A. 2000. *Ethics of the real. Kant, Lacan* (pp. vii–xiii). New York: Verso.
Žižek, S. 2001. *The fright of real tears. Krzysztof Kieslowski between theory and post-theory*. London: BFI Publishing.
Zupancic, A. 2000. *Ethics of the real. Kant, Lacan*. New York: Verso.

Index

FSC
www.fsc.org
MIX
Papier | Fördert gute Waldnutzung
FSC® C083411

Kolibri 360 GmbH
Ferdinand-Jühlke-Straße 7
99095 Erfurt, Deutschland
produktsicherheit@kolibri360.de